IN THE ABSENCE OF THE GIFT

Pacific Perspectives
Studies of the European Society for Oceanists

Series Editors: Christina Toren, University of St Andrews, and
Edvard Hviding, University of Bergen

Oceania is of enduring contemporary significance in global trajectories
of history, politics, economy and ecology, and has remained influential for
diverse approaches to studying and understanding human life worlds. The
books published in this series explore Oceanic values and imaginations, doc-
umenting the unique position of the Pacific region – its cultural and linguistic
diversity, its ecological and geographical distinctness, and always fascinating
experiments with social formations. This series thus conveys the political,
economic and moral alternatives that Oceania offers the contemporary world.

In the Absence of the Gift

New Forms of Value and Personhood in a
Papua New Guinea Community

◆●◆

By Anders Emil Rasmussen

berghahn
NEW YORK · OXFORD
www.berghahnbooks.com

First published in 2015 by
Berghahn Books
www.berghahnbooks.com

Library of Congress Cataloging-in-Publication Data
A C.I.P. cataloging record is available from the Library of Congress.

British Library Cataloguing in Publication Data
A catalogue record for this book is available from the British Library

ISBN 978-1-78238-781-7 (hardback)
ISBN 978-1-78920-806-1 (paperback)
ISBN 978-1-78238-782-4 (ebook)

To Signe and Alfred with love

Contents

—————— ◆●◆ ——————

Figures and Tables

——— ◆●◆ ———

Figures

Tables

Acknowledgements

──── ◆●◆ ────

First I would like to thank Signe for her tolerance, faith and support through the years, and I dedicate this book to her and our son, Alfred. Mbuke people have, with their amazing hospitality and friendship, engaged with my research with more enthusiasm than I could have ever hoped for. To them I am especially grateful. Polongou Kusunan was an extraordinary man who made my fieldwork in the Mbuke Islands much easier by welcoming me into his home; he will be missed by anyone who knew him. Among Mbuke people I would like to give special thanks also to Nialawen and Paula Kusunan, John Tokios, Tatut Selarn, Kutan Albert, Litau Sisky, Niamoto Sisky, Polongou Kisapei, Peter Chakumai, Ponialou Popilel, Kanai, Chalapan Pambuai and many others. To the Mbuke community at large, I extend my *uro* – my thanks!

For comments and constructive criticism on earlier drafts of parts of this book, I would also like to express my gratitude to Ton Otto, Chris Gregory and Keir Martin. Furthermore, I would like to thank James Weiner, Karen Sykes and Steffen Dalsgaard for helpful comments. Nina Vohnsen and Martin Demant Frederiksen provided inspiring advice and criticism during the early process of writing. I also thank Ton Otto for making my stays at the Cairns Institute possible and fruitful. At the Australian National University, I would like to especially thank Mark Mosko and Alan Rumsey for giving me the opportunity to be part of the inspiring intellectual environment at the College of Asia and the Pacific. I am grateful to the authorities in Papua New Guinea who gave me permission to do research there. Finally, I would like to thank my sister and my parents, who have always been supportive of me, even when I have not reciprocated this to the extent that I would have liked to.

The work resulting in this book was made possible by financial support from a number of institutions. Fieldwork was conducted with the support of the Faculty of Humanities at Aarhus University and the Ethnographic Collections at Moesgård Museum. The final writing of the book was done while I worked at the Museum of Cultural History, University of Oslo, and was financially supported by the Research Council at the Museum of Cultural History.

Introduction

◆●◆

'Give me a betel nut!' I looked up from my task, carrying out a small repair to a canoe. Chauka walked towards me along the shore carrying nothing but his flip-flops in his hand, clearly hoping I was in possession of betel nut. As I rooted around in my bag I asked him, 'Where have you been?' 'I have been around the world', he replied, and laughed, while indicating with a gesture that he had walked around the island, a two-hour walk at most. Even bearing in mind that life-worlds in which people live their lives are not identical with the world as a physical globe, his statement was far from true: Chauka's social world reaches far beyond the shores of Mbuke Island in Manus Province, Papua New Guinea (PNG). Chauka grew up on Mbuke, the biggest in the island group of the same name.[1] He left the island aged fourteen and went to high school in Lorengau, the provincial capital of Manus, after which he moved to Port Moresby (PNG's capital city), where he became a banker until he returned to the village and moved into his late parents' house – a house that he had himself funded the building of while he was away.

But it is not only by the token of his personal biography that Chauka's world reaches far beyond the one he had circumambulated that day. He is in frequent contact with his older brother, who lives and works in Port Moresby; he regularly calls his younger brother, who lives in Lorengau, where he works as the local representative of an international NGO; and Chauka also tries to keep in touch with his two sisters, who are 'married to [men in] Australia'. In all his correspondence, a set of quite frequently asked questions among the Mbuke occurs. These may analytically be summed up as the question of 'what about me?' and involve questions such as 'can you send me ...' 'I need money for ...' 'your nieces and nephews are hungry, can you help with ...' Mbuke people tend to categorize these kinds of questions using the Tok Pisin (PNG Pidgin English) term *singaut*, which in this context refers to a request or demand.[2] Apart from extracting remittances and utilities such as fishing equipment and materials for house building from migrant relatives with access to money, these questions maintain, expand and sometimes contract Chauka's social world, a world made up of relations connecting Chauka with other persons and sets of persons. These questions are 'value questions' (Gregory 1997: 7–8), which demand that others respond to the question 'what about me?' by valuing the relationship. Chauka might *singaut* to his brother, who might respond by giving the value he ascribes to the relationship a visible form (such as a bank transfer altering Chauka's bank statement or a shipment of sheet metal for his roof), and thereby confirm to Chauka that they are brothers, and that such a request and such a response are appropriate expressions of their relationship. In Chapters 2 to 4 I discuss various forms of transactions initiated by verbal requests or demands (*singaut*), which all point to limitations in classic anthropological theories of reciprocal gift exchange – and the prominence such approaches have been given in ethnographies of Melanesia – to account for the ongoing production and reproduction of value, relationships and personhood in a contemporary PNG community.

In addition to the 'what about me' question, another question gradually emerged in recent decades among the Mbuke, that of 'what about us?' The social conditions of extensive temporary labour migration have not only given sharing and demands for remittances a central place in the valuing of social relations and in the constitution of personhood, it has also given rise to a new sense of 'us', referred to among the Mbuke with the English word 'community'. The temporary absence of nearly half the adult population has created an inclination for a Mbuke person to think of themselves as part of a social whole, which is not geographically local, and which is not based on specific kin relationships and personal alliances. Directing the question of 'what about us?' to state or government representatives has often led to disappointment among the Mbuke. PNG's state institutions increasingly fail to provide certain services (such as community schools and adequately staffed healthcare posts), which people in Manus – even in its remote parts, like the Mbuke Islands – had become accustomed to during late colonial times and throughout the years after independence. Being both well connected to the national political elite and comparatively wealthy in monetary terms, through having a highly educated migrant diaspora, the Mbuke have taken it into their own hands to respond to the question of the value of their community. During the seven years I have come and gone to the Mbuke Islands, a new school and two healthcare posts have been built in the villages using funds raised by and for 'the community' (see Figure 1). When I did my longest period of fieldwork among the Mbuke in the islands' villages and among Mbuke migrants in PNG's urban centres in 2008/9, discussions about 'social welfare programmes' were beginning to take place in community meetings, reflecting, not least, a widespread hope on the part of migrants that they might ease '*singaut* pressure' from village relatives. The word 'community' has become an important and disputed concept with which to refer to this emerging social whole, a social totality that may take on tangible forms (such as concrete 'community projects') as responses to the question of 'what about us?' that Mbuke people might ask themselves and others.

'Community' as a localized concept refers to a particular kind of social whole in which the constitution of personhood and the formation of value differ from their constitution and formation within the sets of concrete social relationships in which sharing and remittances take place. In Chapters 5, 6 and 7 I deal with the historical emergence of 'community' as an indigenous category of description and level of social organization, with the valuing of actions measured by their ability to 'benefit the community', and the social contestation and negotiation of community vis-à-vis other temporal social wholes.

In this book I provide an exploration of local concepts and practices of value, personhood and sociality by addressing the conflicts, negotiations and transformations relating to what it means to be a person and what can be expected of a relative or a fellow community member among the Mbuke. I address a contemporary situation in PNG in which migration and remittances, sharing on demand and 'community development' are at the centre of relationships and of value formation. Rather than analysing

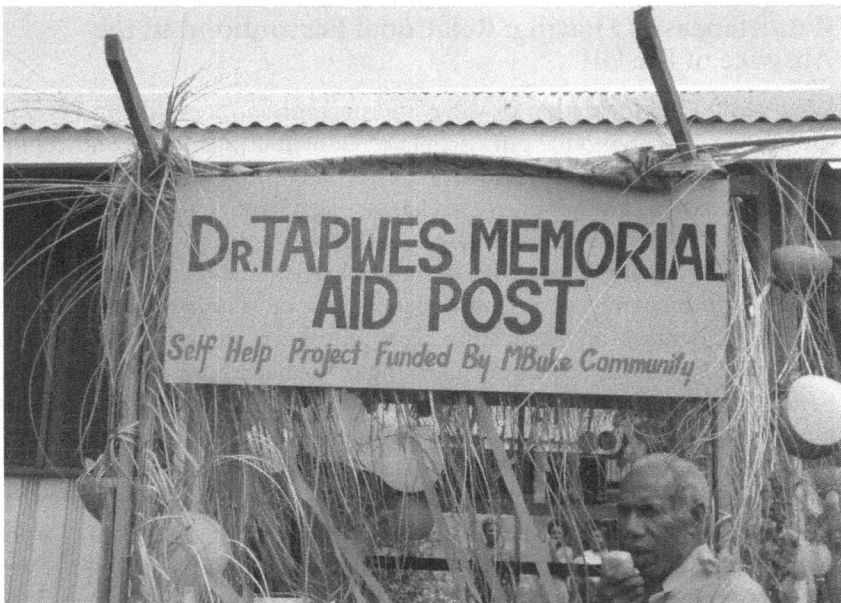

Figure 1: Launching the new healthcare post on Mbuke Island. Photograph by Nia Itan.

social change as a conjunction of cultural systems and fixed standards of value in the transition towards a market economy, I present a processual account of acts of valuation in a composite lived world. I aim to show that value is measured by ongoing and occasionally conflicting human judgements, rather than being determined by social norms and cultural precepts. The title of the book reflects the observation that ceremonial exchange of 'the gift' has gradually lost its significance in the production and reproduction of social relations and personhood. The growing absence of the gift, in this sense, has given way to sharing among close relatives, and an emerging concept of sociality as 'community' that is rendered tangible as 'community projects' in responses to the value question of 'what about us?' The central contention regarding value is that by exploring specific acts of valuing we might better grasp the complex and multiple sets of relationships and other temporal socialities that are produced and reproduced by acts of valuing. I argue that value emerges in transactions and actions that simultaneously reconstitute the sets of social relations by which their value may be measured. My contribution to the anthropology of value is the understanding of value among the Mbuke as formed in the interplay between verbal utterances and visual responses, between questions and answers.

Remittances as Sharing: Relational Personhood in the Absence of the Gift

What would the formation of value and personhood look like in PNG in the absence of ceremonial gift exchange? Contributions to the anthropology of value and social reproduction based on ethnographies of PNG have often focused on ceremonial gift exchange (e.g. Gregory 1982; Munn 1986; Strathern 1988, 1992a), and for good reason, since, as those accounts have demonstrated, many Melanesian socialities have indeed been based on gift exchange in many respects. In the specific case of Manus Province, where levels of migration and education have long been among the highest in PNG, the logic of the gift has been lurking in the anthropological literature. Several authors have noted that temporary labour migrants from Manus remit in order to draw on some kind of reciprocity after their return (see Otto 1991: 247; Gustafsson 1999: 68; Dalsgaard 2010: 231), and those who have written elaborately about remittances have specified that ceremonial exchange in villages has been a major factor in transferring money from migrants to villagers (Schwartz 1975; Carrier and Carrier 1989). Even though the former explanation does play its part among the Mbuke, the contemporary rarity of ceremonial exchange and the widespread absence of (material) reciprocation for remittances on the part of villagers indicate that remittances are most aptly described as 'sharing', not formal exchange governed by the reciprocal logic of 'the gift'.

In my use of the concept of 'sharing', I follow Gell's definition in his discussion of an 'indigenous service economy', where moral obligations to give rather than reciprocal 'debts' motivate sharing (Gell 1992: 152). Rather than making 'sacrifices' that will later be reciprocated by other 'sacrifices' (ibid.), migrants, by remitting, simply avoid losing or jeopardizing, as part of the relational constitution of their person, the relationship indicated by acts of *singaut*, a relationship that might otherwise have been granted to them by birth (such as brotherhood). Sharing is often described, following Sahlins, as the most vague form of reciprocity, namely 'generalized reciprocity', where, among the closest of relatives, transactions are 'left out of account' (Sahlins 1972: 194). But as Sahlins elaborates, '[t]his is not to say that handing over things in such form, even to "loved ones", generates no counter-obligation'; it is rather the case that 'the expectation of reciprocity is infinite' (ibid.). Following this understanding of sharing, people share with others in ways that they expect those others would share, if the situation were reversed, and generalized reciprocity is simply 'what the recipient can afford and when' (ibid.). In the case of sharing among close relatives, on the actual Mbuke Islands it cannot be ruled out by the people involved in it – or by the observer – that over a very long time span, such generalized reciprocal 'debts' might eventually level out. But in the contemporary situation in which much sharing is through remittances, it can, in fact, be ruled out in most cases. My point is, in essence, that the obligation to share is not generated by previous sharing; nor is it primarily motivated by the hope for future reciprocation.

Rather than the infinite delay of reciprocation, which is tolerated because the receiver will do what they can to reciprocate eventually, sharing is – in this context – better described as tolerated consumption.[3] In sharing among the Mbuke, objects and resources shared often 'leak out' of circulation entirely, and value is the result of mutual recognition in which words (such as demands or requests) may play as important a role in valuing as do material things (cf. Keane 1994). Sahlins more recently argued that 'mutuality is the hallmark of kinship' and, drawing on the work of Marilyn Strathern (e.g. Strathern 1988), he defines 'mutuality of being' among relatives as characterized by participation in each other's person, and states that '[k]inship entails an internalization of difference' (Sahlins 2011: 227). If that is the case, and there is no clear distinction of self and other in the transaction, then there is no *hau*[4] residing in the receiver until appropriate reciprocation takes place since, as my Mbuke interlocutors would sometimes put it, close relatives are 'one flesh'. What migrants are faced with, then, when they are subjected to *singaut*, is giving what they owe to themselves, to value a relationship that entails both themselves and the requester.

It is worth noting that sharing among the Mbuke, especially in the context of remittances, is most often on demand, and rarely unsolicited. It is well known in economic anthropology that reciprocity and ceremonial exchange has stolen the thunder at the expense of other less spectacular exchange practices that nevertheless are important in the constitution of social relations. Weiner pointed out that the preoccupation with the norm of reciprocity – starting with Malinowski (1983) and Mauss (1990) – has led anthropologists studying exchange to focus on things in circulation between groups (such as between descent groups who 'exchange' women), rather than on things kept out of such circulation, things which stay within certain groups, but which nevertheless 'act as the material agents in the reproduction of social relations' (Weiner 1992: 3). While in Weiner's analysis, material things act as agents of social reproduction by being kept within a group (and preserved), in the case of *singaut* they do so by being consumed within such 'groups', and are often given in response to requests.

In the context of sharing, Peterson and others have argued that the fixation on the norm of reciprocity has led anthropologists to overlook the moral obligation to respond positively to demands, what he refers to as 'demand sharing' (Peterson 1993). Demand sharing among indigenous Australians (ibid.: 861) and its Manus version, *singaut*, plays an important role in the ongoing constitution of social relations. Demand sharing is suitable for my purposes because, as pointed out by Macdonald, this analytical term depicts the 'moral obligation to respond to demands rather than an obligation to reciprocate a "gift"' (Macdonald 2000: 91). This counteracts the Maussian legacy in economic anthropology (ibid.), while also bringing the role of the verbal demand into focus.

Whether or not it makes sense to say that among the Mbuke 'the gift' is increasingly absent at the expense of other forms of transactions, and to say that as a mode of valuation reciprocity has overshadowed other ways in which non-market transactions produce value, is of course a matter of definition. If one were to follow Gregory's definition of gifts as 'products that are valued according to the non-market principle of reciprocity' (Gregory 1994: 911), which hence potentially defines as reciprocity all transactions that are 'non-market', then nearly all of the transactions described in this book are actually 'gifts'. However, I find it useful to distinguish, as Gell (1992) does, between 'sharing' and 'reproductive gift exchange', and I argue that sharing, which has otherwise been described as generalized reciprocity (Sahlins 1972: 194), may also be looked upon as being 'the absence of reciprocity' (Gell 1992: 152). If it is the case, as Rio notes, that anthropological convention holds that reciprocity is inherent in the term 'gift' (Rio 2007: 450), then it makes sense to say that remittances are not gifts, even if they are clearly non-market transactions. Most saliently absent among the Mbuke is what Gell refers to as 'reproductive gift exchange': exchanges conducted between affinally linked groups (such as inter-marrying descent groups) in conjunction with marriage, childbirth and death, for example (Gell 1992: 143), which I refer to generally in this book as ceremonial exchange. The gift is, in that sense, very much absent, and I shall deal with the historical emergence of this absence in Chapter 1. In the increasing absence of reproductive gift exchange and in a situation of geographical dispersal, informal sharing among close relatives and friends has grown in scope and transformed the ways of achieving social reproduction among the Mbuke. This provided me with a unique opportunity to study the complexities and dynamics of the interplay between *singaut*, what Gregory has referred to as 'the value question' (Gregory 1997: 1–12), on the levels of 'what about me/the two of us', and the way the answer is made manifest in visible, often material forms as the response. Value, then, is formed in the interplay between questions and visible answers.

A central point to be made about *singaut* and remittances is that persons are constituted in terms of relationality in the absence of reproductive gift exchange. The production and reproduction of relationships between those with better access to resources (in many cases temporary labour migrants) and those more dependent on others (in many cases people living in the villages) is analysed as a kind of sharing, rather than in terms of 'gifts'. This is not to say that better-off Mbuke people are always happy with the constant demands for money and goods and with tolerating consumption. Like emerging elites from Matupit and Rabaul in PNG's East New Britain Province, described by Martin, who complain more explicitly about the emerging 'culture of consumption' among their relatives in the village (Martin 2007: 289–90), Mbuke migrants and well-off villagers are looking for alternatives to this growing dependency, one of which is sometimes referred to as 'community projects'. As pointed out by Bille, Hastrup and Sørensen, 'absences are important social, political and cultural phenomena that impinge on people's lives' (Bille, Hastrup and Sørensen 2010: 7), and the widespread absence of material reciprocation for remittances and assistance is very much present among better-off Mbuke people as a motivation for reformulating, in response to requests, the 'what about me' question to a 'what about us' question.

The Value of Community

In a Port Moresby bar, Jacob told me with great enthusiasm about his plans for his return to the Mbuke Islands. After his upcoming retirement from a senior government position in Port Moresby, he was going to start a small business on the island in which he would buy fish from other men in the villages, freeze it and then sell it in the provincial capital. That way, he felt, he could benefit the community by providing a means of income for the villagers as well as himself. Shortly after our conversation, when I was back on Mbuke Islands, the leader of Jacob's clan took up his planned initiative at a community meeting among leading Mbuke men. In response to the proposal one man commented, 'We must determine if that business is just meant to benefit himself, his family only, or if it will benefit the community'. I demonstrate, in the last three chapters of the book, how 'the community' is an emerging standard of value by which both individuals' actions and organized collective action such as 'community projects' may be valued against their ability to benefit and value the community as such. The emergence of this conceptualization of sociality as a social totality ties into a long and complex history, starting in late colonial times and especially involving what was known as the Paliau Movement, a history I discuss at length in Chapter 5.

In the early 1970s, a Mbuke organization called the Sugarloaf Youth Club was established in Port Moresby by young men and women from Mbuke living and working there, and among other things it was the intention from the outset that the club should 'help the villages' in the Mbuke Islands as a whole. In the late 1990s, when those youths had grown older, the club became central in organizing fund-raising events for projects in the villages, such as for the building of a new community school on Mbuke Island. At that time, the club changed its name to the Mbuke Islands People's Association (MIPA), and the association came to cover 'Mbuke people' as a totality – whether they lived as labour migrants outside Manus Province or lived in the villages. In the late 1990s, as dependence on remittances increased in the villages and state institutions began ceasing to provide services like schools and healthcare posts in villages, migrant members of the MIPA decided that the association needed a regular income of its own to provide money for 'community projects'. A company owned by the association, named MIPA Holdings Limited (MHL), was therefore established with the explicit aim of earning money to be used for 'community projects', an example of which was the plan of building new healthcare posts in the two biggest villages in the Mbuke Islands. The hope was to earn money in a variety of ways, such as organizing the collection of sea cucumbers around the islands for onward sale to Asian buyers, and by running a small cargo ship chartered from the Manus provincial government. In 2006, many Mbuke people told me with great enthusiasm that they were now doing something for themselves, as they were 'tired of waiting for development'.

During the Christmas holidays of 2006/7, the population of Mbuke Islands nearly doubled due to the many labour migrants who came 'home' from PNG's urban centres for their Christmas leave. When the festivities were at their peak, the small cargo ship run by MHL arrived on Mbuke Island. Nearly everyone in the village on the island walked towards the beach while the ship dropped anchor in the shallow waters, and the bow door opened directly onto the beach.

It was the first time the ship had been to the Mbuke Islands, since it normally operated out of Rabaul (in East New Britain Province). Mbuke men started unloading numerous barrels of petrol and other things. I joined the crowd going aboard the ship, and many of my companions repeatedly told me with obvious pride 'this is our ship', and that it was 'run by the community'. But there were also those who kept their distance. One of them was a Mbuke *lapan* (traditional leader), who I spoke to later that day. He expressed concern that the ship had been used to transport the petrol, which, as it turned out, was intended for a local man's political campaign around Manus villages. 'That's just one man's company, you know', the *lapan* said, pointing towards the ship. This same *lapan*, like many others, had previously often assured me that the community company (MHL) would add to the 'good of the community', that it would benefit everyone. Meanwhile, each action and every social event (such as the arrival of the

Figure 2: The *MV Manus* on Mbuke Island. Photograph by Ton Otto.

ship and the unloading of the petrol) provides the possibility of socially negotiating and evaluating actions as well as organizations and their ability to benefit the community, while at the same time disputing the appropriate perceptual form that the community should take. As reflected in such debates and disagreements, 'the community' does not simply exist; rather, it is 'made to appear' in perceptible forms by (community) projects that claim to benefit it – like gifts render specific relationships visible, but also make claims about those relationships. MIPA and MHL are in that sense organizational 'visual appearances' of community, possible answers to the value question, 'what about us?'

Like the *lapan*, there were people who felt that MHL was not successful enough in allocating funds for community projects. For example, many people complained that the promise of building new healthcare posts was not being honoured, and some suspected that those Mbuke men who were running the company from a small office in Rabaul (mostly highly accomplished migrants now employed in the company) were 'eating the money' themselves, rather than using it for the benefit of the community. In 2008, one migrant couple took matters into their own hands and organized a large-scale fund-raising dinner in Port Moresby, to which they invited members of their urban elite network, as well as fellow Mbuke migrants. The money raised on that occasion, along with other donations from Mbuke migrants, was used to build two new healthcare posts (see Figure 1) without the direct involvement of MIPA or MHL. While 'the community' has emerged as a kind of social whole, a standard of value, among many Mbuke people, the tangible forms – both in terms of organizational structures (e.g. MIPA) and specific actions and events – by which 'the community' may be valued are subject to ongoing contestation. Some would say that the plans laid out by leading members of MIPA were 'mere talk', while the actual building of healthcare posts was evidence that certain people were genuinely 'benefiting the community'. Yet others felt uneasy about bypassing MIPA, as this placed the couple who organized the fund-raiser in a potentially privileged position in the community. We might say that by organizing donations to the community, the couple constituted themselves as persons in terms of an idea of membership of an abstract social whole (community), rather than revealing themselves in their relational constitution by sharing with specific relatives. The problem for the sceptics then became that they revealed themselves in a particularly important membership position vis-à-vis others, not simply in that particular project, but in the community as such, which the project rendered tangible.

Community is not a clear and single shared or agreed upon standard of value among the Mbuke, but a temporal and contested social whole, and several kinds of actions may give tangible form to it. While acts of remitting money to village kin might be valued in, and give specific value to, the sociality of particular kin relations, a community project is valued for its ability to benefit the community, its ability to value the community. Here the person who conducts projects that 'benefit the community' does not reveal specific relationships with specific relatives through their actions and donations, but rather reveals themselves as a member of a more abstract community. But just as the person requesting remittances and the person responding to that request might not agree about the appropriate guise of the relationship, so too does a project like building a healthcare post provide a site for negotiating the community as such. The person as a member of the community as opposed to a person in a specific kinship network ties into current discussions about the emergence of forms of individualism as opposed to the 'relational person' in contemporary Melanesian ethnography. In this book I discuss these changes not as a radical rupture, but as ongoing and long-term negotiations between different concepts of sociality and personhood – persons and socialities that are only temporarily constituted when transformed into visible forms.

Value and Temporal Wholes

Discussions of value in anthropology have often dealt with part–whole relations in ways that are relevant to the way in which Mbuke people value things and actions as answers to value questions that imply certain temporal social wholes. In this book I develop an understanding of valuing among the Mbuke as a dialectical process of questions and answers in which both value and the standard by which it is measured are outcomes of the transaction, not its precursors.

Dumont (1980) is perhaps the most radical, in terms of defining valuing as closely associated with holism. He argues that the value of an entity (or context) is relative to its position or encompassment in a larger context or whole (Itéanu 2009: 339). Here, an entity's value is relative to the context in which it is hierarchically situated from the point of view of another entity therein (Dumont 1980). This fundamentally structuralist understanding of the relationship between value and social wholes is similar to what Graeber describes as a linguistic understanding of value: the value of a sign vis-à-vis other signs, or meaningful differences within a system of signs (Graeber 2001: 2). The problem with Dumont's approach, for my purposes is that it assumes the existence of the social whole as prior to actions producing value within it. Graeber's more action-centred theory of value also presupposes certain part–whole relationships: 'forms of value can only be realized on some sort of larger stage … [F]or the actor, "society" is simply the audience one would like to impress' (ibid.: 78).

The use of the concept of community among the Mbuke seems to invite a similar understanding of value as related to a social whole.

However, conceptual totalizations of sociality like 'community', 'culture' and 'society' have been widely criticized in anthropology (cf. Bubandt and Otto 2010: 2). In Melanesia, such critiques have highlighted that Melanesians do not necessarily conceive of themselves as individual members of a social whole that exists beyond specific persons in specific relationships (Wagner 1975). Most famously, Marilyn Strathern has argued that the conceptualization of society vis-à-vis the individual carries certain assumptions about the relationship between parts and wholes, which entail that the whole encompasses its parts (Strathern 1992b). She argues that such part–whole relations are misleading when applied to Melanesian local conceptualizations of sociality, which are allegedly based on the assumption that 'there are no principles of organization that are not also found in the constitution of the person' (ibid.: 86). Society and similar analytical categories cannot be assumed to have 'indigenous counterparts' (Strathern 1988: 3), and rather than conceptualizing the person as an individual member of the abstract social totality of society, the person is, according to Strathern and others, a model of the concrete social relationships in which it is entangled, and hence the part is not a fragment of its whole but a microcosm of that very whole (Strathern 1988; see also Wagner 1991).

This issue of personhood has given rise to the now famous Melanesian 'relational' or 'dividual' person, constituted out of that person's concrete relationships. Through exchange, this person is continuously composed of 'parts' which may be understood as those relationships with others that are 'made [to] appear' by gifts (Gell 1999). The same person is, in conjunction with death, symbolically decomposed, for example in mortuary exchanges (e.g. Mosko 1983; Strathern 1992b: 76; Mimica 2003), when the deceased person is 'finished' with regard to otherwise ongoing exchange relations (cf. Foster 1995a: 97). Hence the social whole in which the person lives is temporary and changes with specific acts of exchange, when people reveal relationships to themselves. For Strathern, 'the moment of exchange renders value visible' (Keane 1994: 606; cf. Strathern 1992b: 172). The concrete sets of social relationships, which are constituted or reconstituted in that moment, are the source of value. As Gell has phrased it, Strathern has proposed a framework for understanding how Melanesians make visible that which is otherwise invisible through what Gell calls 'appearances', such as gifts embodying relationships (Gell 1999: 37). Borrowing Gell's meaning of the term 'appearance', actions and things transacted are analysed in this book as visible answers to value questions. I analyse both acts of remitting and 'community projects' as 'appearances' whereby actions can be said to make statements about (or be embodiments of) the sociality in which they unfold, as well as about the nature of being a person in (or as a social microcosm of) such a temporary social whole. In this way I develop an action-centred approach, and take the concept of 'appearances' to contexts where 'the gift' is absent, and to where relationality is not the only way in terms of which persons are constituted.

My understanding of 'community' as a shared but contested standard of value, for example, deals with that which is considered good, valuable or meaningful within a social totality as it is revealed by acts that claim to benefit it. The idea of a 'standard' of value might indicate a degree of fixity, a structure in which certain things or actions have fixed value relative to other things and actions therein, but, as Gregory points out, 'human valuers are the means by which values exist' (Gregory 1997: 13). Considering the example of *singaut* and response, the point of comparison (standard) is the outcome of the inter-personal interaction when, by means of the dialectical process of questions and answers, human valuers reciprocally recognize and negotiate the form of the relationship. A Mbuke migrant might see a request for remittances from the village as recognition of the fact that they have a valuable relation to the person making that request. On the other hand, the person making the request will see the money they might receive in response as recognition of the same relation. In this way, the same value is produced (or the relationship confirmed or constituted), although a phone call and a banknote are not easily conceived of as equivalent or comparable in other contexts. Value is an outcome of the transaction, not a precursor of it, and so is the standard. This contrasts with the model of value derived from the 'barter model of value' in which specific things have value vis-à-vis one another (e.g. Strathern 1992a: 176). Transactions, in this sense, also involve a change of personhood and mutual obligations, as they are implied by the act of *singaut* and the response it might conjure, as well as involving a change of socialities embodied by persons and changes in the temporary social whole in which value is formed.

It is worth comparing the contemporary Mbuke situation with a classic case of exchange in Melanesia, namely one from the Kula ring. I said earlier that Chauka's world reaches far beyond the shores of Mbuke Island, because of the specific relationships that connect him with places as far as Sydney, where one of his sisters lives. Munn has argued, in the case of Gawa, an island in the Kula ring, that value is the result of actions that succeed in extending the person or the community in space and time, such as through newly established connections in Kula exchanges (Munn 1986: 9). To the Gawans, as described by Munn, value is the ability to create new social relations. For Munn, the social whole that provides a standard in the light of which acts are valued is that very whole as expanded by those acts (the expansion of 'the fame of Gawa'). In that sense, all acts are measured by the same standard, even if those acts themselves transform it. Among the Mbuke there is no clear agreement about the appropriate social whole by which to determine the value produced by a particular action. Among the Mbuke such temporal social wholes often come into conflict, and distinctions between them become unclear and are socially disputed. Is Jacob's fish project really going to benefit the community? If so, does that place Jacob in too privileged a position in that community? Or might it end up only benefiting his specific kin relations?

The relationship between social wholes and value is understood here as the temporary social wholes by which human valuers value their actions and relations. These wholes are constantly reworked and therefore changed when transformed into perceptible forms (appearances) in a process of action and recognition.

Personhood and Social Change

Those questioning Jacob's fishing project and insisting that 'it must benefit the community' testify to an emerging concept of a social whole beyond specific relationships, a social whole in which actions can be valued and a person can be socially constituted as an individual member of a 'community'. This indicates a move away from the more relational understanding of the person and of sociality. While in recent years a number of anthropologists have pointed to the emergence of individualism in Melanesia, this book draws attention to the emergence of a social whole of which such individuals conceive of themselves as parts (fragments rather than fractals, perhaps). Numerous accounts of personhood and forms of relationships in Melanesia have pointed to the emergence of individualism, as opposed to dividual or relational personhood, and discussed its consequences for forms of exchange (e.g. Foster 1995b; Robbins 2004, 2007; Martin 2006, 2007; Sykes 2007a, 2007b). While Martin associates individualism with those who are successful in the commodity economy (the 'Big Shots') and less successful persons with relational personhood (e.g. Martin 2007), the situation is rather different among the Mbuke. In the case of the Mbuke, the local concept (*eh mo ye*) that appears to come very close to Macpherson's (1962) definition of possessive individualism is associated with selfishness and is mostly used in moral critiques of others (cf. Sykes 2007a). Among the Mbuke, possessive individualism is not often a legitimate perspective held by certain persons in certain situations (as in Martin 2007). 'Community', on the other hand, is a new way for Mbuke people to construe themselves as individual parts of a whole. It is a way of relating to others which must also 'appear' in a perceptible form such as organizational structures made concrete by actions conducted in accordance with them.

Recent critiques of the 'Strathernian' position on issues of personhood and sociality in PNG have focused on the way in which persons are in fact conceived of as individuals in certain contexts, for example as Christian 'sinners' who are individuals vis-à-vis their God (Robbins 2004, 2010), or as successful businessmen who pose as possessive individuals when attempting to limit the scope of reciprocal obligation towards village relatives (Martin 2006, 2007). These critiques have argued that there are certain contexts in which it is not reasonable to talk about the person as 'relational' or 'dividual' (Robbins 2010; see also Errington and Gewertz 2010; Knauft 2010). In doing so, they have paid comparatively little attention to the concept of the social whole of which such individuals must consequently form part (although see Foster 1995b). In this book I deal with the emergence of what appears to be such a social whole, and I compare the type of personhood which it entails with the one reflected in the transfer of remittances and day-to-day sharing that mostly take place between kin. Rather than viewing this 'new' kind of social whole simply as a break with past understandings of sociality, I show that although part–whole conceptions may vary, some of the concepts by which social action reveals the temporal social whole within which it takes place do form a good basis for understanding many different forms of sociality among Mbuke people. Thus, rather than rejecting the idea of a social totality beyond specific relationships, I argue that different socialities are relevant to different people in different situations, as also revealed by their internal disagreements about the specific relevance of various socialities in specific situations. As Rio puts it, 'if we can no longer hope to approach society as a "coherent whole", then we can at least trace empirically how people themselves conceptualize their social life world' (Rio 2007: 1); moreover, I argue, with Martin, that 'there is more than one way to constitute a person in contemporary PNG' (Martin 2007: 297).

Value and Personhood in the Absence of 'the Gift'

The central focus of this book is twofold. First, it addresses relational personhood in a situation where ceremonial exchange plays a minor role compared to other places in PNG and shows instead the significant role that the informal sharing of money has come to play in the ongoing constitution of persons in terms of relationality. Secondly, the book addresses an explicitly stated concept of a social whole which appears initially to be an 'indigenous counterpart' to the idea of 'society', namely that of 'community' as a meaningful social whole in which Mbuke people conceive of themselves as individual members. This is not to say that Mbuke people have now finally reached a 'stage' of development (nor to say that such a universal stage can be identified) in which a person is an individual member of society, but rather that they too have ideas about a kind of social totality. Following Rio, I argue that 'they' might have concepts of social wholes even if anthropology has left them behind (Rio 2007: 7), and that such ideas may be of assistance to an anthropological concept of the social wholes that people nevertheless live by.

In the absence of ceremonial gift exchange, value and personhood are formed in other contexts, in which actions and things render sociality and personhood tangible and create value. This is a book about questions asked and the value of the answers. Answers and questions may differ, valuers may disagree, and often answers tend to rephrase the question. For instance, when a relative in the village calls and asks for money the answer might be 'we are working to find solutions for you people in the villages'; thus, the book also provides insights into the dynamics of social change.

Rather than approaching value as specified by particular fixed standards of value or as relative to the hierarchical ordering of entities vis-à-vis paramount values within a particular social whole, I argue instead that the comparative basis ('standard') for valuation is implied, negotiated and contested by acts of valuation, when temporal social wholes are transformed into perceptible forms. Visible forms enable a reciprocal recognition and negotiation in which people can value relationships and actions by reference to temporary social wholes suggested by such actions and contested by their responses. Hence, it is by actions that 'settle' the obligation to 'benefit the community' that the person 'appears' as an individual member of that community, while it is by sharing with relatives that the person appears as an embodiment of their relational personhood. While a relationship between a labour migrant in the city and a village relative can take on the perceptible form of a banknote or a changed number on a bank balance, 'the community' can take on the form of the unfolding of organized action, such as felling a large tree for a 'community canoe' or organizing a village business. In such 'appearances', the constitution of social relations as abstract (and invisible) wholes appears in perceptible forms. It is such appearances that others may contest, recognize and misrecognize, and it is in this dialectical process between actors and 'audiences' of action that value as well as the social whole in which value takes form are socially negotiated, changed and reproduced. In this sense Mbuke people do not have a conceptual counterpart to social scientific concepts such as 'a society' or 'a culture' (or even 'a community' as it is sometimes understood) as fixed wholes, since their social wholes are of a provisional kind. In this book I make the claim that such local ideas about the properties of social wholes and their formation can be of assistance to an anthropological understanding of sociality and value.

Fieldwork and the Scope of a Captive's Perspective

On my very first morning in Lorengau, the Manus provincial capital, I was woken by the sound of someone banging on my hotel door while shouting my name. My great confusion about the fact that someone in this part of the world not only knew my name but was able to pronounce it exactly like Danish people do was resolved when I opened the door. I recognized Francis, whom I had got to know when he was in Denmark as part of an exhibition about Manus at a museum where I was working at the time. Having heard of my arrival, he kindly offered to take me to his village for my fieldwork. I politely declined, explaining that I had planned to study the building of outrigger canoes and therefore intended to go to the Mbuke Islands, where such canoes are built in great numbers (cf. Rasmussen 2013). Over the following two days, similar scenes occurred. Another man who I got talking to in the hotel told me that I was very lucky because they had just cut down a tree for a canoe, and that I should come and live with his family on his island. When I first arrived in Manus, I was clearly not the first anthropologist there. In the large village of Pere they have even named a village hall the 'Margaret Mead Hall', and people from there told me with great pride about the many anthropologists who had come to their area. 'Anthropologist' is a far better known category in Manus than it is, say, in Denmark, and having 'their own anthropologist' is something that Manus people take pride in.

After Francis's visit I walked to the large roofed market in the middle of town. The hotel bartender had told me that I would find a few Mbuke women there, selling betel lime (a white powder made from coral, which is chewed with betel nuts), but to my bewilderment half the stalls in the market sold betel lime. In despair, I asked two women in a random stall if they knew of anyone from Mbuke, and in an amazing stroke of luck that neither of us have yet entirely got over, they happened to be the Mbuke women I was looking for. I told them who I was, and they must have spread the word because over the following days Mbuke men started finding me at the hotel. First came a man who introduced himself as what I understood as 'the chairman of Mbuke' (later I found out he was the 'chairman of MIPA'), explaining that he would organize a boat for me to go to Mbuke. The following day, however, without having heard from the first man, there was a knock on my hotel door again, this time by a rather wide and tall man wearing sunglasses followed by two small and thin men. They entered my room and, after a brief conversation, the large man finally said, 'I will take it from here'. And so it happened that I sailed off towards the Mbuke Islands – after, on this man's instructions, having spent all my cash on petrol and canned food – into a bit of a gale in a small open boat.

In many ways, in doing fieldwork among the Mbuke, I have allowed for them to 'take it from here'. This has got me deeply involved in relations and transactions among the Mbuke, but it has in turn tended to limit me a bit in terms of Mbuke people's relations with non-Mbuke people.

In any period of ethnographic fieldwork there are certain limitations as well as benefits attached to the roles and social positions, and hence the knowledge, that a particular researcher manages to access. In turn, the roles and social positions that a fieldworker manages to achieve depend in obvious ways on the researcher as a person (e.g. Jenkins 1994: 445). The more trivial aspects of the researcher as a person are those such as gender, skin colour (at least in PNG) and age. Had I been a woman I would have gained access to other spheres of Mbuke life; had I not been as young as I was the first time I arrived on the Mbuke Islands, I might have had greater difficulty in getting acquainted with young people; and had I not been so European in appearance I might not initially have been associated with 'ol masta' (TP: white people, lit. 'the masters') and the high status often ascribed to them that the term reflects.[5] My own adoption by a specific family and kinship group, along with the role of being a member and representative of the Mbuke community outside PNG, indicates the multitude of ways of being a 'person' among contemporary Mbuke. Common to them both, however, was that I was understood as 'belonging to Mbuke', and during my initial periods of fieldwork this made me feel a bit like a captive.

On my initial arrival on Mbuke Island, I was provided accommodation in a household that, in fact, turned out to be that of a close relative of the man who had taken me there. And so I was thrown right into a potential conflict between kinship relationality and 'community' by being snatched out of the hands of the MIPA chairman, who might have had other plans. Not long after I had moved in with Polongou and Linda, a middle-aged couple, and their teenage daughter, Paula, they gave me a local name. After this the terms of reference changed. Not only did people start referring to me and addressing me as Mwaton (my new name), they also acted to a degree in accordance with the associated kinship relation, of me being the son of Linda and Polongou. For example, my male cross-cousins started joking with me in ways that came as quite a surprise after having been addressed as 'masta', 'big man' and even 'sir' by younger men until then. The relationship between male cross-cousins among the Titan, the ethnic and linguistic group to which Mbuke belong, is often characterized by competition and jesting of a somewhat abusive (though joking) nature, often with sexual connotations (see also Mead 1934: 250–52). Men who had previously addressed me in an overtly respectful manner suddenly began to use every chance they had to insinuate sexual relations between women of the village and me – a common joke in that sort of relationship.

My becoming an adopted member of one particular household made me a son, a cousin, a brother and an in-law, and meant that I had a meaningful place in terms of kinship relations. This made interaction with me much easier because kinship relations often help determine appropriate behaviour, and my being 'someone' among Mbuke people made this possible. Going along with these new relationships meant that I was sometimes instructed as to whom it would be appropriate for me to go and live with, when going to Port Moresby for example, which in itself was a source of insight; likewise, being a relative I was trusted to carry envelopes with money back to people in the villages and otherwise get involved in things that a more distanced observer might not have been able to do. Ton Otto, who did fieldwork on Baluan, also in Manus Province, described his adoption as a moment of social recognition and, indeed, a methodological breakthrough (Otto 1997). Otto looks upon the role that he was given by local people as a kind of 'role play', as we (anthropologists) cannot fill the role we are given fully or properly, and both parties know this (ibid.: 98). This kind of role play may have been what my cross-cousins were doing, although using the word 'play' might erroneously indicate that such actions are not the same as the 'real' actions taking place between cross-cousins who are 'real' Mbuke people. But not all Mbuke people know how to fulfil their role properly either, for instance in ceremonial exchange (as I discuss in the following chapter), and adoption is in fact extremely widespread in Manus, and even adopting someone from another language group is not entirely unusual.

Another way of understanding my adoption may be that by being adopted I filled a void in relationships, replaced a 'road' that had in fact been cut off by death. Mwaton was the name of a son of the couple with whom I lived who had passed away some years before my arrival. He was a university student, as I was at the time, and I was even told that I reminded everyone of him because of my abstracted air and heavy smoking, among other things. A similar kind of replacement has, in fact, been observed in the sphere of leadership among Titan elsewhere in Manus. In some of these cases, if the ageing chief had no suitable children himself, or if they had not survived, members of other families, 'may have taken the places of missing men of the lineage' (Schwartz 1963: 70). The adoption of strangers from other villages or islands further indicates that biological descent was not a prerequisite for a person to become a member and even leader of a family or clan, and the anthropological literature on Manus reports how the kidnapping of children for adoption was widely practised (Schwartz 1963: 86; Fortune 1969: 107, 313; Otto 1991: 59, 74–76; Gustafsson 1999; Mead 2001). In fact, there was indeed a sense of being kidnapped in the way I first went to Mbuke.

Reflecting on his own adoption, Otto has said that certain people had a specific interest in adopting him because the land he was living on could more easily be claimed after his departure by those who were his relatives (Otto 1997: 99). I cannot identify such direct instrumentality in the way I was adopted, but it was clear that initially Mbuke people saw me as a kind of investment, both as a white person assumed to have privileged access to money, but also as a chance to enhance the 'fame' of Mbuke in the wider world by my writings. Mead noted how most adoptions among Titan people in Pere village were carefully planned, and they were often a means to 'widen economic roads' in a network of trade relations: 'adoptions [were] carefully planned to meet deficiencies in the economic strength of the household' (Mead 2001: 58). As discussed in the following chapter, highly educated temporary labour migrants providing remittances is a crucial determinant of the economic strength of most households in the Mbuke Islands. A 'white man' from a Western European country would seem perfect for such a purpose since the few 'white people' who make their way to Manus (NGO workers who distribute money, for example) are often roads to resources. But clearly, I was also seen as a suitable replacement for the son who had died, both in terms of potential future remittances (and in that sense also an asset, although a more local version), and a person who did in fact resemble Mwaton in terms of personality.

Being meaningfully conceived of as a Mbuke person and entering into relationships of the kind that Mbuke people engage in amongst themselves gave me the role of an apprentice (e.g. Wadel 1991: 45). Being Mwaton, I suppose, is a case of what most anthropologists experience during the long process of fieldwork: gradually learning to be a proper person as they are perceived among the people with whom one lives. From my brothers' actions and responses to me, I learned to be an appropriate brother to them. To people in the periphery of the network of relations I came to occupy I am perhaps simply 'the white guy' attempting to behave like a Mbuke man. Migrants and certain village leaders occasionally consulted me on funding applications for NGOs and other funding agencies, when planning 'community projects', and I tried my best to be of assistance. In that sense, I became both a node in a kinship-based network and a migrant member of 'the community'. As I discuss in Chapter 7, my different roles as, on one hand, a person of a particular descent group and, on the other, a member of the community at large, occasionally came into conflict in a similar way to the case of Jacob and his fish project, described above. I also faced restrictions in certain situations as a man whom some might suspect is politically affiliated with certain kinsmen.

Having been 'captured' for adoption by one particular family, and thereby by one particular clan among Mbuke people, I make no claim to be able to see all perspectives. But after all, an ethnographer's perspectives are always partial and positioned (cf. Haraway 1988), although perhaps differing from one situation to another, in which the personhood of the researcher also might differ accordingly. This sort of partial perspective is not a disadvantage as much as it is an advantage, since being meaningfully conceived (or captured) as a certain person among Mbuke people meant that I had to participate in relationships and transactions 'as Mwaton' and that people acted towards me 'as though' I was a 'real Mbuke person'. I saw no point in retaining the role of 'masta' (including 'researcher') since in participant observation that would have mostly taught me about the relationship between 'white people' and local people in PNG, which was never my focus of enquiry. In this book, when I speak of 'Mbuke people', I have no illusions of being able to represent *all* Mbuke people, a few of whom I have never met, since such a task would have been highly difficult (if not impossible and meaningless) and would have prevented me from forming strong relationships and trust with certain persons. Although I try like other anthropologists to account for certain general tendencies in one way or another, the perspective is partial and 'captured' – but this is a consequence of the fact that the tool of the research in question is a human being with certain personal properties.

When Margaret Mead left Pere after her first period of fieldwork there, 'the death drums were beaten', and she argued that at that time Manus people had only a very vague idea of a world outside their own, and so leaving it was in that sense similar to death (Mead 2001: xxvii). As she herself noted (ibid.) following her second visit after the Second World War, much had changed since the 1930s, and places like Denmark are now part of the world of Papua New Guineans as much as Papua New Guinea is part of the world of Danes. Even today, several years after I lived in the Mbuke Islands, I am addressed on the phone and in online chat situations as Mwaton, not as Anders who once came around and played the role of Mwaton for a limited period. For this reason too, I have only changed the names of informants in cases that are particularly conflict ridden, since changing the names of, say, the people I lived with in the village would really only seem odd – everyone knows who I am and where I lived.

In summary, much of my fieldwork was done in the channels through which my Mbuke friends and relatives 'sent me', which hence has limited my insights into, for example, Mbuke people's interaction with other Papua New Guineans in Port Moresby. Whether deliberately or not, I have thereby lived up to the 'collaborative ideal' valued in much anthropological fieldwork (cf. Marcus 1998: 112). This in turn means that this account deals more or less strictly with relations and transactions among Mbuke people themselves, and less with Mbuke people's relationships with others. By noting this I do not mean to blame Mbuke people for possibly superficial accounts of their memberships of diverse religious groups or elite networks in Port Moresby, or friendships with people from neighbouring islands. But I would claim that for the specific questions I have set out to answer here, these issues are of lesser relevance and that their exploration would have been undertaken at the expense of both the depth of the answers to the questions I addressed as well as the social role I gained by being Mbuke's own anthropologist.

The study is based on a total of twenty months of fieldwork among Mbuke people carried out between 2006 and 2012 in periods ranging from one year to a few months. Apart from those on the actual Mbuke Islands, the network of people who identify themselves as Mbuke people living in Port Moresby has been my main field site (for between four and five months), and it is on them that I base my understanding of Mbuke people as migrants. While most of my fieldwork has been conducted in Tok Pisin, I did eventually manage to learn Titan well enough to understand it. All Mbuke people, like most Papua New Guineans, speak Tok Pisin entirely fluently, since it is the daily lingua franca of this province of only 50,000 inhabitants, where thirty different languages are spoken. In some households, such as those that involve intermarriage with other groups, it is even the preferred language of everyday communication.

Book Outline

Chapter 1 serves as an introduction to the historical and ethnographic setting, providing an overview of historical processes during the late colonial era and throughout the years after PNG gained independence, which contributed to making money and remittances a crucial part of the livelihoods of the Mbuke, and the ethnic group to which they belong – that is, the Titan, previously referred to as 'Manus' (cf. Fortune 1969; Mead 2001). Here I argue that sharing on demand among close relatives plays a key role in drawing remittances to the villages. The Tok Pisin word for request or demand, *singaut*, is employed analytically to highlight how a kind of 'demand sharing' (Peterson 1993) plays an important role in the constitution of personhood and social relationships, especially between migrants and non-migrants. In other words, while it has often been pointed out that ceremonial exchange plays a key role in the 'social reproduction of persons' in PNG, informal sharing between close relatives, by contrast, plays a major role in these processes among the Mbuke. *Singaut*, I argue, is the verbal demand of another to value a relationship by making it visible in the form of a response to that request.

My focus in Chapter 2 is an attempt to theoretically develop local concepts of visibility and value. I discuss how *singaut* is acknowledged with acts of sharing, all of which are conceived of as the visual appearance of personhood and relationships – that is to say, visual forms of value. Following Mbuke concepts of vision and visibility used in the context of sharing and other kinds of transactions, I argue that giving is not only a way of seeing, but also of 'making seen' persons and relationships as they are constituted and valued socially. Although the need for visual 'appearances' points to a degree of distrust in words and is analysed as a way of transcending 'the opacity of other minds' (Robbins and Rumsey 2008) I show that particular kinds of verbal utterances do play a role in these same social processes.

Chapter 3 is about the exchange of words. I discuss how gossip and curses, in the form of statements, are ways of reconfiguring relationships in their right order through attempts to draw appearances from others by questioning their will and ability to make such appearances. As a disputed standard of value, the obligation to respond positively to *singaut* is an important indicator of *tawian*, a person's value, as reflected, among other things, in the person's (visually) apparent valuation of others. As this local concept of human worth connotes, value is essentially reciprocally and interpersonally constituted, even if material reciprocity may be completely absent. In this chapter I give examples of ways of responding to a lack of sharing, as well as responses to sharing that cannot be materially reciprocated; that is to say, the problem of value that cannot take visual form.

Conflicts between *singaut* and business are the focus of Chapter 4. I show how attempts to do small-scale business in the villages easily become difficult when customers are friends and relatives with whom one is expected to share. Central to such conflicts of interest is the accusation of selfishness. I argue that these critiques are often ways of manipulating the relevance of kin solidarity. In line with the discussion of reciprocity and sharing above, I point out that the social obligation to give and the social obligation to return are not always fundamentally interrelated; they may even be rhetorically presented as radical opposites. Given that different transactions reveal different kinds of relationships and that most Mbuke people engage in a number of different kinds of relationship, even with the same person, the nature of a specific transaction may not always be entirely clear and therefore open to manipulation. It is this difference that is being manipulated when people who run up debts in other people's trade stores, forever deferring the 'tomorrow' of repayment, present the obligation to return a loan as the refusal of a relationship characterized by the obligation to share. In this chapter it becomes particularly clear that the extent of obligations to help relatives is far from agreed upon, being subject to constant social negotiation in a changing economic situation.

The next three chapters deal with the social negotiation and conceptualization of 'community' as a meaningful social whole that is beyond

◆

specific kin relations (and their concomitant *singaut*) and in explicit opposition to possessive individualism. Chapter 5 addresses the idea of community, both as a level of organization and as a specific concept. I expose its historical roots in the colonial encounter, such as in cooperative plantations, and in past and ongoing social movements such as the Paliau Movement in Manus. I show that community is not simply a pre-colonial social form with a new English label. On the other hand, new kinds of socialities among Mbuke people are not simply deliberate radical ruptures that betoken cultural abandonment since Mbuke people have been highly selective in their appropriation of certain organizational forms from colonial times.

I offer examples of how certain organizational forms and events act as visual 'appearances' of the social whole that is 'the community' in Chapter 6. Here I argue that others may judge a person by their success in meeting 'community' goals: a good person supports a good community, regardless of their obligation to specific kin. I further argue that it is by actions that 'settle' the obligation to 'benefit the community' that the individual 'appears' visually as a member of that community. Such actions are likewise the means by which the community appears in visible forms, in the same way that sharing and remittances reveal the social whole embodied in a relational person understood as a microcosm of relationships (Strathern 1988). But the 'community' is a bigger social whole within which value can also be produced by actions that reveal the person as a part rather than an embodiment (or fractal) of a social whole. Acts of donating to the community show the means by which the constitution of the person – which is revealed as relational personhood by remitting to kin – becomes individual membership in that context.

Chapter 7 centres on a single case of felling a large tree for a 'community canoe'; I discuss the ways in which this reveals the social negotiation and contestation of 'community' as such. As I show, 'community' is not simply 'new lives for old' (Mead 2001), and Mbuke people have their own ways of theorizing totalities and their own dialectical practices of social negotiation. Drawing on a local concept of totalizing and valuating social relations, I argue that organized social actions reveal communal value visually, along with the standards by which such valuation is accomplished. The unfolding of 'community projects' makes claims about what is good for the community, and by doing so about what 'community' involves and contains: claims that may be denied, disputed or recognized by others who exert forms of agency in response to a project as it unfolds. Like other standards of value and acts of valuing, the community and the actions aimed to benefit it are conceived and contested when they are transformed into visible forms.

Notes

1. The name 'Mbuke' tends to be hard for native English speakers to pronounce. While intuitively they might be inclined to pronounce it '*em*-buke', I find that with the specific dialect of the Titan language spoken among Mbuke people, simply pronouncing it 'buke' is a better approximation.

2. Tok Pisin is the most widespread lingua franca of Papua New Guinea, a form of Pidgin English also occasionally referred to as Neo-Melanesian. In the spelling of Tok Pisin terms I follow Mihalic (1989), though this is not always possible, since this language is continually evolving, with new words being incorporated all the time. Where a Tok Pisin word or phrase is recognizably English in origin, the word is given in roman type; other Tok Pisin terms are given in italics. Hereafter, I indicate Tok Pisin terms with the abbreviation TP; words in the other locally spoken language, Titan, are indicated with the abbreviation T.

3. 'Consumption' refers here to the word in the sense of 'eat up, devour, waste, destroy or spend' rather than its more recent meaning in the 'anthropology of consumption' and its application to 'consumer societies' (Graeber 2011: 491).

4. That is to say, there is no part of one person residing in the other until reciprocation (Mauss 1990: 12), if the very distinction between self and other is blurred.

5. The Tok Pisin term 'masta' derives from the English 'master' and reflects, if not racism, then at least ethnocentrism on the part of previous colonial powers in the area who introduced such terms.

1

The Historical Roots of a *Singaut* Economy

———— ◆●◆ ————

On going to Papua New Guinea (PNG) for ethnographic fieldwork, I admittedly nurtured somewhat exotic hopes of experiencing life in a village built from palm leaves populated by people who conducted elaborate ceremonial exchanges. When I first arrived in the Mbuke Islands I had already visited a few other villages in Manus Province. These had lived up to my expectations concerning the appearance of PNG villages, since most houses were made of what Manus people refer to as 'bush materials' (locally harvested sago leaves, branches and logs, for instance). The Mbuke Islands constitute a small group of islands situated off the southern coast of Manus Island, the large main island of Manus Province, which is to say, I had travelled to one of the most isolated provinces in the country, and gone even further to some of the more isolated islands therein. But what first caught my eye in the village on Mbuke Island was an extremely large satellite dish that stood on a pole next to a house. As I was to find out, the villages on the Mbuke Islands are somewhat unique by Manus standards. Almost all the houses are built with what Manus people call 'modern' or 'permanent' materials, such as sheet metal, cement board and sawn timber. When I started enquiring into ceremonial exchange practices in conjunction with childbirth, marriage and other life transitions, I was repeatedly told that such things were 'the ways of the ancestors' and were, in fact, 'a waste of resources'. In this chapter I historically trace how the people of the Mbuke Islands have become so relatively different from many other rural Papua New Guineans, focusing in particular on the gradual emergence of an economy heavily reliant on education, migration and the remittances that play a key role in the reproduction of relationships and personhood in a situation with an increasing absence of ceremonial gift exchange.

Three of the eleven islands that constitute the Mbuke archipelago are permanently populated.[1] In 2009, between 600 and 700 people lived in the village on Mbuke Island, 10 people lived on the nearby island of Pokali, and 150 to 200 people lived all in one village, on the second-largest island of the group, Whal Island. But in addition to this population, between 300 and 400 people who refer to themselves as Mbuke people live in Port Moresby (this includes children and youths born there), and another 100 to 200 are dispersed among other cities and towns of the country, such as Lae, Madang, Rabaul and Manus's provincial capital, Lorengau; and finally, there are a few in some places in Australia. A rough estimate would be that 600 Mbuke people live outside the Mbuke Islands, while approximately 900 live on the islands. This means that approximately 40 per cent of the Mbuke people are absent in conjunction with labour migration. This is not completely surprising since Manus is the province in PNG with the highest degree of 'out' migration, and between 1970 and 2000 approximately 15 to 19 per cent of people born in Manus lived outside the province (Dalsgaard 2013: 285). Nevertheless, Mbuke islanders constitute an extreme case, and by comparison to PNG as a whole this situation is fairly unique, especially considering the level of education and thereby level of income that most Mbuke migrants achieve. Very few are casual labourers; more often they are lawyers, government bureaucrats, politicians or skilled labourers.

Rumour has it that some of the people living on the southern part of Manus Island, who occasionally travel to the Mbuke Islands in small, heavily loaded dinghies to sell their garden produce, call these islands 'the ATM of the south coast'. In other words, if all other options have been exhausted, the Mbuke Islands are a safe bet as far as acquiring some cash is concerned: people are always in need of betel nuts and sago, and more importantly, always in possession of money. Regardless of whether the rumour is true, it says much about the ostensible monetary wealth of these islands. How is it that a small group of islands, relatively far from the provincial capital, has acquired the reputation of being an ATM? The short answer is: remittances, and in the following section I discuss the historical processes, during the late colonial era and the early decades following independence, which made money a crucial part of subsistence, especially among the ethnic and linguistic group to which Mbuke people belong, the Titan. I historically trace how barter with other groups has gradually been replaced by a village economy which is highly dependent on money for a variety of things, including subsistence, and finally the historical roots of how requests (*singaut*) and remittances have largely replaced ceremonial exchange in the reproduction of social relations.

A Historical Overview

According to oral tradition, around the turn of the twentieth century, seven men living in the large village of Pere on Manus Island had 'got tired of being stolen from' and tired of ever more frequent conflicts within the village.[2] Led by a man who later became known as Niachili,[3] they migrated to the Mbuke Islands.

From Pere, the seven men sailed in large seagoing outrigger canoes characteristic of Titan (see Rasmussen 2013) to the Mbuke Islands, where, around 1900, they settled in houses built on stilts over the shallow waters of reefs close to the islands (see Crocombe 1965: 44). Whether they brought their wives from Pere at a later time, or whether they intermarried with the small population which was at the time already living on the highest land of Mbuke Island itself remains unclear in the oral tradition upon which this early part of Mbuke history is based. Since both accounts are given in oral tradition, it might be the case that it was a combination, also because there still are a few Mbuke people and families who claim some kind of descent from the 'original' population of Mbuke Island. The small original population lived as far from the coast as they could – on highest point on Mbuke Island – and spoke a different language from the new arrivals and, according to oral tradition, interaction between the two groups began as 'silent trade', with one group laying out on the beach whatever they wanted to barter for something else and the other group replacing these things with their own produce once their counterparts had hidden themselves away. Eventually, the pre-existing population of the Mbuke Islands became extinct or was assimilated as part of the seven decent groups originating

Figure 3: Map of Manus Province, excluding Wuvulu-Aua, Ninigo and Hermit Islands. Map by the author.

from these seven men. This also means that all Mbuke people speak the language of – and identify themselves as – Titan, the ethnic and linguistic group of Pere and other villages in southern Manus, all of which were in the past built on stilts over the shallow waters of reefs or on small islands.

During the period when the anthropologists Reo Fortune, Margaret Mead and Ted Schwartz conducted their respective periods of fieldwork in Pere and its vicinity, the Titan, who constitute the biggest ethnic and linguistic group in Manus Province, were known as the Manus or 'Manus true', and the province was named after them (see Schwartz 1962; Fortune 1969; Mead 2001). Later they adopted the name 'Titan', which means 'that's right' or 'all right' in the Titan language. In the early colonial and pre-colonial period, Titan people were part of a widespread regional 'system' of ecological specialization in which different kinds of products were bartered between different groups in the area. Titan people themselves still often distinguish between three overall ethnic groups in southern Manus based on this specialization: the Titan, who specialized in seafaring, transport and fishing, and who were more or less landless; the Usiai, who specialized in gardening and rarely came to the shore, and who lived mostly inland on Manus Island; and the Matankor, who practised both fishing and gardening, and who populated larger islands such as Lou and Baluan. These overall categories reflect Titan classification, and the Titan themselves are the only group amongst the three who share one language (Mead 1934: 193; Schwartz 1963: 60). Mbuke people are obviously aware of this, and I have often been told that 'Usiai', for example, include many distinct groups, and that it is a bit rude to address them as Usiai, rather than their specific group names (cf. Schwartz 1962: 211; Crocombe 1965: 4).

In the system of ecological specialization, Titan as well as other groups with similar specialisms, such as the Ponam of northern Manus (see Carrier and Carrier 1989, 1991), harvested fish and other marine products in exchange for sago and other sources of starch, as well as acting as middlemen and traders due to their privileged access to the seafaring technology of large, seagoing, outrigger canoes (see Mead 1930; Schwartz 1963; Rasmussen 2013). While access to land, gardening and domesticated animals are major concerns for many rural Papua New Guineans, Titan based their livelihood on fishing and trade. Not only did they specialize in fishing and seafaring, they actually had something of a monopoly on the technology needed for it – that is, the building of large seagoing sailing canoes – and this 'monopoly' was previously subject to strict ownership rules and was, if necessary, defended with violence and the destruction of canoes (Schwartz 1995: 117; Rasmussen 2013: 84–85).[4] Being in control of open sea transport provided the Titan with a privileged position in the exchange system as middlemen, as well as giving them an advantage in warfare (Mead 1930). As middlemen and people without land, however, they depended on trade and exchange with groups who had access to land, and thereby garden produce as well as materials for the building of houses and canoes. Up until after the Second World War, Titan people lived near small islands or on coral reefs where their houses were built on stilts; there was little production in the villages, and fish was, with few exceptions, their only contribution to the exchange system, apart from transport (Mead 1934: 189).

In many ways, Titan people were the most powerful and the most privileged group in the system of ecological specialization. But this position also made them the most vulnerable to the changes brought about by colonialism, which prevented the respective groups from defending their monopolies and specialisms, which gradually diminished from 1900 onwards (Otto 1991: 131). As ethnic divisions and specialization diminished, other groups began fishing and started demanding money for their garden produce instead of bartering it for fish (see also Carrier and Carrier 1989; Otto 1991). Money gradually became important to subsistence, and especially for people like the Mbuke (cf. Otto 1991: 197). Although monopolies on certain practices such as transport and fishing were broken, the same has not been the case for landownership to the same extent. Titan still have comparatively little land and limited knowledge about gardening. Production in the villages on the Mbuke Islands is still fairly limited apart from that intended for direct consumption, and so the options for making money among people living in the villages are relatively small. Meanwhile, it is now difficult to obtain sago and other sources of starch as a supplement to fish without money. Clearly, one reason why Mbuke people chose education and migration as economic strategies is that they are a necessity in this particular historical situation.

Mbuke people all affiliate themselves with one of seven patrilineal descent groups, which are referred to in Tok Pisin as 'clans', and in Titan as *tali* (see Mead 1934; Fortune 1969). Each 'clan' is based on descent from one common male ancestor (one of the 'first' seven men), and each clan contains between two and five patrilineages, some of which are also called in Tok Pisin 'sub-clans'. The clans are exogamous, and hence women would appear to leave their original clan and become members of their husband's clan after marriage. In this sense, clans among Mbuke people, as among other Titan, may be defined as 'patrilineal unilateral groupings', as Mead (1934: 206) put it. However, it has also been pointed out for Mbuke people that it might not make sense to try to decide whether descent is patrilineal or multilateral since, for example, certain powers over other natal clan members remained with women after having 'left' the clan on marrying. For instance, women inherited specific spiritual powers to affect the destiny of their brother's children, a power which was inherited through the maternal line of their father's *tali* (Gustafsson 1999: 16). I shall return to these spiritual powers in Chapter 3.

Nevertheless, it is fair to say that most activities of ceremonial exchange in the past were based on exchange relationships between different patrilineal descent groups, transactions which were initiated by intermarriage and re-emerged on occasions such as childbirth and eventually in mortuary exchange. The basic formula in mortuary exchange, for example, involves transactions between the natal clan of the mother and the clan of the father of the deceased person. On such occasions, Mbuke people explain that relations between the clans are 'straightened out' (TP: *stretim*) or reconstituted now that a 'road' between the clans has been cut. This idea, that ceremonial exchange 'refashions' social relations, is widespread in the literature on Papua New Guinean mortuary practices (e.g., Strathern 1994: 208; Foster 1995a: 97).

Ceremonial exchanges of this kind are nowadays extremely rare among Mbuke people themselves. On those rare occasions when they do get involved in them – for example, in interaction with other Manus groups with whom some are intermarried – they look for elderly men to oversee their part of the exchange, simply because, as they openly admitted to me, they have very limited knowledge of the specific workings and complexities of ceremonial exchange. When I enquired into ceremonial exchange I was referred to such elderly men who 'know the ways of the ancestors', but even these elderly men themselves told me that they dreaded being involved in such activities out of fear of humiliating themselves by not knowing what to do and in what order. During the approximately sixteen months I have spent on the actual Mbuke Islands, I have seen only two elaborate exchange events, both in conjunction with the death of a person whose specific kin relations caused people from other Manus villages to become deeply involved, which, considering the number of people who passed away while I have been there (more than fifteen), indicates that such exchange events are no longer mandatory or normative. I saw no notable (public) ceremonial exchanges taking place in conjunction with either childbirth or marriage. And many Mbuke people told me that they habitually refrain from such exchange ceremonies, referring to them as 'a waste of money'. This apparent indifference to ceremonial exchange ties into the specific history of periodically radical and rapid social change that has taken place in Manus, especially after the Second World War, but which started, if slowly, around the time when the seven men from Pere migrated to the Mbuke Islands.

It was probably not until after independence from Australia in 1975 that the extent of labour migration and the level of education among

Manus people began to result in remittances becoming an important part of village livelihoods, as is currently the case in the Mbuke Islands. Nevertheless, local people with incomes, from whom money entered village life, have been there much longer. Labour and personal incomes arrived with extensive colonial administration from the beginning of the 1900s onwards, when unskilled contract labour became an option in Manus Province (see Otto 1991: 131–42). For people in Manus, skilled wage labour, especially outside the province, could be availed of from the 1950s onwards (Schwartz 1975: 314–15), but before the Second World War being a 'police-boy' was the most prestigious position obtainable for local men (Otto 1991: 139–40).

Otto asserts that the most profound effect of early labour migration and the presence of 'white people' such as colonial administrators and missionaries was perhaps that, through knowledge about other people's *kastom* (culture, traditions), Manus people were enabled to take a more distant look at their own (ibid.: 139), which in the long run facilitated the process of the 'objectification of tradition' (ibid.: 143). In this process of becoming collectively self-aware, it became clear to Manus people, Otto argues, that 'white people's ways' were generally different from the 'ways of the native' of PNG generally (ibid.: 145). A significant effect of this realization was the observation among Manus people that, '[t]he way of the white man appeared to be more powerful and the lives of white people seemed easier, healthier and wealthier' (ibid.). This led a large section of Manus people to turn against their own way of life as they saw it, and this happened at an especially early stage among labour migrants, some of whom came home from urban centres to promote change (ibid.).

Paliau Maloat, the founder of Paliau Movement for reform in Manus that started a few years after the end of the Second World War, was one of these returning migrants, and he turned especially strongly against 'traditional culture' (ibid.: 147).[5] Returning to Baluan, his native island in Manus, after having worked for, among other things, the colonial police force, Paliau Maloat managed to convince many people in Manus that they should do away with traditional exchange feasts, saying, for example, that ceremonial exchange was a waste of the money that migrants sent home, and that the conflicts and social tensions that exchange feasts tended to create only served to make people sick and die (Otto 1992: 432–33). After the Second World War, such feelings gave rise to what Otto has termed 'the Paliau revolution' (Otto 1991: 150), during which many of the strongholds of the Paliau Movement deliberately abandoned ceremonial exchange between clans since 'old clan divisions did not have a role in the new organisation, which stressed village unity' (ibid.: 166). I shall return to this ideology of 'village unity' for social organization and the emerging idea of 'a community' in Chapter 5, but it is clear from the many accounts of this movement that the move against ceremonial exchange tied directly into an idea of larger social entities than particular kin groups. The strongly articulated hope for, and successful attempts at, leaving behind past 'ways of the ancestors' and becoming more like 'white people' made Manus people – and especially the Titan, many of whom entered the movement – somewhat famous for their quick adaptation to the new economic situation caused by colonization and the presence of foreigners in their midst (see esp. Mead 2001).

Schwartz asserts that after the war a 'whole generation of young men' deliberately tried to adopt what they considered a 'European lifestyle', focusing on achieving literacy, numeracy, English language skills and so on as part of the movement (Schwartz 1975: 315). The movement converged with the colonial administration's introduction of schools in Manus villages, which in turn were especially well received in villages where the Paliau Movement was strong, many of them Titan villages, and Mbuke was (and still is) one of the movement's strongholds. Manus Province became one of the most highly educated provinces in PNG, even though it is among the most isolated ones, and the 'Paliau Movement villages' became the best-educated ones therein. As Schwartz noted, 'young men and women from Manus are disproportionately represented in the educated work force all over Papua New Guinea' (ibid.: 316), and the Mbuke Islands constitutes an extreme example of this to this day. Even today, many Mbuke people echo statements made by Paliau Maloat more than fifty years ago, when they say that big exchange ceremonies are 'a waste of money' (cf. Otto 1991: 149; 1992: 433).

The fact that ceremonial exchange is very seldom observed in the Mbuke Islands today, and the fact that often it is simply not conducted at times when it would have been appropriate, clearly comes – at least partly – from the continued faith that many Mbuke people still have towards the current form of the Paliau Movement. Meanwhile, the absence of ceremonial gift exchange must also be traced to the growing importance of remittances and daily sharing motivated by requests, which, as I demonstrate below and in the coming chapters, plays a large role in the social reproduction of social relations and personhood, perhaps partly in the place of ceremonial exchange.

Get Out Before It's Too Late

Every so often a young woman from the Mbuke Islands arrives in one of the Mbuke households in Port Moresby to act as a maid and to look after a migrant couple's children. While this provides her with the opportunity to experience life away from the small islands of Manus Province, and while it helps ensure that the children of the migrant couple get further exposed to their native tongue, the young woman's parents might also have more cunning plans in sending her to the city. Many admitted openly to me that in encouraging daughters to go away – both to work as maids and in pursuit of education – they hoped to avoid her becoming involved with and potentially becoming pregnant by young men in the village, alliances that often result in many children and hard living conditions. Generally, women living in the village bear children at a much younger age than those who move away for education or work, and the strategy of sending young women to Port Moresby (or other urban centres) also reflects the hope that they might get involved with men from Mbuke enrolled in education or working there during the many gatherings and social events in the large urban Mbuke community. Whereas in the past marriages were often arranged by parents while the couple were still children, plans which were tied into ongoing alliances between clans, a major concern for Mbuke parents today is to ensure that their children are successful not only in becoming educated but also in other ways, particularly by 'getting out of the village' before it is 'too late'. Both hopes for a better life for the young person and the enhanced prospect of remittances from them are given as explanations. Such 'marriage strategies' provide an example of new forms of social relations and economic 'alliances' that people strive for in the context of the growing absence of ceremonial gift exchange and a still more heavy reliance on remittances.

In her book on changing gender roles in the face of 'modernity' (her term) among Mbuke people, Gustafsson describes how the arranged marriages of the past had in the 1990s been partly replaced by a new form of 'arranged marriage' (Gustafsson 1999: 88–91). These appear to reflect an earlier stage in the gradual switch from a focus on inter-clan exchange towards solidarity between cognates. In this new kind of arranged marriage, parents that Gustafsson spoke to hoped that an uneducated daughter might marry an educated Mbuke man as a new form of economic alliance through marriage (ibid.: 89). But the parents of the educated and working man might also see this as an attractive option, as Gustafsson notes, because such a marriage would ensure and enhance the young man's attachment to the village, by preventing him from marrying a woman from another part of the country. Such an enhanced attachment would strengthen a sense of obligation towards village kin, that is, towards the parents themselves (ibid.: 89–90). These marriages were presented not as enforced but as 'helping' their children or 'suggesting' partners for them (ibid.: 91).

The new form of arranged marriage which Gustafsson describes, and the current practices and hopes of Mbuke parents, indicates a tendency towards a greater emphasis on 'the extended family' (ibid.: 23), a term which has entered Tok Pisin and which Mbuke people use themselves. In the past, marriages among Mbuke people – and other Titan – were arranged as alliances between separate clans, sometimes without regard for the preferences of the couple in question (ibid.). Breaching betrothals led to fierce conflicts and large claims for compensation (Fortune 1969: 41–42), since all ceremonial exchanges were more or less related to these alliances, based on 'long-term delayed reciprocity' between clans that continuously confirmed these alliances, which were also highly economic in nature (Gustafsson 1999: 80–82). Marriages constituted economic 'roads' between clans (ibid.: 23).[6] Such alliances between clans have become less important as they are no longer economic in nature (ibid.: 83), and migration and dependency on money from external sources have become a crucial part of the economy. Furthermore, the contemporary hopes and strategies on the part of parents aim at strengthening alliances within certain descent groups rather than between them. The alliance which had become very important in the early and mid 1990s, Gustafsson points out, was that between parents and children, and since parents were losing control over children due to geographical separation and by their no longer having arranged for their marriage as in the past, they now expected 'repayment' for their investment in the child's education (ibid.: 81). Thus, we might say that long-term delayed reciprocity was now between cognates rather than affines.

As noted above, parents do not simply hope that their children will 'get out' out of self-interest – that is, anticipating the prospect of receiving remittances from them; they want their children to have a successful life, and that is less likely to happen by staying in the village. In Dalsgaard's recent account of remittances in Manus, he points out for the nearby island of Baluan that those who have been away as migrants without keeping up with the affairs of the village – such as participating in ceremonial exchange – are said to be 'lost in the bush' when they finally come back (Dalsgaard 2013: 294). For example, Dalsgaard describes how a man who was considered the obvious candidate for taking over the leadership of a clan was bypassed in favour of a man who had lived in the village precisely because he was 'lost in the bush' (ibid.: 295). On Mbuke, by contrast, the vast majority of 'clan leaders' (*lapans*) are returned migrants and, in fact, in 2009 two of them still lived in Port Moresby after having become leaders. One key difference between Baluan and Mbuke is that Baluans are 'Matankor', that is to say, they have gardens and depend less on money for buying foodstuffs, and therefore depend less on remittances. As I demonstrate in the coming chapters, among the Mbuke, the social reproduction of social relations and personhood (including establishing oneself as a potential village or clan leader) is tied up with sharing with one's family, and making donations to the community (cf. ibid.), and so having a successful life among the Mbuke is closely tied up with access to money that may be used for such purposes. If one does not ever 'get out', one is less likely to become a 'traditional' leader.

Most, if not all, households in the villages depend on money for buying petrol, rice, sugar, biscuits, canned meat, tobacco and similar products, bought either in the outlets and trade stores on the islands or in Lorengau, the provincial capital. The most crucial need for money is probably the large amounts used for buying sago (the daily staple, eaten in conjunction with fish) from other groups in the province. Other large expenses are school fees, petrol for the outboard engines of their boats, which are used for transport and fishing, hospital bills and medicines. There are a few seasonal and otherwise highly fluctuating means of making money on the actual Mbuke Islands, including harvesting sea cucumbers and sharks for shark fin from the sea, which are sold in town to buyers for export to Asian markets. Other village produce sold mainly at markets within the province are fish, lime for betel chewing, coconut oil and eggs from wild birds. Finally, some households run a trade store or a petrol outlet in the villages, but these largely depend on an external input of money which cannot be generated by the limited amounts made in local markets. Money has become a necessity, and there are indeed those in the villages who struggle to get by. Parents have good reason to hope that their children 'get out'.

In overall terms, there are two categories of people who 'struggle' in the Mbuke Islands. One of these consists of people who have spent their whole life in the village and do not have many migrant children or siblings to send them money. The other category consists of migrants who have lost their jobs and returned before they had saved any money, and who had not yet built a house in the village. As Dalsgaard points out, Manus migrants make an effort to prepare for their return, for example by building houses and making investments in the village (Dalsgaard 2013: 292–94), and, as I shall demonstrate in the coming chapters, by remaining 'visible while away' through remitting money, and therefore not having to rely on relatives whose requests for help have previously been ignored. A number of unfortunate 'untimely' returnee labour migrants included those working in Rabaul (East New Britain Province) until it was destroyed by a volcanic eruption in 1994, as well as those who had found employment linked to the large Panguna copper mine (in Bougainville), which closed down in the 1990s. In some of these cases, this meant that migrants did not manage to obtain an education for their children, leaving them with relatively small prospect of receiving remittances, while at the same time lacking skills in fishing and other means of subsistence and income available in the village. It also seems clear that Mbuke migrants tend to intensify their involvement

back in the village as they grow older, which is probably partly a consequence of increasing incomes as their careers develop, but possibly also the
corollary to the fact that they plan on going back to the village. There are
many other reasons for dissimilarities with regard to access to money; and
as I suspect is the case in any village, there are those who are hardworking
and successful and do well while living their whole life in the village, and
those who find it more difficult to get by for a variety of reasons. However,
most villagers share the need for an external input of money.

Yap is the term Mbuke people use for temporary labour migrants.
Yap means 'far away' in Titan, and in the colonial period the word often
referred to the places from which white people came, or simply to white
people in general (cf. Mead 2001: 22). Today, *yap* refers to the same thing
that in some contexts is referred to as 'out' in Tok Pisin, a general term
for 'outside Manus', including everything from Port Moresby to Denmark;
in daily discourse, however, it mostly refers to the cities in PNG outside
the Manus region to which Mbuke people usually migrate for work. In
addition, *yap* refers to migrants themselves. In the plural, 'the *yap*' (TP: *ol
yap*; T: *ala yap*) are those Mbuke people who temporarily live elsewhere.
Among Mbuke *yap* there are those who live in big, expensive houses
near the beachfront in Port Moresby, and those who live in more humble
dwellings and share houses with other families, but they tend to live in the
better-off districts of the national capital, and none that I know of live in
the so-called 'settlements'.[7]

The Mbuke migrants in Port Moresby are mainly academics, senior
(and junior) government officials, highly educated professionals and
skilled labourers, such as electricians and carpenters, but there are also
a few informal sector betel-nut sellers and a few casual labourers. In
her discussion of gender roles among Mbuke people in Port Moresby,
Gustafsson asserts that very few Mbuke women living there had formal
employment, and that most were 'housewives', due to the fact that parents
preferred to invest in the education of male children (Gustafsson 1999:
99). Although some Mbuke people (especially men) today confirm this,
and told me that they prioritize boys if they cannot afford school fees for
all their children (school fees are gradually increasing), this seems rather
normative when compared with actual practice. Among Mbuke people in
Port Moresby there are quite a few very successful women in high positions, and although there are many 'housewives' or homemakers, there are
also many women who are both educated and have jobs. To give a few
examples, there is a Mbuke woman working in a management position
for Coca-Cola, one who runs a rather successful private company and one
who is an air traffic controller. The few Mbuke men in Port Moresby who
have no paid job (apart from those still at school or who are retirees) are

in many cases living with Mbuke relatives and more or less formally 'work for them'. But the vast majority of Mbuke people in Port Moresby do work, and tend to be quite well paid, which makes remittances to the villages possible, and in some cases quite extensive. Mbuke migrant incomes are high enough for them to play a significant part in the livelihoods of people back in the villages, not least due to the types of jobs they do.

Mbuke people help each other to get good jobs, and since the older generation (say, those aged forty-five and above) tend to have very high-status, well-paid, white-collar jobs, they also tend to be in positions where they can employ – or influence decisions concerning the employment of – new employees in their workplaces. As Reed notes, it is not unusual to find that employment and promotion in Papua New Guinean workplaces are to some extent effected by what is generally referred to as the 'wantok system' (Reed 2003: 165), referring to a tendency to favour people of one's own language group (*wantok* means a person of the 'same language' in Tok Pisin). In many cases, *wantok*s are people from the same village as oneself in a country of more than 700 different languages (in fact 'indigenous language' is referred to in Tok Pisin as *tok ples*, which literally means 'village language'). For example, one of my closest young informants got his first job as an economist in a government body where another Mbuke man was in a leading position. The *wantok* system permeates much of life in urban PNG and covers everything from booking domestic flights to help during periods of unemployment or being materially supported in paying compensation after having been in a conflict or a fight with a person belonging to another language group in Port Moresby. In that sense it works as a safety net among Mbuke migrants in Port Moresby. The flip side of this involves not having 'same language' persons in the right places, as exemplified by one Mbuke man who had to wait for several weeks for some simple treatment at a hospital because no one from Mbuke had any connections among the hospital staff, and he kept being passed over for patients who did. Younger migrant informants increasingly refer to similar dynamics with the English idiom 'who knows who', which indicates that networks not associated with kin or regional origins also play a role in similar forms of favouritism. While many of the highly educated Mbuke migrants in Port Moresby would often refer to the *wantok* system as the reason for the slow pace of 'development' in PNG, in many cases they also felt that refusing to help fellow Mbuke people get jobs if they could would marginalize them socially and even, in the worst case, alienate them from the village to which they hoped one day to return. Similarly, remitting money to relatives in the village places migrants in a moral conflict between wanting to be able to support their urban family sufficiently and keep up with kin and community obligations back in the villages.

Remittances and Social Reproduction in Manus

It is probably fair to assume that up to 40 per cent of Mbuke people are currently migrants.[8] Working migrants provide a constant input of money to which the village economy has adapted and without which it would have to change radically – otherwise hunger could potentially become a serious problem. Robbins and Akin have pointed out that Melanesia provides a unique opportunity to study the effects of the introduction of general purpose state currencies at an early stage (Robbins and Akin 1999: 2), but obviously, as time goes by, this becomes less and less true. Money has played a significant role in Mbuke people's lives for more than fifty years, and throughout this period remittances have been an increasingly significant source of money in the villages. In this section I provide an overview of previous writings on remittances in Manus, which interestingly all point to aspects of ceremonial exchange as playing a key role in motivations for sending remittances. This raises the obvious question of why and how extensive remittances have 'survived' in the increasing absence of ceremonial exchange among the Mbuke.

Schwartz (1975) provides the earliest description of remittances in Manus in an article about relations among generations among the Titan of the south coast of Manus Island, in the area where the village of Pere is situated. Like most Titan, people in Pere joined the Paliau Movement more or less en masse, but Schwartz stresses how aspects of 'their old culture' (ibid.: 322), as he terms it, had persisted in new forms in the face of the radical changes taking place during the time of movement, and that was what made it impossible for migrants to resist demands for money from home. One of these aspects of the 'old culture' in particular involved exchanges between clans (of the kind described above). Here, Schwartz stresses significant exchange events such as 'buying teeth', an ongoing inter-clan exchange practice in which money (or other wealth) was given to the clan that provided a woman to the patrilineal group to which the givers belong.[9] Such 'payments', which upheld good relations with other clans and reproduced the migrant as situated in their own clan by supporting it were, according to Schwartz, one of the two main ways for remittances to be drawn to the village (ibid.: 318–21). Another way for remittances to be extracted was the money demanded from young migrants by their parents under the threat of being cursed, demands that were hard to resist (ibid.: 320), something which I discuss in Chapter 3.

In 1963, the cash earned from village produce was very little and did not, according to Schwartz, yield change to practices of exchange or economic relations (ibid.: 318), but in exchange ceremonies the presence of money and expensive goods was nevertheless increasing. The source of this wealth was young migrants working elsewhere, who shipped or otherwise sent the necessary articles back from urban centres (ibid.: 319). It would seem that an important factor in drawing wealth from city to village was formal 'inter-clan' ceremonial exchanges, in which such resources were subsequently circulated. Schwartz does not go into great detail on the remitting of money and goods that did not enter ceremonial exchange, but he does note that in the period from 1967 to 1973 the number of outboard engines in the village had gone from 'only a few' to thirty-nine, and that they were mainly paid for by money from the 'salaried progeny of the village' (ibid.: 319). There is no indication that these engines, which were hugely expensive in comparison to people's incomes and other monetary expenses, were drawn into exchanges between discrete clans in the villages. I was told by some of the older Mbuke migrants that back in the early days of their labour migration (1960 to 1980) it was the 'goal', especially of migrant men, to provide both a house and an outboard engine for their parents or close kin (such as brothers), which might indicate that these items did not, at least in the Mbuke case, enter the village through inter-clan exchanges.

In what remains the most thorough description of remittances in Manus, Carrier and Carrier (1989: esp. 62–96) described a situation very similar to that of Mbuke on Ponam Island in the northern part of Manus Province. Ponam is populated by people who occupied a similar position to the Titan in the system of ecological specialization, and previously specialized in fishing. Ponam migrants became, like the Mbuke, highly educated 'elite migrants' who made enough money to send vast amounts of it back to relatives in the villages (ibid.: 167). Ponam in the villages had similarly come to depend to some extent on the input of money after the system of ecological specialization was undermined by historical changes during and after colonization (see ibid.: 62–96). During the Carriers' fieldwork on Ponam Island, they found that one important way for money to be drawn from temporary migrants living and working outside Manus was through requests by close kin, who needed it for participating in ceremonial exchange on the island. According to the Carriers, there were two such ways in which this was done: one involved islanders requesting money from migrants for use in ceremonial exchange on the island, and the other involved money coming directly through migrants' own participation in these exchanges when, on occasion, they returned to the island (ibid.: 213–14).

Carrier and Carrier make it clear that the particular kinds of exchange that were at that time significant were actually significant because of historical processes following colonization, and assert that 'tradition depended on modernity for its survival' (ibid.: 235). This was underpinned by the fact that a large part of the money circulating in exchange ceremonies in fact consisted of remittances from migrants. At the time of the Carriers' fieldwork, Ponam people as a whole spent money totalling an estimated K25,000 annually, but only made around K5,000 themselves (ibid.: 167).[10] This was bound to cause changes. The biggest change that remittances caused to ceremonial exchange, according to Carrier and Carrier, was that 'Big Men' were no longer able to impose debts on younger relatives or allies by funding their bridewealth; relations among generations had changed so that many people had come to depend more or less on children or siblings in towns, from whom they accessed money for a number of things, including ceremonial exchange (ibid.: 195).[11] In this way, the 'patron–client relations' (Carrier and Carrier's term) that Big Men were previously able to impose on others were no longer possible; thus the introduction of new sources of wealth (wage labour) had promoted equality by undercutting and altering the connection between power and wealth (Carrier and Carrier 1989; cf. Otto 1991: 138).

Carrier and Carrier do not describe how the role of these new 'mediators of wealth' (migrants) had developed, or how they managed to connect privileged access to wealth with gaining authority over others, as traditional leaders had managed to do. It seems likely – since most migrants were young – that they did not enter directly into a similar role to the one that 'Big Men' had previously held, which is also confirmed by Schwartz's argument for another part of Manus (that is, the area around Pere) that the older generation still had authority over young people. Carrier and Carrier provide another conclusion that may help explain the apparently small amount of authority gained by migrants when they sent money home, compared to previous mediators of wealth, which also takes us back to the question I raised earlier in this chapter regarding the role played by money transfers in social reproduction.

Gregory identifies two overall ways in which social reproduction takes place, upon which the Carriers draw: one involving the production, consumption, distribution and exchange of things, and the other involving the production, consumption, distribution and exchange of people. Together, the two would work as a structured whole (Gregory 1982: 30). According to Carrier and Carrier, this whole had split into its two parts among the Ponam because the site of the entire process of the social reproduction of persons, taking place in various exchange events, was Ponam. Migrant Ponam had no choice but to contribute or somehow participate in ceremonial exchange back in the village in order to maintain a social position and identity in their community. The other aspect of social reproduction identified by Gregory, that of things, referred to the contribution of migrants who injected money and things bought with money into the local situation on the island. Money was converted into gifts even though it came from the commodity sector outside the island. In that way dependency operated both ways, and ceremonial exchange became crucial in drawing home remittances (Carrier and Carrier 1989: 224–27).

According to Carrier and Carrier, a Ponam person's greatest responsibility was seen as the obligation to help their close kin, and their close kin's biggest obligation was to contribute in ceremonial exchange. So what drew money to Ponam from migrants was ceremonial exchange. Based on this, the Carriers conclude that ceremonial exchange on Ponam was one of the main ways of drawing money from town to village, from migrant to island resident (ibid.: 204).

One might argue, however, that it is the obligation to close kin in the first place that draws in money, regardless of what that money might be used for afterwards, and that is indeed what the situation on Mbuke today indicates, where very little ceremonial exchange is conducted, but the obligation to close kin is important nonetheless. Among the Mbuke too, one of a person's greatest social obligations is, as we shall see, to help their immediate kin, which is not the same as participating in or contributing to elaborate exchange events. The obligation to help kin is mostly practised outside the sphere of ceremonial exchange. Among Mbuke people, social reproduction does not just take place on the island, as was the case for Ponam at the time of the Carriers' fieldwork. The fact that there are so many Mbuke people living in cities like Port Moresby means that Mbuke migrants can retain a social identity as Mbuke people among themselves, and remittances have become a way of upholding social relationships with people back in the village. In 1980, around the time of the Carriers' fieldwork, there were only thirty Ponam people living in Port Moresby (ibid.: 192), whereas Mbuke migrants in the national capital in 2009 numbered more than 300.

Carrier and Carrier do note that requests for money sprang from day-to-day needs for buying food and so forth as well (ibid.: 168), but they leave it at that while placing their emphasis on ceremonial exchange, probably because they see that as the main mechanism for making money travel. By focusing on ceremonial exchange, they run the risk of making it seem as though even money that travels *within* families and clans does so only to be exchanged *between* clans back in the villages, and that inter-clan exchange is what is socially reproductive. However, as we shall see with regard to Mbuke people, it might also be the case that *singaut* (TP: request, demand) and positive responses to it are equally important in a situation in which migration and remittances are significant parts of social life.

A *Singaut* Economy

During my longest period of fieldwork on the Mbuke Islands in 2008/9, I conducted a household survey, which consisted in visiting all households in the Mbuke Islands and asking certain standard questions about overall aspects of livelihoods and life stories. On one such occasion, I visited a man in his thirties who had grown up as the son of a migrant couple outside Manus, but who had not himself been successful in education and had therefore moved back to the village. As a result of growing up elsewhere, he explained, he was not very good at fishing. I asked, 'How do you get food and money and those things, then?' After a pause he said: 'The truth is, I live mostly on *singaut*; sometimes I *singaut* inside the village, but mostly I *singaut* to my family in *yap*'. Strikingly, in nearly all of the households of the Mbuke Islands, I was told that remittances played a significant role in livelihoods, and that most often these transfers were made in response to *singaut*.

Based on estimates made by people residing in the villages, the average Mbuke household receives K1,200 in remittances annually.[12] This figure does not include school fees for children, which are quite often paid by migrant relatives. Additionally, many migrants visit the islands during their holidays and annual leave, and they usually pay for food, petrol and other necessities for themselves and the relatives with whom they stay. Most houses are funded by and built with money from migrants, who also finance most of the outboard motors and fibreglass boats that people own. Even big logs for building outrigger canoes are bought with, or using money from, remittances from migrants. Furthermore, Mbuke migrants contribute money to the many fund-raising activities that take place in the city for 'community projects' in the village (discussed in Chapters 5 to 7). In Manus Province itself, there are relatively few options in terms of wage labour, and the few jobs available (for example in the provincial government) are generally not as well paid as the jobs available in the central state bureaucracy in Port Moresby and other larger urban centres. The entire village economy depends on the external input of money, and this has caused a situation in which a big number of people depend on others. Even those who do not receive remittances themselves depend on them indirectly, by asking those who do for money, by eating in their households or by selling goods and services to them. Mbuke people have adopted the Tok Pisin word *singaut* to describe the overall 'problem' (the word 'problem' is occasionally used by migrants in particular to describe this situation) of people asking for money and other things from those in more privileged economic situations.

The word *singaut* comes from the English words 'sing' and 'out', and it is generally used to mean 'call upon', 'invite' and 'summon', but is also used to mean 'request' and 'demand' (see also Mihalic 1989: 174). The terms 'request' and 'demand' are the relevant translations when the word *singaut* is used with reference to money and other significant resources requested from others among Mbuke people. While I often heard complaints among migrants saying *planti singaut tumas* (TP: 'there is too/very much *singaut*') and similar sentences in which *singaut* is used as a noun, there is also a verbal form, as in *brata blo mi save singautim mani* (TP: 'my brother usually *singauts* for money'), but for the sake of clarity I shall simply use *singaut* for both. There are many different ways to *singaut*, varying in accordance with the concrete relationship in which it takes place. But what they all have in common is that *singaut* refers to the attempt to make other people share when they do not do so unsolicited, and in that sense *singaut* is very similar to what Peterson (1993) has described as 'demand sharing': sharing initiated by the receiving party. *Singaut* is a general term which covers diverse kinds of demand that are deployed in different situations and different kinds of relationship. Remittance transfers, for example, are mainly drawn to the village through requests from receivers who stand in relation to migrants in terms of specific kinship relations, such as parents and children or siblings. As the following case of a set of siblings from Mbuke exemplifies, *singaut* is an important part of what draws remittances to the villages.[13]

Andy is a skilled labourer but, he told me, he got tired of working for other people, of the long working hours and of getting paid so little. He felt he was wasting time living in Port Moresby, and with the help of a wealthy older brother he started his own small business in the city. He does not seem to accumulate much, and even though the business makes a good profit, it still took him more than one year to save up for a new windscreen for his old car. This, he says, is because he sends too much money to his relatives in the village. When his parents were still alive he mostly sent money to them, and they distributed it further as they wished. Now he sends money mainly to his siblings, but also more generally to other people who *singaut*. The premises of the small business are physically conjoined with his rather large house in which a number of other Mbuke people also live more or less permanently. One young woman is employed to take care of Andy's young children, and three young men who, in terms of classificatory kinship, are Andy's sons (because they are sons of brothers or classificatory brothers) also live in his house. These young men occasionally work for Andy, while one of them is also enrolled at college. I asked Andy to try to calculate his 'expenses' in relation to people back in the village over one year, and the estimate he arrived at was K10,000. In this he included both direct remittances and money donated to a number of fund-raising activities that had taken place among Mbuke people in Port Moresby during the period in question. Together we calculated that this was nearly half his income (after deducting expenses for electricity, the mortgage on his house and so on), something that also surprised him.

Andy sends money to the village quite frequently; this is confirmed by those who receive his remittances, and I sometimes acted as a carrier myself. One sister who lives in the village calls him regularly, and on such occasions he sends her about K200. He also pays the school fees for her two youngest children. Andy also has a sister who lives in Lorengau with her husband, who also works there. She also *singauts* to Andy occasionally, even though her husband earns an income, but she and her husband are, in turn, also subject to a kind of *singaut*. Living in Lorengau they receive many visitors from the islands when these are 'in town'. I often went to their house when I was in Lorengau, and I have not yet been there without there being people from the islands hanging around – and eating – there, while being in town on other errands. This has resulted in a situation where Andy's sister and her husband are always short of money and food. Paul is Andy's older brother, and now lives in Manus after having retired from a senior government position, and he too occasionally *singauts* to Andy for money. The problem for Paul is that even though he has children, who are usually the primary senders of remittances to elderly people (see Table 1), they are all women and married. Paul's daughters do not work themselves, and therefore he finds it hard to *singaut* to them because it would in reality be their husbands' money he would receive, and Paul explains that he finds it a bit shameful to *singaut* to an in-law (T: *kayo*). As indicated in the discussion of marriage strategies above, not everyone shares this view.

Another way to *singaut* that was increasingly becoming a challenge for Andy and others in Port Moresby at the time of my fieldwork was people sending text messages asking for credit for their own phones. This took place at a time when a feature making it possible to transfer credit from one phone to another was introduced – which suited *singaut* almost too well.[14] While on the subject of mobile phones, I have heard about people who keep changing their phone number to limit the number of relatives who have it, and I have observed Mbuke migrants not answering the phone when they recognize a Manus number in the display, simply to avoid *singaut*, the problem being that you need to have a good excuse ready if you are going to say no to certain kinds of kin – especially classificatory siblings and classificatory parents. When people from the Mbuke Islands arrive at the beach in Lorengau, they all hasten to find a place where they can charge their mobile phone, and once that has been done the text messages of *singaut* start going out. It is not unusual to send the same request to a number of people in *yap*. I know that siblings who are migrants sometimes check up with each other when someone asks for something, enquiring 'Did that person also call you?' or 'How much did you give her?' and so on.

Nearly all the Mbuke migrants I spoke to told me that they only send money to people when asked for it, and 'if they need it'. It was often a subject of laughter and anecdotes during gatherings of migrants to talk about how to react when a Manus phone number appeared in the display of a mobile when it rang. 'Oh no, not again', was the reaction of one migrant man. On the other hand, there is a certain ambivalence towards *singaut*, because not being subjected to it might indicate that village relatives are losing faith, both in the migrant's financial abilities and in their willingness to maintain a relationship with them. In this sense, *singaut* is not simply a necessary evil; it also constitutes a form of much needed social recognition. Migrants also take great pride in helping relatives, and in being trusted to be able to help. For example, on one occasion I overheard a conversation in an exclusive club in Port Moresby between a Mbuke migrant and another member of the club, during which one of them said, 'So, how many people depend on you, back in the village?' The query shows that a migrant's relationship with the receivers of remittances is not the only social setting in which a person can produce a particular social identity by remitting. In this sense, when someone says 'oh no, not again' it is probably important to note the 'again', and to note the fact that they say it out loud for others to hear.

What is clear from the case of Andy and other Port Moresby migrants is that the sharing of money on demand – on *singaut* – is a big factor in the process of transferring money from migrants to the villages. What is also interesting when inquiring into remittances among Mbuke people generally is the fact that nearly all of this money is transferred between people with specific kinship relations, that is, within relations of close kinship who need the money for immediate consumption. This observation runs counter to previous accounts of remittances in Manus, which have emphasized exchange between distinct descent groups (inter-marrying patrilineages in particular) as the vehicle for the transfer of money. This indicates that sharing on demand is an important aspect of the ongoing social reproduction involved in transactions.

Table 1: Primary senders of remittances in terms of kinship relations.

Man's brother	Man's sister	Couple's children (unspecified)	Couple's daughter	Couple's son	Woman's brother
16%	12.5%	12.5%	10.4%	8.3%	8.3%
Man's siblings (unspecified)	Man's cousin-brother	Woman's sister	Woman's siblings (unspecified)	Woman's parents	Man's parents
8.3%	6.3%	4.2%	4%	2%	2%

Table 1 illustrates relationships to the primary senders of remittances based on household surveys. Although this is based on only on statements collected from a sample of forty-eight households in the Mbuke Islands, it does indicate one thing: people seem to receive remittances from immediate relatives (siblings, children, parents). The 'respondents' here were asked to account for who they mostly *singaut* to, so the results do not include unsolicited sharing or infrequent *singaut*. The figures are striking nevertheless.

As Annette Weiner pointed out, the preoccupation with the norm of reciprocity has promoted a focus in economic anthropology on things in circulation between groups, rather than those specific possessions that are kept out of inter-group circulation, but which nevertheless 'act as ... material agents in the reproduction of social relations' (Weiner 1992: 3). Weiner points to the role that 'keeping' certain things within a group plays in the reproduction of a group's connection to ancestral, mythical or divine authority, making it 'retention not movement, [which] bestow[s] value' (ibid.: 4). She states that this aspect of social reproduction mediated by material things has been overlooked because it often took place in what was associated with 'the domestic sphere', which has been seen as separate from 'the public sphere' in which ceremonial exchange took place (ibid.: 7).

Focusing on *singaut*, I mean to point to a similar area of transaction that has been overlooked in favour of a preoccupation with ceremonial exchange, namely less formal sharing among close relatives of the same patrilineage. Such sharing often takes place on demand, something that Mbuke people usually refer to as *singaut*. There is a sense in which *singaut* operates in the domestic sphere more than the public sphere because it takes place between people who have at some point been part of the same household (parents, children and siblings). One popular idiom often used to morally explain both *singaut* and the sending of remittances is precisely that the relations involved are those between people who used to 'eat out of the same bowl', referring to how, particularly in the past, the whole household in the Mbuke Islands would gather around one large wooden bowl in which sago was served.

As Peterson has pointed out, there is a general tendency among anthropologists to focus on unsolicited giving in contexts where generosity and sharing are important ethical values. This focus means that the role played by sharing on demand, or generosity that is activated by active request by the receiving party, has been overlooked (Peterson 1993: 860). Peterson's term, 'demand sharing', has been widely adopted to describe such practices (e.g. Macdonald 2000; Peterson and Taylor 2003). Accounts of this phenomenon – and the concept as such – have their roots in studies of indigenous Australians, and 'sharing' more generally has usually been associated with studies of people categorized as hunter-gatherers (e.g. Macdonald 2000; Wenzel, Hovelsrud-Broda and Kishigami 2000; Peterson and Taylor 2003; Jiménez and Willerslev 2007); meanwhile, Melanesia has been associated with exchange and spectacular distributions governed by ongoing reciprocity. The importance of *singaut* among Mbuke people, as I show in the following two chapters, shows that a kind of demand sharing is also present in Melanesia.

Both demand sharing and the Mbuke version, *singaut*, play important roles in social reproduction, that is, in the ongoing (re)constitution of social relations and personhood. Peterson argues that generosity and sharing in 'small-scale societies' should not be confused with connotations of unsolicited and altruistic giving that 'generosity' has for 'Westerners', and states that 'more emphasis should be placed on the constitution of social relations through social action' of such sharing (Peterson 1993: 861). In the case of Melanesia and PNG specifically, I might add that ceremonial exchange has received a great deal of attention in discussions of how transactions help constitute social relations (e.g. Gregory 1982; Strathern 1988), while the small-scale, informal and pragmatic sharing of daily life and its role in the constitution of social relations and personhood needs further attention. This is not to say that anthropologists, such as the authors cited here, for example, leave no space for sharing or transactions within particular descent groups or households rather than between them. Rather, I want to point to the socially productive and reproductive role played by sharing, which has occasionally even been contrasted with ceremonial exchange precisely on the grounds that the former is not productive of social relations: 'domestic reciprocity contrasts with the social productivity of ceremonial exchange where wealth mediates new relationships' (Strathern 1988: 262). Strathern obviously makes this point for a part of PNG where this is presumably the case, and she further explains how domestic reciprocity simply reveals the multiple kinship origins of a person (in both maternal and paternal kin) that such transactions 'simply confirm' (ibid.). However, among the Mbuke, as I demonstrate in the next chapter, even very close relatives can turn entirely invisible (even when physically present) to one another in the absence of sharing. Furthermore, in the classificatory kinship system of the Mbuke, whether someone is a brother or a cousin can in a sense be a matter of choice, since people in this relatively small group are related to the same person in a number of different ways, one of which may be foregrounded depending on which 'road' of kinship one chooses to reveal, for example through transactions.

Mbuke provides a good case for exploring social reproduction through informal sharing (including remittances) among close relatives because ceremonial exchange plays a relatively small part in daily life by Papua New Guinean standards, and because money (especially from remittances) has become such an important part of village subsistence. Demand sharing is a good place to start because, to repeat the quote from Macdonald provided in the Introduction, this particular term refers to the 'moral obligation to respond to demands rather than an obligation to reciprocate a "gift"' (Macdonald 2000: 91), thus counteracting the legacy in economic anthropology of focusing on exchange relations involving the obligation to reciprocate (ibid.). While Peterson and Macdonald see demand sharing as a kind of cultural practice that exists despite change – that is, as something which is potentially threatened by the market economy (ibid.: 108) – among Mbuke people it seems that to have grown in extent as a consequence of the historical processes that began with the colonial encounter and the introduction of a commodity economy.

Why Do Migrants Return?

In 2009, a conflict arose over a dead body. The deceased had retired from a senior army position, and his son felt that it was appropriate that he be buried in the army cemetery in Port Moresby. Village relatives, on the other hand, argued strongly that he should be buried in the village, and when finally this was agreed upon, 'the community' organized the cleaning of the village seafront and set up fences and decorations for a parade in which the casket was carried from the house where it was temporarily placed to the cemetery outside the village. As I noted in the Introduction, while social affiliations and networks involving Mbuke people with non-Mbuke people largely fall outside the scope of this study, they nevertheless increasingly compete with Mbuke migrant identity as, for example, a 'Moresby-Mbuke' person, or in this case compete with a workplace identity. In time it must be assumed that a decreasing number of migrants, or children of migrants, will return to the islands, perhaps not even after death. As it is, however, nearly all Mbuke migrants I have spoken to in Port Moresby plan to return at some point. Before I conclude this chapter and go on to consider the more specific concepts of value and personhood involved in remittances and sharing in the next two chapters, it might be useful to briefly consider why Mbuke migrants return to the villages after retirement or earlier. The plan to return after retirement obviously has a part to play in causing a continuous need to be 'socially reproduced' as a Mbuke person while absent (cf. Dalsgaard 2013).

Most Mbuke people living away from the islands say that they mean to return after retirement, and throughout the seven years I have visited the islands, I have seen many cases of them doing so. There is a variety of reasons for doing so: one is that they will no longer have an income and will therefore find it difficult to survive in the city; another reason (and the reason most Mbuke people stress) is that they prefer village life, that they would like to die back home, and that there will be somebody to look after them when they grow old. I have never heard of any Mbuke person being buried outside the Mbuke Islands, and in 1999 neither had Gustafsson (1999: 78). The fact that most migrants plan to go back naturally plays a major role in motivating remittances, since they are interested in maintaining good relations back home (cf. Otto 1991: 247; Gustafsson 1999: 68; Dalsgaard 2010: 231). In this regard, the Mbuke situation is very similar to the situation Carrier and Carrier describe for Ponam Island: here, the actions of migrants were also affected by their wish to return eventually to the island and their corresponding need to maintain good relations with the family back there (Carrier and Carrier 1989: 190). Based on fieldwork carried out around 1980, Carrier and Carrier predicted that the need for migrants to go home to their village might be about to change, because pensions were introduced, and the houses owned and provided to public servants by the state were sold off at a rather low price to residents, offering them the chance to stay in the city permanently (ibid.:198–201). If Mbuke migrants are anything like Ponam migrants, this prediction has not yet come true, although the new practical possibilities have probably had some impact. There are other reasons, apart from economic ones, for people to go back to the village when they grow old. Among Mbuke people, staying in the city after retirement has only happened in a very few cases.

Many of the more highly accomplished Mbuke migrants have in fact bought property and now have a place to stay in the city, even to the extent of being able to rent out their property or selling it to go and live in a smaller house and live off the profit for the rest of their lives. Pensions, on the other hand, have proved highly unreliable for many retired Mbuke people, with pension payments (from the army, police, fire department and 'works department' in particular) being hard to actually get disbursed. Economic considerations alone (such as housing and pensions) do not take into account the fact that both Ponam around 1980 (ibid.: 200) and Mbuke people in 2010 tended to agree that they preferred life in the village to life in town; such explanations were also given to Otto by Baluan labour migrants in the late 1980s (Otto 1991: 247). It is not surprising that they identify with the village in which they were born, because often a Papua New Guinean city-dweller's identity is very much tied up with their village of origin (see Carrier and Carrier 1989: 200; Errington and Gewertz 2004: 92), and most Papua New Guineans I have met in Port Moresby bring up the subject of their place of origin (TP: *ples*, often referring to their village) within the first few minutes of a conversation (see also Hirsch 2010). This attachment may be, as Carrier and Carrier assert, a matter of a material need for clan rights and membership after returning, but as they also say, it is a matter of social identity as well (Carrier and Carrier 1989: 200). In addition, it may also simply be the emotional bond that many Mbuke people do, after all, feel for the place where they grew up and the relatives and friends they have there. And village life is, to be fair, cheaper, less stressful and in some senses safer than life in, for example, Port Moresby. The young generation, however, particularly those born outside the Mbuke Islands, may turn out not to feel the same degree of affiliation to the islands they may have only visited a few times or even never. A growing number of Port Moresby residents refer to themselves as 'Mosbi Mosbi', that is, a Port Moresby resident who originates from Port Moresby, rather than, as is otherwise often the case, as for example 'Mbuke Mosbi' or 'Mbuke *yap*'.

Conclusions

When the 'first' seven men took off from Pere, Titan people were still part of a more or less closed regional economic system in Manus, but this is no longer the case, and what determines the economic strength of a house-hold on Mbuke has long been affected by colonial history and national politics in the postcolonial nation-state, as well as things like the demand for dried sea cucumber in Hong Kong. This does not mean, however, that Mbuke people are simply victims of such a history, since they have been more successful than most in responding creatively to their circumstances by getting an education, jobs and access to money. The aim of this chapter has been to provide a historical overview and introduction to the context of the study, a history to which more detail will be added in Chapter 5, in which I deal with, among other things, the historical emergence of the concept of 'community'.

I have indicated in this chapter that remittances often take the form of sharing on demand, and that social reproduction mediated by transfers of money is no longer tied to 'traditional' kinds of transaction such as cere-monial exchange. In the accounts of Schwartz and the Carriers, money was very much drawn back to the village following demands, typically from older relatives who used it in ceremonial exchange; as Carrier and Carrier point out, this was important for the social reproduction of persons and groups. Ceremonial exchange revolving around alliances between 'clans' in particular was underlined as an important factor in drawing money from cities to villages in these earlier accounts. What I have indicated in this chapter is that demand sharing, or *singaut*, between close relatives (rather than ceremonial exchange) is currently the most significant factor in the social reproduction mediated by the circulation of things such as money. More detail will be added to this claim in the following chapters.

This means that while the relationally constituted person has often been associated in Melanesian anthropology with ceremonial exchange, another way of making a relationally constituted person 'appear' and be constituted involves informal sharing practices involving less formal reciprocity and less spectacular transactions. While I have indicated in this chapter that *singaut* and sharing are important in social reproduction, the way this is related to personhood is not yet clear. In the following two chapters I aim to provide more detailed discussion – exemplified by remittances and other kinds of sharing – of the constitution of personhood and processes of value formation more specifically. I especially want to draw attention to the concept of the person and the person's constitution in social relations, and how this is reflected in the concepts, metaphors and practices of giving as well as making others give.

Notes

1. This number depends on what size of island one includes. The number does not include the unpopulated Perdy Islands, of which Mbuke people also claim ownership.
2. Pere is the original village from which Titan migration throughout Manus started, according to oral history. Pere is referred to as Peri by Mead (1934, 2001), Fortune (1969) and Schwartz (1962), who all did fieldwork there or in its proximity.
3. Niachili means 'that which cut [the village]' (T: *nga*, from which *nia*, 'cutting device'; *chilli*, 'to cut'). This refers to the fact that he 'cut off' a part of Pere by initiating migration.
4. Using terms such as 'monopolizing' and 'ownership' for describing specialized and 'possessed' knowledge is a bit of a simplification here. I have discussed the form of property relations concerning canoe-building skills elsewhere (see Rasmussen 2013: 73–111), where I conclude that canoe builders in the Mbuke Islands look upon their skills not as a possessed object separate from an alleged individual subjectivity of theirs, but rather as an inalienable part of their personhood that may in particular ways be passed on within the patrilineal descent group.
5. For detailed accounts of the Paliau Movement, see Schwartz (1962), Otto (1991, 1992) and Mead (2001).
6. On relations and alliances as 'roads', see also Mead (1934: 228) and Fortune (1969: 94).
7. 'Settlements' are more or less slum-like unregistered areas of Port Moresby, where the crime rate is said to be highest.
8. Both the number of people living in different locations, which is mostly based on estimates made by myself in collaboration with Mbuke people, and the percentage of migrants among Mbuke should here be seen mainly as indications, since exact numbers would not be easy to produce nor particularly crucial for my purposes here.

9. 'Buying teeth' might literally have referred to pre-masticating the food for her children (who genealogically belong to the giver's group), which might in a sense wear down her teeth (Schwartz 1975: 318). Today, these payments are called *baim blut* (TP: 'pay-off/compensate the blood') on Mbuke, a term explained by referring to the fact that women bleed while giving birth, and have to work hard to bring up children that are members of another clan. The maternal clan will be given the most in distributions because they gave something that one could say they 'reproductively' have no gain from.

10. The national currency of PNG is the kina (K). At the time of fieldwork 1 kina was approximately equivalent to 0.3 Euros.

11. Carrier and Carrier's use of the term 'Big Man' largely follows Sahlins: a Big Man is a man who becomes a leader by his own efforts and builds his name through accumulation and distribution (Sahlins 1963: 291). In this book I do not use the term Big Man for Mbuke leaders since, as Dalsgaard (2010: 106) and others have pointed out, traditional leadership in the southern part of Manus is a combination of achievement (like Sahlins's Big Men) and hereditary leadership 'received' from others. See Rasmussen (2013: 83–95) on receiving aspects of personhood.

12. This figure is based on a survey of all households on the Mbuke Islands.

13. In the following, I have changed the names and other defining features of this set of siblings to avoid potentially damaging significant relationships among my informants – such as by revealing specific complaints about someone's endless requests or lack of generosity, complaints that would have been put differently if those complained about were addressed directly.

14. My longest period of fieldwork (2008/9) was conducted at a time when mobile phone usage was spreading rapidly in PNG.

2

Visible While Away

Concepts of Vision in Exchange Practices

———————— ◆●◆ ————————

During my longest period of fieldwork (2008/9) I decided to map out the kinship relations of all living Mbuke people. This turned out not to be as straightforward as I thought it would be, as the following example illustrates. I was asking a young man how many brothers he had. He told me he had two, both of whom were away as labour migrants. It so happened that I had also interviewed his parents, who had informed me that they had four sons, three of whom were labour migrants. I asked the young man again, presumably looking suspicious or confused, if he had just two brothers. He replied, 'Well, there is another one, but I don't know about him, he doesn't know about me, he never sees me. Maybe he's dead or has become a criminal or something'. I argue in this chapter that it was no coincidence that the young man used the word 'see' when criticizing his third brother, and that in fact there is a problem of invisibility between them, explaining why he did not mention him initially.

Requests and remittances in response to them are ways of valuing relationships, even determining the qualitative existence of the relationship and the aspect of the involved parties' personhood that constitutes the relationships. But the question is not simply one about the existence of the relationship, for it involves the value of the relationship and of the persons involved. My informants frequently expressed the notion that in knowing what another person knows and feels and what relationships a person recognizes, words alone are questionable; rather, relationships and the value ascribed to them should show in visual form. In that sense, words cannot fully be trusted to reveal the invisible, but can only, in such contexts, refer to that which has become manifest in visible form.

Rendering invisible things such as intentions, relationships and the interior aspects of one's personhood visible in actions of giving, and as things given, are ways of making others see what is in one's own mind, helping illuminate what has been termed 'the opacity of other minds' (Robbins and Rumsey 2008). I argue that this is what remittances are in this case; they are persons and their relationships appearing in perceptible forms, even if the people involved are far away from where they assume appearance in social relations. Remittances are familial love, relations between kin and, ultimately, personhood in perceptible form; they are one among many ways for concrete persons' personhood and the nature of their relationships to be transformed into temporary material or visual forms.

This chapter addresses the ways in which personhood and relationships are constituted in practices of sharing in particular, and exchange more generally. Thus it helps to explain why and how flows of remittances are maintained. Among Mbuke people, a number of local concepts of seeing, visibility and vision are used to describe ways of and motivations for giving. In this chapter these concepts are mostly discussed in terms of remittances, but they are also related to other exchanges which take place in the villages. Using such concepts Mbuke people point to the ways in which certain actions make visible that which is otherwise invisible. I argue that this need to make social relations visible comes from a general distrust of words, and also points to a certain concept of the person. The need to make intentions, relationships and one's person visible by means of sharing and giving points to ways of accessing 'other minds' by observing their actions, and points to how actions are ways of making others see what is in one's own mind. I argue that such actions are embodied perspectives as they appear in perceptible forms (such as money transfers) which help constitute and contest social forms (persons and relations, for example). This chapter theoretically develops local concepts of visibility and value, concluding that value results from a dialectic between questions and answers.

Karen's Christmas

As I pointed out in the discussion of my own adoption on Mbuke in the Introduction, kinship is not fixed and tied to biology among Mbuke people. Adoption is widespread and kin relationships are subject to continuous confirmation, constitution and negotiation; or, to use the analytical term that I wish to elaborate on here, they are 'made to appear' as visual embodiments. For example, mortuary exchange among Manus people often gives rise to discussions of what the kinship relations of the deceased were, since these relations are reflected in the way money and other exchange items are distributed (see Suhr, Otto and Dalsgaard 2009). In line with this point, I have observed – during the few mortuary exchanges that took place during my time on the Mbuke Islands – how discontent with the 'share' received is expressed with reference to having a closer relationship in terms of kinship than that indicated by the 'share' received relative to the total sum of money and other things distributed. Here arguments such as 'I used to feed him, so I should have a bigger share' may be heard, which indicates that bringing up and feeding children establishes and constitutes kin relationships as much as biological descent (cf. Carsten 1997). Here we see how in ceremonial exchange a fairly clear reference to formal reciprocity is made: some people feel they should be reciprocated for having contributed to a person's upbringing by the close relatives of the deceased. Such elaborate exchange events are very rare among Mbuke people, and, as I indicated in the Chapter 1, more informal sharing among relatives now plays a central role in social reproduction. In other words, actions of sharing more often constitute the visual 'appearances' by which persons are constituted in terms of kin relations. While it might be common practice to share with close relatives elsewhere, here I want to point to how relationships and persons of particular kinds are redefined, questioned and confirmed by even the smallest and seemingly most insignificant actions of sharing. The following example involving a young Mbuke migrant visiting the village for Christmas illustrates this well.[1]

Unintended pregnancy is not unusual among young Mbuke women. It is often the case that relatives living in the village adopt the children resulting from it, especially if the young couple in question are enrolled in education and therefore live in one of the bigger cities of the country. One such couple are George, a man who later went on to become a successful and highly placed civil servant in Port Moresby, and Margaret, a woman who lived and still lives in the village and never migrated, or 'went to yap'. When they were younger, the couple had a daughter, Karen, but since George lived in Port Moresby (except during the holidays) and was enrolled at the university, the child remained with Margaret in the village. Later, when she married, her husband Jeff adopted Karen as his daughter.

During my first visits to Mbuke Island, Karen attended high school in Lorengau, and for holidays and on weekends she came to the village and stayed with her parents. In high school she did quite well, and was an obviously capable of going on to higher education in Port Moresby, but her parents could not afford the school fees involved. As is often the case in situations like this, they looked towards wealthy migrant relatives to sponsor the significant tuition fees that university education requires. In this case, the young woman's biological father stepped in; he is now a wealthy man living in Port Moresby with a family of his own. He said that she could live with him in Port Moresby and that he would pay for her education.

When I met Karen during her first Christmas back in the village after she had moved to Port Moresby, I noticed that while she had in earlier conversations with me referred to Jeff in Tok Pisin as 'papa' (T: *papu*), she now referred to George as 'papa' as well. I should note that it is not unusual in a classificatory kinship system for the same person to refer to many men as 'father'. However, in this situation the two would seem to preclude one another, seeing that they are not brothers nor even members of the same clan. George was also back in the village that Christmas; in fact, he had paid for Karen's trip and given her some cash for her to use in the small trade stores in the village. One day during that Christmas holiday I went to George's house to see his younger brother, who lives in the house permanently. As the brother was not around I sat down and started chatting with George. As we sat there Margaret, Jeff and Karen turned up and sat down. In contrast to the direct and confident attitude I otherwise associated him with, Jeff seemed nervous from the outset. The conversation took place mainly between Jeff and George, while both Margaret and Karen sat looking down most of the time. Jeff said that he thought it was a problem that Karen walked around the village just as she wished, and that she should stay with her parents instead. In his opinion, George should have come directly to Jeff and Margaret's house and delivered Karen to them when he and Karen arrived on the island a few days earlier. By doing so he would have made it clear that she should live with them during her stay, and that they would be the ones to take care of her when she was in the village. Jeff continued by saying that her visits to other households would then have been under their supervision. I later found out that the problem was that Karen had not gone directly to her parents' house after arriving on the island, and that Jeff and Margaret felt that this questioned their parenthood. Instead, she had been 'going around' the village on her own and had bought food in trade stores, rather than eating in their household.

Jeff said, 'If she has money she must give it to her parents, she must recognize her parents, she must love her parents!' George responded that he had simply given Karen a bit of money in order for her to be able to buy 'a few (small) things for herself', to which Jeff – who was becoming increasingly vocal – responded that such things were 'the parents' job' (TP: *wok blo papamama*). George responded by saying, 'there is nothing of what you are saying that I disagree with', and after a while he added that the money was simply intended for her to buy 'women's things' (sanitary towels, he later explained to me). Without commenting directly on that statement, Jeff repeated his argument that they as parents should look after her when she was in the village, and George repeated that he agreed. While Jeff was obviously tortured by the situation, George answered the criticism in a calm tone, seemingly unaffected by what seemed to be of utmost significance to Karen's parents. Eventually Jeff and George shook hands, and Jeff, Margaret and Karen walked off towards Jeff and Margaret's house.

On the face of it, this might seem simply to be a case of co-parents disagreeing about the strictness required for raising their teenage daughter, but I would suggest that it actually reflects the way in which even small actions 'make' kin relationships 'appear'. Had Karen been 'turned over' directly to Jeff and Margaret by George, his action would have acknowledged that they were the parents. In equipping her with money and failing to take her to her parents, he was seen by Jeff to be questioning this fact. It probably did not help that Karen had spent large quantities of time in George's house. To Jeff and Margaret, the situation was especially sensitive, since by failing to take her to them and by giving her money George could be seen to be claiming back his fatherhood of Karen. To them, this would not only be emotionally distressing, it also questioned their parenthood in terms of authority over her whereabouts. And notably, it questioned the principle that they should be given some of the money to which she had access, money that she instead had used in trade stores, 'making appear' for others to see that she had her own money. Everyone in the village knew that she could not have been given this money by Jeff and Margaret, who are not very wealthy. Karen, for her part, had failed to 'recognize' (TP: *luksave*) them as her parents, not only by not giving them the money that she had brought to the village, but also by buying food elsewhere rather than eating in their household, thereby depriving them of the chance to establish further grounds for saying that they are her parents by feeding her.

Visual Proof and the Opacity of Other Minds

It has been pointed out that in many Pacific contexts there is a particularly strong belief that one cannot know what is in the mind of another person. Robbins and Rumsey have termed this issue of the inaccessibility of other people's thoughts and feelings 'the opacity doctrine' (Robbins and Rumsey 2008: 408). In a special issue of *Anthropological Quarterly* on 'the opacity of other minds', a number of authors give examples of this in Pacific contexts including cases from Papua New Guinea (PNG). For example, Rumsey explores the role of confession among the Ku Waru of PNG (Rumsey 2008), and Schieffelin shows how in language socialization of among Bosavi (also PNG) children, adults do not teach children to speak by guessing what the child is trying to say – as they might do elsewhere – because they work on the assumption that one cannot read the minds of others and should not try to do so (Schieffelin 2008: 431–32).

These authors focus on 'the opacity doctrine' in relation to 'language ideology', that is, local ideas about what language 'can do' (Robbins and Rumsey 2008: 411), on how ideas of opacity are reflected in language and in the use of language. The relevance of 'the opacity of other minds' for my purposes, on the other hand, is to show how a similar assumption about a degree of opacity of other minds is reflected, but also overcome, in social action, and that it is this kind of action that metaphors of vision in exchange practices refer to. Certain kinds of actions are ways of transcending the opacity of other minds, ways of overcoming the opacity of one's own mind from the point of view of others, and ways of transcending the opacity or informality of social contexts in which they unfold.

Among the Mbuke, as in some of the cases brought out by the aforementioned authors (e.g. Rumsey 2008: 455), it is often assumed that mere words are questionable sources of knowledge about the feelings, motivations and knowledge of others (both about those who speak them and about third parties spoken about). When Mbuke people use metaphors of vision in exchange practices, they do so, I argue, because visual 'appearances' are important not only as moments when the minds of others can be accessed, but also as moments when they can be affected. Actions of the sorts referred to as ways of 'seeing' are ways to 'make appear' the nature of social relations in dialectical (or reciprocal) negotiation with others. In this latter sense, social action makes visible one's view (feelings or thoughts) on a social form (such as a person), while also recognizing the views of others of that form, and since such perspectives that are 'made appear' are reciprocated one way or the other, they form ongoing negotiations about the nature of social relations which, in this reciprocal or dialectic process, are subject to constant revision.

Much like the anthropologist who is taught not to take people's claims about social life at face value, and to hold them up against what people actually practise, so too do Mbuke people assume that one cannot know what the other knows, what the other is capable of, what relations the other has or recognizes, unless these aspects (this personhood) become visibly manifest. This is not unknown in Manus ethnography, where Otto has pointed out how in 'Baluan epistemology' the most valid kind of knowledge is the one of which one has personally seen the effects. Talking, on the other hand, and second-hand statements, are viewed with much scepticism: 'In general, knowledge which is not based on experience may be accepted as true if the effects of that knowledge are manifest' (Otto 1992: 437). The thoughts and feelings of another person must become manifest by being 'made to appear' by the actual person, and so too must the constitution of the person become manifest in their actions and in the products of their actions. For example, money given as remittances to relatives makes relationships with and compassion and love for such relatives visibly manifest.

To turn back to the case of Karen: if she had gone straight to her parents in the village and given them the money she had been given by George, it would have 'made appear' not only her love for them ('she must recognize her parents, she must love her parents!'), it would also, as an act of giving, have made the child–parent relationship appear in an appropriate guise. Regardless of the fact that George said 'I agree with everything you say', this was a claim which was contradicted by what had appeared – as a result of his actions – not only for the parties involved to see, but also for the trade store owners to see when Karen came and bought food with large denomination banknotes which her parents in the village would be highly unlikely to have given her. The parent–child relationship between George and Karen, on the other hand, had appeared in effects that were visual (banknotes and her whereabouts).

A note should be made here that one of the bases on which parents claim parenthood, and thereby may legitimize *singaut* on the basis of the obligation to give in response to requests for remittances, is having paid for a migrant's education. This put Jeff and Margaret in an already problematic situation because they could not do this for Karen, and it made it particularly important for them that she and others 'made' their parenthood 'appear'. Even though caring for and feeding a person throughout their childhood, as they had, is the strongest claim to parenthood, both Karen's and George's behaviour appeared to be a serious challenge to this claim. They did not, notably, argue that Karen should reciprocate their hard work, but rather, in line with the logic of sharing outlined in the introduction, complained about Karen not showing affection.

Concepts of Vision in Exchange

The actual terminology used both in Titan and Tok Pisin regarding a variety of exchange practices reflects the way in which actions 'make' social relations and the constitution of the persons involved 'appear'. For example, on one occasion, Polongou (the man whose house I lived in on Mbuke and who became my adoptive father) was heading off to a mortuary exchange ceremony. Mortuary exchanges in Manus often involve (as part of a longer process) close paternal relatives of the deceased pooling money from a number of people related to the deceased, and afterwards this money is distributed, with the biggest part being allocated to relatives constituting the deceased's maternal kin (members of the deceased's mother's original clan). This particular exchange was being conducted on the occasion of the death of a man whose mother was from Polongou's clan, making Polongou among those who would receive the most. As he was leaving to go to the place where the exchange was to take place, he said to me, 'I shall go and see them with 50 kina' (T: *Yo po kula lisi ala me 50 kina*). Using this kind of wording ('to see with money') is not unusual among Mbuke people, a wording in which a term referring to sight, seeing or perspective is used for giving. Although such expressions may be figures of speech, they point to the importance of making visible that which is otherwise invisible, as well as indicating ways of overcoming the opacity of various aspects of social life.

Polongou's giving of money in this case 'made appear' the fact that he was maternal kin, as well as recognizing (T: *lele-awian*; TP: *luksave*) the receivers as paternal kin through the money he gave. Naturally, in such situations people present themselves and enforce that appearance on the other party, who in many cases already know both parties' genealogical relation. But such actions ensure that they see this, and reconfirm it, thereby working on the assumption that what is in the mind of another can only be known if it becomes manifest. He went to 'see' (T: *lisi*) his kinship relation to the deceased and the bereaved by giving to those conducting the exchange (the deceased's paternal kin), and in the final stage of the exchange (which takes place over several days) they 'saw' back, by giving the biggest part of the money that had been gathered to the maternal kin of the deceased, among them Polongou.

As I noted in the previous chapter, ceremonial exchange between 'clans' (T: *tali*) often revolve around, in simple terms, the ongoing reciprocation for the 'gift' of a women's procreative abilities to her original patrilineal descent group or clan. These ongoing reciprocal relations between descent groups entail a long series of gifts and counter gifts, even within one specific event of exchange. In the specific exchange event that Polongou took part in, the paternal kin for their part would explain giving money to Polongou as 'we see Polongou's "good seeing"' (T: *yota lisi lele-awian e Polongou*). The verb *lele-awian* is translated by Mbuke people into Tok Pisin as *luksave*, or the English 'recognize', while literally it means 'view good' or 'perspective good', *lele* being the substantive form (view, perspective) of the verb *lisi* ('to see'), and *awian* or *wian* meaning 'good', 'right' and 'valuable'.[2] In this sense, giving and receiving such as this could be described as a kind of reciprocity of perspectives confirming and recognizing relationships. Giving something or acting in a certain way 'makes appear' certain relations, while they may also recognize an appearance in response to the actions of the other party.

The aim of this chapter is not to discuss mortuary exchange but to show the relevance of these concepts of vision in contexts of sharing and remittance; but it should be noted that how exactly someone is related to another is never completely clear-cut and final (and not always agreed upon), and exchanges are always continuations of ongoing relations of exchange and other things between persons and groups, something which becomes particularly clear during mortuary exchanges when relationships are, as Strathern has put it, 'refashioned, for the living can no longer embody them' (Strathern 1994: 208). The parties involved knew that George was Karen's biological father, but it was only when he 'appeared' as such (especially in Karen's actions) that this became a potential threat to especially Jeff's claim of parenthood.

Since ceremonial exchange plays such a small part in daily life, the situations in which these 'appearances' of persons and relationships most often occur are those of a more mundane nature, as in the case of Karen. The important point here is that for social relations to exist they must be 'made to appear' – made visible, thereby transgressing opacity – by actual action, in this case by giving, and they must be recognized by such 'appearances' by both parties. If Polongou had not presented himself at the event and given, he would have been given nothing in return; and he had to go there not only to see them, but to make himself seen by contributing, otherwise he would not have recognized the relations, and the paternal kin on their part would have had no way of 're-recognizing' that recognition. Polongou's action not only constitutes him as a maternal relative, but implies the sociality of kinship relations in which actions such as his may be valued, and may be value in themselves (T: *lele-awian*). Looking at the details of these conceptualizations, all of which refer somehow to vision, and the way they are used, reflects the way in which visual 'appearances' help in negotiating, contesting and presenting the meaning of social actions, as well as the nature of the contexts of social relations in which they unfold.

The word Polongou used on this occasion, *lisi*, is one among many terms for 'see', and can in its substantive form (*lele*) also refer to perspective, view or opinion of certain things. Interestingly, *lele-awian* also means reciprocation in certain contexts, and people might say, 'I did this for him so maybe one day he might reciprocate (*lele-awian*) me'. Here *lele-awian* also means acknowledge and recognize, but not the action as such but that which it made appear: the person. What is interesting here is that the concept refers to a state in which a person can be or a way of seeing things; but it also implies an action in response to this. Reflecting an assumption of the 'opacity of other minds', a person cannot in that sense be perceived to feel love unless one makes that love visible by action, and here we recall Jeff saying that Karen 'must love her parents', while indicating that this was not the case because her actions had not made this appear since she had failed to give them her money and go to their house. A perspective here is a (perceptible) response to that very perspective simultaneously.

Assumptions about the opacity of other minds make it necessary to 'make appear' a perspective for it to exist socially.

Remittances: Persons and Relationships Made Visible

As we saw in the Chapter 1, on the Mbuke Islands many people rely on remittances. For migrants, '*singaut* pressure', as they sometimes term recurrent demands for remittances, is a constant problem of life in the city. On one occasion, during an interview, I asked one Mbuke migrant man why he and other people from Mbuke send so much money home to the villages, and he responded in Tok Pisin, but also used the Titan word *lele-awian*:

> Because we see [it] that way, when we help them and when you go to the village they will look at you – help you. When we go to the village on leave, they cannot talk, they know about my helping. If I stay in the village, they bring – take [my classificatory brother] for example, I usually send him money, and I just sit there [in the village] and he brings me fish. They come and see you, because they know that you too usually recognize (*lele-awian*) them. *Lele-awian* [he says by way of explaining to me] – you look good at them by helping with money or something, in their times of need.[3]

As in the example of Polongou, who said that he would go to the people who conducted the mortuary exchange and 'see them with 50 kina', it is shown here how one can 'see by giving', but also how one can make oneself seen. Money in this context is a perspective that is 'made appear'.

'Seeing' is way of making social forms appear in perceptible forms, such as banknotes given in mortuary exchange as recognition of a certain relationship between clans previously connected through the person now dead, but also as a way of reconfiguring those relationships to fit the changed situation. In such cases, relations need to be reconfirmed, or even contested, by gifts given or not given, small or big. By seeing by giving, persons have the chance to make themselves seen by others, to make relations seen by temporarily making them into amounts of money. During one mortuary exchange, I heard a complaint that 'we looked after him when he was a child, but they have hardly seen us [TP: *luksave long mipela*], we should have received as much as those'. As the case of Karen indicated, kinship is not biological by definition, and having looked after someone and having 'fed them' are ways of establishing kinship.

Meanwhile, we see also in this statement how a very literal understanding of the reciprocity involved in ceremonial gift exchange is articulated. In making such complaints, people are not simply disputing what the appropriate amount should be; they are underlining what the relations are, what part they had in the deceased. In a documentary filmed on Baluan Island in Manus Province, Suhr, Otto and Dalsgaard (2009) show that the unfolding of exchange events is also a site for the social negotiation of their content, as can be seen in a comment made by Sakumai Yep, one of the central characters in the film: 'I myself perform the culture, I myself can change it' (57.12) (cited in Poltorak 2010: 915). So while social action is a 'scene' on which relations and persons are constituted and contested, the scene itself is also contested, by being made 'seen' and see-able by that which unfolds on it.

To Mbuke migrants in particular, who are cut off physically from the village, appearing in other forms, such as in the form of money transfers, is particularly appropriate. Migrants often explained that they had to see (T: *lisi*) their relatives in the village by way of sending money, because otherwise they and their relatives would become invisible to one another. In downtown Port Moresby, I visited Twain, a man from Mbuke, in his office on the sixth floor of a large office building. He works there as the director of human resources in the National Agriculture Council. He explained the following in English – which some 'elite migrants' speak rather than using Tok Pisin in their daily work – pointing out that he often felt that he had to give money in response to *singaut* because otherwise, 'if I go to the village – I will find a way to avoid them … because I cannot face up with them, I cannot face them, and they will also be feeling the same'.

Explanations like this point towards having to be able to actually look at the other person again, and that they would not know how to look at the other if they had not 'seen them' in the past. Other migrants explained likewise that, if they do not give to village relatives they will have to avoid meeting them back in the villages (which would entail not going there), because they would, by not having 'seen' them, put into question whether or not they cared about their relatives, whether or not they considered them relatives in the first place. If a request is an 'appearance' of a relationship between the person who requests and the person who is met by it, and if meeting that request with remittances is a reciprocation of that (same) relationship, ignoring or denying requests without a proper excuse (such as having no money) is the same as saying that the other does not exist in the form that they attempt to 'make appear' through their actions. Such a refusal would cause serious offence on the part of the requesting party. Twain continues:

The thing is, we have this bond. After living here [in Port Moresby] you are going back to Manus, eh? You are going back home. Do you want to create that resentment? By not giving you are actually widening the gap. So even when […] I am also feeling the pinch – you know, if they suffer we will suffer. Because eventually at the end of the day I am going home [...] and if I don't give, and I go to the village, no one wants to ... They will feel hesitant to come and visit. It will probably take a while, because they will want to find the reason why I was refusing them. And unless you tell them [why you were unable to meet requests ...] they will still think that you are just ignoring them. And at the end of the day they will say that you came out from the village and your parents were the ones that looked after you, and they made you who you are. So it is those thoughts, and also that [...] I cannot refuse because if I go to the village I will have to have a reason for having been selfish.

As this quote makes clear, remittances as a form of sharing are not seen from every social perspective and in every situation as 'the absence of reciprocity' (Gell 1992: 152). But it is a very different kind of reciprocity from the more calculated reciprocity of ceremonial exchange, in which people may complain that they should have received more in return for what they have previously invested in a relationship. Rather, *singaut* and remittance constitute a reciprocity of perspective, of 'good seeing' and making seen. In this sense, giving is a recognition (a seeing) of the very existence of the other, manifested as that particular kind of relative that they make themselves appear through their *singaut*, their value questions. Giving in response to requests (and requests as well) is an 'appearance', a social recognition of a relation, while not giving is a refusal of the relation. The latter might make it hard for both parties to know how to behave towards the other, or hard to even conceive of the other in a meaningful way. It might create resentment and shame. Persons who send large amounts of money are often the ones who go to the village often, while those who send small amounts often go to the village rarely.

Outlining her perspective on Melanesian gift exchange in contrast to 'the barter model of value', Strathern argues that the exchange of unlike things in terms of labour time – one shell for one pig, for example – would be meaningless unless value or equivalence were outcomes of the transaction, not prior to it (Strathern 1992a: 171). This may run counter to the image of large exchange ceremonies in Melanesia, where counting is obvious and a matter of great discussion (as I mentioned above, 'they have hardly seen us' and so on). They do count, but Strathern argues that we have to 'calculate their calculations'; we need to find how the analogy between values in exchange is established. This may mobilise a different set of assumptions from those of the 'barter model of value' (ibid.: 176). Analogy in this sense means that one entity can appear as a form of another, persons can appear in the form of gifts, brides in the form of bridewealth, and in certain contexts there are 'equivalences between what we would otherwise separate as persons and things' contrary to 'the barter model of value, which assumes the intrinsic and separate qualities of persons and things' (ibid.: 177). In this sense, brides have no price; the exchange is one to one (ibid.: 188), the same in diverse forms, because bridewealth is a bride in the form of wealth. The exchange must always be a match – it defines the relationship (makes it appear in perceptible form), and although there may be much calculation and discussion during exchange events, in the end it is a match, and the parties must see themselves in new forms (ibid.: 187), forms that constitute answers to value questions. In this sense, one's act is what is returned, but not as a direct reflection; it may be qualitatively enlarged or diminished by the perspective of the other.

In Strathern's sense then, things may be persons appearing in a different form, while in the case of 'seeing' among Mbuke people, actions are like-wise not conceptually separate from persons as their 'makings', but are aspects of acting persons appearing in perceptible forms. Rather than acts being reflections of perspectives, perspectives take the form of acts, referred to as ways of seeing. But if the number is always one, in the sense that one perspective appears in the embodiment of its counterpart – the act of giving is a seeing of a seeing, as in 'I see their good seeing' (T: *yo tu lisi lele-awian e ala*) – wherein lies this reciprocity of appearance between migrants and villagers? How might money given be reciprocated by requests for more money?

Singaut as Persons and Relationships Made Visible

As one of the migrants cited above pointed out, a migrant's relatives in the village are able to somehow reciprocate remittances with assistance when the migrant visits the village. They may do so by way of helping them out, bringing them fish they have caught or making available their canoes and other things during the migrant's visit home. But in fact, migrants often complain about the expenses incurred in buying food to bring to the village, as well as about all the gifts they feel obliged to give people there. But in this case, the action of 'seeing the other' is what is valued. And villagers also continuously 'see' their relationship with migrant relatives, but do so by requesting money. The villager possesses fairly few things, in a material sense, that the migrant desires or needs, other than recognition of their belonging to the village and their kin. And the relationship between close relatives is one of love and compassion, in which material reciprocity or the expectation of it at some point – 'what the recipient can afford and when' (Sahlins 1972: 195) – is less relevant, even morally problematic. I might give an example from a conversation I had with a married couple from Mbuke, both highly placed civil servants living in Port Moresby.

Tommy and Molong live in a relatively small house in Port Moresby, but outside the house two brand-new four-wheel drive vehicles are parked.

One of them is theirs, the other is provided by Tommy's workplace for his personal use. This couple exemplify the fact that both men and women can have careers and make money, and they are both quite highly placed in the workforce. Molong and Tommy are relatively young and are both members of rather big families back in the villages (they have many siblings, and their parents are still alive). During an interview conducted in Tok Pisin, when confronted with the question of whether they would expect some sort of reciprocation from the villagers for their remittances, they responded as follows:

TOMMY: These days, that is sometimes the case with people from outside – not inside your family, but outside. Like if it is someone from Mbuke and he asks for help, and you see him (TP: *yu lukluk long em*) and you help, then he will think of it when I come to the village, he will help me somehow.[4] But that is only the case with those from outside, from other families.

A.E.R.: What if he does not?

TOMMY: If he does not, then he will be [feeling] guilty, and also it will stop him from making demands (*singaut*) again – because he knows, because he is ashamed.

A.E.R.: Is that the same in the family?

TOMMY: No! That would never happen! Not unless I had borrowed the money and had to pay it back, but with money that is already in my pocket – never! If he wants to look back (TP: *lukluk i kam bek*) at what I did at some later time, that is his own choice. It all depends on my relation to the person: that causes me to think … If I should expect him to return it, you know [looking up into the air, moving his head from one side to the other, indicating thoughtful consideration] … no, no that guy is like, 'You're my brother' […] But otherwise it's like that [i.e. not expecting anything in return].

MOLONG: It is like liking one's parents – I do love them you know. And when they *singaut* to you, you feel obliged.

TOMMY: And also, in the end you will have to go to the village. And if we are not nice to them [they will say], 'We used to *singaut* to you, and you never send anything, but now you come here […] and want all sorts of things from here'. But we usually consider/remember them, and when we go to the village people usually look at us (TP: *Tasol mipela save tingim ol, na taim mipela go long ples ol i save lukluk long mipela*).

MOLONG: And even if you do think somebody should [reciprocate] – I can't say it, it is for them to say – but I can say it like this too; it also depends on who you are [as a person].

> We here [in Port Moresby], we have security. In the village it is a different scenario; that may be the only money s/he (TP: *em*) has. So if they borrow from me – and they want to reciprocate (TP: *bekim*), it's up to them.

The idea of reciprocity in terms of obligations being generated by previous transactions is clearly problematic, especially 'inside' the family. Perspectives are reciprocated, one for one, but these are perspectives that look at the same relation from very different economic situations. However, these economic situations do not determine or change relationships between brothers for example; lack of recognition, on the other hand, might do so. Although migrants lose out in material terms, they need to be seen by their relatives as much as the villagers do. Reciprocity in material terms is not in this case a precondition but a possible outcome, a possibility which might not be realized (and often it is not).

I was often puzzled about why one of the men in whose household I resided in Port Moresby was seemingly happy and proud when he told me that the phone call he had just ended was with a sister or 'cousin brother' (Tok Pisin for a classificatory brother) of his in the village who had asked him to send money. How could requests for money be a good thing, as they appeared to be? Another migrant's statement (in English) might help answer that question:

> They request for money, but it is okay, it is not too much. And if they do not request? Then I usually call them and ask, 'Why aren't you asking for money?' [laughs loudly] […] [I]t is something that you like to do, and at the same time you don't want to do it. You don't want to do it, but when it gets a bit too long [since the last request] you feel a bit … 'I have to do this kind of thing' [i.e. give money].

There seems in this statement to be an uneasy tension between wanting to keep your money to yourself and wanting to 'keep yourself' as a particular kind of person. Requests for money are clearly not simply a necessary evil, brought about by the moral obligation to help less fortunate kin who ask for help; but simultaneously *singaut* is that which provides the migrant with the possibility of 'appearing' as a person in a particular guise, that is, in the form of the act of transferring money. In that sense, requests for money are relationships and persons that are made to appear, and it is important for migrants to be met with requests like it is important to villagers that migrants send them money. These requests are made and fulfilled not merely to meet material needs. Even though requests sometimes lead to problems in migrants' personal finances, they still occasionally call village relatives on the phone to ask them how they are doing, thereby providing them with a chance to request some money. Often they will not ask directly if village relatives want money (as the man cited above indicated), or transfer it without request, and it might be argued that this is because under such circumstances there would be no reciprocity of perspectives, no recognition on the part of the villager by requesting, thereby implying that it would be appropriate for that particular person to help them out. To those who are absent it becomes particularly important to be present by way of seeing (giving) and being seen (met by requests) to avoid becoming socially invisible to certain relatives.

Being a migrant from Mbuke in Port Moresby is comparable with the situation of Papua New Guinean prisoners described by Reed (1999). They conceive of themselves as hidden in the prison rather than as illuminated and exposed – as argued by Foucault (1977) in his study of imprisonment – because they are cut off from relationships of which they form part, and out of which they see themselves as constituted (Reed 1999: 47). Among other inmates in the prison, on the other hand, they do much to remain 'invisible' (by hanging up blankets around sections of their beds, for example). Reed's prisoners try to avoid exchanging gazes with other inmates because such an exchange might acknowledge a relation, and hence obligations for transactions, such as sharing tobacco (ibid.: 49) that cannot be met.

Migrants from Mbuke, on the other hand, do the opposite by calling village relatives, attempting to give the other a chance to 'see' them by requesting things, because they are people with whom they would like to maintain a relationship. Even though requests and responses to them might seem to be two very different social perspectives, in fact that which is (made) seen by different kinds of actions (requests as well as money transfers) is the same, namely the social relationship. In other words, money and requests for money 'are relations'; they are the same thing appearing in diverse forms. Those in the village who had lost contact with migrant relatives sometimes said that they 'must have died', or say that 'he must think that I have died, that I do not exist', if they fail to provide remittances. 'He never sees (T: *lisi*) me' is a common way of complaining about a lack of remittances. But these are not simply metaphors, as they do connect to actual vision, and as one migrant said during an interview, some migrants worry about what will happen if they do not give: 'You go to the village and you see them. The eyes will go down, look away, because you don't know about [or acknowledge] others' (TP: *Yu go long ples na yu lukim ol. Ai blo ol bai igo down because yu no save long ol narapela*). As in the case of the prisoners, 'seeing' is both metaphorically a way of recognizing a relationship while also being related to the actual visual operations of looking at one another, just as Polongou's going to the mortuary exchange was both a matter of his actual physical presence and recognition, and his metaphorical 'seeing' by giving.

As kinship is often subject to discussion and is not a clear reflection of biology (as in the case of Karen), it is not assumed that others indubitably 'know' (or recognize) that they are your brothers, for example, if they do not act accordingly by providing remittances (make kinship appear) in response to *singaut*. Again, 'seeing' and 'making seen' are necessary if relationships and personhood are to be regarded as what they are claimed to be. Persons have to show that they know, and show who they are, by 'making it appear' with 'visual effects' (such as money transfers). The reciprocity of perspectives is important especially because one perspective needs recognition of its appearance in another form. If a person keeps requesting money from another person who never complies with these requests, then the requester will at some point have to accept that the other is refusing the relationship which the request implies. Perspectives in that sense are always inter-personal. So as appearances of perspectives reappear in reciprocal appearances of the other's perspective, the person can see themselves in the actions of others. Making visible is one thing; being assured that one did so successfully is another. By exchanging perspectives, every action also contains a 'statement' towards those acted upon, and if exchange is understood as actions making persons and relationships appear (rather than as the transfer of material entities), a request like other statements is a donation too. When the person makes their perspective visible by 'giving it', they make the constitution of themselves visible, since they are also constituted by the relationships that they are 'suggesting' by their action.

Appearances, Value and Audiences

Things exchanged, such as money, have no intrinsic calculable value here, but are valued with regard to the relations between transactors that they make visible. If there is discussion and counting during exchange events, it is because of this. People negotiate their relations (not the absolute value of certain things as entities in themselves), and they do so by objectifying their relationships in their action. When someone requests large amounts of money, they might receive smaller amounts both as a reflection of the money available to the giver, and as a statement about the relation and the obligation in reciprocations of the statement entailed in the request. The exchange of perspectives is also a change and negotiation of personhood and mutual obligations. When through 'seeing by giving' a Mbuke migrant gives money to a village relative, such a perspective implies in itself a view back onto itself as a particular kind of relative to the receiver. As Munn pointed out in the context of Kula exchange in the Massim region of PNG, value transformations presuppose the inter-subjectivity of 'space-time'.

Value is caused by action and otherness is the arena of self-constitution: 'social relationships can be seen as engaging the actor's perspective on an outside other that implies a perception of the other's perspective of the self' (Munn 1986: 16). Munn argues that the act of exchange unfolds in 'inter-subjective space-time', but as that action is social it creates that very space-time as it unfolds. The very same meaningful order that constitutes the persons who act in it is constituted by their actions (ibid.: 12), and, as I have argued here, relationships and persons constituted therein are con- stituted by making them seen by seeing them. What is implied in action is more than the person acting, always at least including one other who, rather than being the object of an action, is embodied along with the actor in the relationship appearing in that action.

As Graeber has pointed out, the value-producing actor always acts with an audience in mind, whether imagined or present (Graeber 2001: 78), those who are meant, one way or another, to respond to (recognize) a perspective made to appear (in Mbuke terms: see what is made seen). Graeber takes inspiration from Munn when he states that: 'Value emerges in action; it is the process by which a person's invisible "potency" – their capacity to act – is transformed into concrete, perceptible forms' (ibid.: 45). This action-centred approach, which Graeber advocates, takes relation- ships to be results of action. People evaluate their actions as they perform them, and hence value as such is constantly subject to transformation. The importance of 'otherness' stressed by Munn is reproduced by Graeber, who argues that value can only be social as there are few pleasures which are enjoyed in solitude: 'we' conduct our value-transforming action with reference to an audience whether concrete or imagined. 'Society', Graeber argues, is a process through which activity is coordinated; it is the potential audience of one's actions. In this respect, Graeber finds that there is some kind of whole – a constantly shifting or provisional one – and there may be more than one on different social levels (ibid.: 76). The actor pursues value through actions on a 'stage', a stage which is being formed by those very actions. For the actor, 'society' is an audience that has to recognize the value of their actions. In the case of remittances, the audience is the receiver, but audiences can be wider and more abstract as well.

There is a third way in which concepts of vision play a role in the making and remaking of relationships and personhood among Mbuke people. One of Jeff's arguments against Karen having her own money to spend in trade stores was that 'it did not look good' (TP: *lukluk blo dispela i nogut*) when other people, such as trade store owners, could observe her having money, buying her own food and staying with George, rather than staying and eating in her parents' household. While in basic terms 'appearances' constitute persons through reciprocal recognitions between, for example, the person who makes a relationship appear by *singaut* and a person who responds to such an appearance by giving money, appearances often involve an audience, in whose eyes things appear in a particular way. Graeber is useful here because he does not – like Strathern – oppose a concept of society altogether; he operates quite explicitly with the idea of a whole, a whole which is not as concrete as the one presented by Strathern (the sum of actual personal relationships, reflected in the person as a social microcosm, see Strathern 1992b: 86), but simply the potential audience of value-producing action (Graeber 2001: 76). While Strathern's argument is that there is no society but only open-ended and concrete networks which are not bounded wholes (Strathern 1992b; 1988), to Graeber wholes are present, but they are in a state of temporality and exist only as patterns of actual action; and importantly, wholes are imagined by the actor who conducts their creative action with reference to them, and hence trans-forms them (Graeber 2001: xii). In this sense, as the appearance which is constituted by transfers of money is a 'working theory' of a social relation-ship, and is imagined until it is made visual and reciprocated (recognized), so too may the actor imagine other social wholes then the receiver (the audience).

To use Graeber's terminology: performers perform in a way that tells the audience how to be the audience, reflecting how the performer conceives of the relation between them. The audience constitutes the 'imagined whole' to the person; they are the recipients of exchange, and the evaluators ('valuers') of actions. Strathern brings forth the assertion that exchanging parties are not just exchanging things – they are also exchanging parts of themselves and perspectives. But they do so in certain ways and have to 'make things appear in their appropriate guise' (Strathern 1999: 14). This proper guise, I would argue, is worked out with reference to an 'imagined social whole', but at the same time the 'proper guise' is redefined by each event of social action. This may change the idea of what a proper guise is, in the mind of the actor as well as in the imagination of the other(s), provided that the action is acknowledged as 'appropriate' in the dialectical process of the reciprocity of perspectives that are made appear by actions. In this sense, an action involves a statement about the 'standard of value' (however temporary) of that very action. Should the 'receivers' of that action acknowledge that statement about the value of the action (the definition of what that action is) – by reciprocating the exchange, for example – then the standard of value (made) relevant for the particular type of action has been transformed temporarily and becomes a working theory to inform future action.

For instance, if a resourceful man from Mbuke working in the city is back home in the village and gives a donation for the renovation of the local healthcare clinic through the Mbuke Islands People's Association, rather than giving money to his direct kin, he gives his perspective of his obligation towards the island to those on the island objectified by his gift, which makes appear a different audience (the 'community') differing from the perspective invoked when giving money to direct kin. And by doing this, the giver asks for recognition from that audience, a recognition he might not get from his direct kin, who might have preferred to receive the money themselves.

Conclusions

My answer to the question of why concepts of vision are used in exchange practices is that they are concepts referring to a kind of 'seeing' which 'makes appear' persons and social relations in a reciprocity of perspectives which constitutes an ongoing 'theory' of the social relations in which appearances (actions) unfold. Social relations and persons are made when they appear for participants to see in a context in which that which is not manifest as visual evidence is often considered questionable. Appearances of perspectives help Mbuke people solve the problem of the opacity of other minds as well as the opacity of the social forms in which such minds attempt to operate. In this sense, actions of sharing, such as sending remittances in response to *singaut*, are socially reproductive in that they confirm, contest and negotiate relationships as well as persons.

The aim of this chapter has been to develop a possible explanation for the continuous flow of remittances to the Mbuke Islands from temporary labour migrants. I have argued that persons 'appear' as actions and that persons appear as embodiments of constantly changing socialities, networks of social relations, appearing differently, seeing differently according to the context of their actions. When a perspective appears, it defines (or makes claims about) a receiver and audience for that action; and if reciprocated, this context (whether a social relation, a clan configuration or a power structure in a business) is socially accepted, and it becomes a revelation of the reality people will henceforth live by. The important thing to note about many of these concepts of vision in exchange practices (such as *lisi* and *lele-awian*) is that seeing and giving are in this respect the same thing: giving is a way of seeing. When a person makes their perspective appear by 'giving it', they make the relevant part of the constitution of themselves visible, since they are also constituted socially in terms of the relationships that they are 'suggesting' by their action. 'Things' given have value only with regard to the relations between transactors, and therefore a request for money and a transfer of money into a bank account is the same (relation) appearing in diverse forms. It might seem to make little sense to say that money is reciprocated by requests for more money, but the logic of such a transaction will depend upon what is being transacted. What I have argued here is that people exchange perspectives on their mutual social relationships, thereby constituting themselves relationally. In transactions (requests and remittances) among close relatives, the person is relationally constituted by being seen from the point of view of the other.

At the beginning of this chapter I asserted that words are often not considered a reliable source of knowledge among Mbuke people, and that this helps to explain why making things visible in different ways is important. On the other hand, 'talk' of different kinds does play an important role as well, including in the context of ensuring sharing. Even if people for some reason do not need (or want) to maintain good relations back home, even if they do not care about their relatives, or do not plan to go home ever, there are still ways for people in the village to reach out to the migrant or moneyed person and try to affect their priorities: gossip, curses and blessings are some of the ways of doing this, and I turn to these in the next chapter.

Acknowledgements

A different version of parts of this chapter has previously been published as 'Visible While Away: Migration, Personhood and the Movement of Money amongst the Mbuke of Papua New Guinea', in Ø. Fuglerud and L. Wainwright (eds), *Objects and Imagination: Perspectives on Materialization and Meaning* (Berghahn Books, 2015).

Notes

1. In the following case I have changed the names of the parties involved because my written version of the 'conflict' – which is ongoing – might cause further conflict and distress for those involved. It might be argued that I should use local names rather than English-sounding names, but such a choice might cause even further problems, since this sort of situation is not unusual and hence might give rise to misunderstandings. In fact, I have used 'Christian names' that are not unusual in combination with indigenous ones.

2. The Danish or Norwegian speaking reader will note that *lele-awian* is quite similar to the verb for a kind of giving, *tilgodese* (English: 'for-good-see'), also a contraction of forms of 'see' and 'good'.

3. Tok Pisin: *Mipela save lukluk olsem, taim mipela i halpim ol – taim yu go long ples ol bai i lukluk long yu – help you. Taim mipela go long ples long leave, ol i no inap toktok, ol i save pinis long halpim blo mi. Mi stap na ol i kisim – olsem* [name of person omitted] ... *mi save salim mani long em; mi stap tasol, na em*

i kisim fish i kam. Ol i kam lukluk long yu, because ol i save you save leleawian long ol tu. Leleawian – you lukluk gut long ol long way blo halpim, long mani na olsem long taim blo, taim ol i nidim.

4. I have translated the Tok Pisin *em* (he, she, it) as 'he' for the sake of clarity and in order to stick to the singular tense used.

3

The Power of Words

Cursing and Blessing Relatives

———————— ◆●◆ ————————

After many years of labour migration, Polongou and Linda returned to the Mbuke Islands. Linda continued her lifelong occupation as a teacher in the village community school. She eventually became the first female headmaster there, until she retired a few years back. This meant that until recently they had an extra income in addition to what they earned from the small trade store that still run from their house. In the village they are still among the wealthiest inhabitants, both in terms of access to money and in terms of owning material assets, such as two houses, a small speed-boat with an outboard engine and several large seagoing outrigger canoes. This means that they are often subject to *singaut* for money and food from others within the village. It is often the case that former migrants and those few who hold jobs in Manus Province (such as teachers) constitute the monetary elite in the village. While in previous chapters I have focused mostly on migrants as the subjects of *singaut*, wealthier villagers are also the subject of requests, as we shall see in this chapter.

During an interview, I asked a recently returned migrant, who is also the wife of a village clan leader (*lapan*), 'Why don't you just say no?'

> I would feel bad about that. In the village we depend on each other for survival, you know. And what if later they say [to others] that I am not a good person? You know gossip [...] It would not be good if people were saying that the wife of the *lapan* ... is a rubbish (TP: *rabis*) woman.[1] And also, you know, people believe that you can be cursed if you do not help other people. It can work in many ways; like your things won't last long or your money, and it can harm you too. People believe in these kinds of things you know. Those of us who have a bit of education, we know – I mean, I

◆

don't believe in it, but other people do. And if one day you need something that they have, they might say 'no', and say 'you never help me'. It is not good to end up being all alone.

This chapter deals with the role of 'talk' in ensuring sharing. While I pointed out in the Chapter 2 that words are considered questionable as descriptions of the relationships and personhood they delineate, in this chapter I discuss the role that certain statements nevertheless play, especially in summoning an 'audience' for recognizing 'appearances' or the lack of them. Cursing, blessing, and gossiping all take the form of the utterance of statements, and I argue that they all share the feature that they address and call upon the effects caused by a third party, an audience, both in the form of the social context for concrete acts of speech and for recognizing the social form, such as relationships, that are made to appear by that action itself. This means that an audience may be concrete others who are present, but it may also be an audience summoned, or defined by the act of speech, such as the Christian God or ancestral spirits. Concerning 'seeing others' by way of actions of sharing and their reciprocation discussed in Chapter 2, the statements described here refer to 'appearances' of social relations – or the lack of them – in the sense that the statement is a way of questioning or forecasting social relations and persons, but made with reference to and the hope of recognition by a third party, an audience. Curses as well as blessings, I argue, are statements describing a person or a relationship, but it is believed that such statements will come true, not as foretelling but as an active attempt – through the agency of an audience – to affect the future of which statements speak.

Particular statements are here also a kind of embodiment of sociality in the sense that they attempt to produce that which they describe as they describe it (Austin 1962). Take, for example, the following statement: 'He does not see me, so he might as well lose his job and come back to the village and live – here he might be able to see me'. This could be a statement made by an aunt (father's sister) or a parent, about a migrant, and it may well have an effect resulting in that person (nephew or offspring) losing their job. Therefore people do what they can to stop people from 'talking', and we may recall the statement of one migrant quoted in Chapter 2: 'When we go to the village on leave, they cannot talk (TP: *toktok*), they know about my helping'. 'Talk' in such contexts can refer to gossip, which by nature has to do with talking, but it can also refer to curses fuelled by a specific power held over a person by certain relatives.

Curses as well as blessings among Mbuke people take the form of the utterance of a statement in the presence of others. In this sense, their unfolding in social action is similar to gossip in being the 'morally laden verbal exchange concerning the conduct of absent third parties' (Besnier 2009: 13), although, as I shall discuss shortly, in blessings the 'victim' is not necessarily absent. All these kinds of 'talk' involve another kind of third party apart from the person spoken about, namely the audience of gossip as well as of curses and blessings. For instance, when a blessing is uttered, the statement addresses a third party beyond the person doing the blessing and the person who is being blessed, namely the Christian God or ancestral spirits. In these contexts, value is not produced by the exchange of perspectives between two persons or groups, but by recognition by an audience not directly involved in the specific relationship which the 'talk' addresses, and the value in question is that of a particular person as reflected in their actions, a value which for various reasons has failed, become disputed or cannot be produced reciprocally between the talker and the person who is subject to talk.

Bringing certain things into being by describing them in spoken words immediately brings speech act theory to mind (e.g. Austin 1962; Searle 1969). However, as has been noted, the understanding of intentionality in the classic formulations of speech act theory reflects, in the words of Michelle Rosaldo, an understanding of 'doing things with words as the achievement of autonomous selves, whose deeds are not significantly constrained by the relationships and expectations that define their local world' (Rosaldo 1982: 204). More recently, it has been argued that the concept of 'intention' in speech act theory relies on Western folk models of the person (Duranti 2006: 34; Girke and Meyer 2011: 9). As we shall see, the 'doing' involved in 'doing things with words' is not simply authored and implemented by an individual. Even if the intention of a person may be that certain effects or events occur, such as in the cases of gossip, curses and blessings discussed here, the intentional agent relies on a third party – that is, an audience – to ultimately cause those events or effects to appear, much as their own intentional acts are caused by the other (the victim). That is to say, if we were to define the agent, following Gell, as 'one who "causes events to happen" in their vicinity' (Gell 1998: 16), then intention is in this case split from the effects caused by the intentional act of speech. In fact, the agency (here the intention of making things happen and the actual causation of those happenings) involved in a single act of speech is socially distributed both among living persons and among the living and the dead, as we shall see in further detail below. A Mbuke person calls upon a third party to 'implement' their intentions as reflected by forms of 'talk'. The third party, in this sense, provides an alternative answer (visual effect, happening) to the value question that might previously have been misrecognized, for example by refusing or ignoring an act of *singaut*. I start here with blessings as one of these kinds of 'talk'.

♦

Hurting Eyes, the 'Free Gift' and the Third Party

During their time as migrant workers, Polongou and Linda sent money to relatives in the village. To begin with, they sent remittances to their parents in particular, because back then siblings and other relatives did not ask for money from migrants to the extent that they do today, Linda explained. Later, Polongou and Linda paid the school fees of many of their siblings and some of their siblings' children, and they built a house for Polongou's older brother. Now they live in the village, but that does not mean that they are not subject to *singaut*. Since Linda and Polongou constitute one of the wealthiest households in the Mbuke Islands, they are often subject to *singaut* from other people in the village. People come around knocking on their kitchen door asking for a bit of rice, or simply show up to eat with members of the household. It often puzzled me to see the quantities of food in storage and in prepared form that were not consumed by members of the actual household in which I lived, but which in large part were 'consumed by *singaut*'. I was often told that this was because the sharing of food is important, and refusing to share would reflect poorly on 'the good of one's person', one's *tawian* (T: a contraction of *te*, *oy* and *wian*; TP: *blo yu good*; English: 'belonging (to) you good'). During an interview, I asked Polongou why the sharing of food was so important, and why he never turned away the many people who came to his kitchen doing these kinds of *singaut*. He answered in Tok Pisin, but used the Titan *mata-moma*, the meaning of which he had recently explained to me:

> You know, when somebody comes to you, and speaks low, and he does not speak loudly – and you know that when a man speaks low that he has tears in his heart. His tears, you must help his tears. You must feel sorry for him, you must *mata-moma* for him. No matter if you are not able to give a lot, you must give a little.

In addition to appealing to feelings of pity, as Polongou and others often did when I asked them why in certain situations they were not concerned with material reciprocation, they would also refer specifically to a sense of wanting to cry when others were suffering, or when others looked sad and might want to cry. In that sense, pity is conceptualized specifically as the pain and distress of seeing something which is painful or distressing in appearance.

Literally, *mata* means 'eye' or 'eyes', while an equivalent of *moma* in Tok Pisin is *bagarap* (from 'buggered up', i.e. ruined, wrecked, spoiled; see also Michalic 1989: 62) or, in this context, 'hurting'.[2] *Mata-moma* can thus be translated as 'eyes hurting'. In spoken usage, *mata-moma* refers to unselfish actions of helping others without any hope of reciprocity, acts of giving out of an allegedly genuine sense of pity, but also to the sense of pity as such. In this sense it also implies a sense of superiority, a sense that the other (as opposed to the person giving) is unable to make it on their own. In a sense, *mata-moma* is seeing something which in your perspective is not right, not the way it should be, and it is – like *lisi* and *lele-awian* – a metaphor of vision used in reference to giving, while it is translated as pity. Interestingly, it is also (on much rarer occasions) a term for jealousy, another sense of seeing something which it is painful to see. It refers to feelings but entails a response to that which is seen or felt. Again we might recognize the centrality of visual evidence, overcoming the opacity of other minds, both in the sense that the eyes need to recognize the other's need, and in the sense that feeling some-thing is always already a response to that feeling as the visual appearance making the feeling exist. Relations of familial love cannot simply be said to exist if they do not 'appear' as action, and the same is the case for pity.

As a kind of sharing, *mata-moma* can be described as giving out of pity without expecting anything in return. It is a 'real gift', I was told.[3] It is a gift given to someone who will not be able to reciprocate, but also to someone with whom one does not necessarily have a relationship which might be appropriate to reveal by giving, which is often the case with remittances and other transactions referred to as *lisi* or *lele-awian*. Examples of *mata-moma* include giving food to elderly people, helping elderly people by carrying water or firewood to their houses, helping children in need, and helping those who suffer and make you feel pity and distress by the sight of them. One example often given is the sight of an elderly person strug-gling to carry their firewood back to their house. Even helping complete strangers is brought out as an example. Mbuke people tend to assume that active responses to pity for those in great and hopeless need is universal for the human race, and often seem to find it somewhat disturbing when confronted with the question of why they would help if they will never get anything in return. Regarding *singaut*, the appeal for sharing might also be an appeal for *mata-moma*, a 'cry' for pity.

The following statement was made by a wealthy migrant, Andrew, one day when I was sitting with a group of people on a veranda on Mbuke Island: 'Oh, I have no betel nuts. I am a poor, poor man, so poor I do not even have a betel nut to chew. I wish I had a betel nut. I travelled so far from *yap* (T: 'far-away', in this context) but no one is seeing (TP: *lukim*) me, no one feels sorry for me (TP: *save sori long me*)'. Andrew is a migrant worker living in Port Moresby who was in the village on Christmas leave, and he is one of the wealthiest Mbuke migrants. In response to this clearly ironic outcry of his, I gave him a handful of betel nuts from my string bag. Excessively loudly he responded, 'Ooh, thank you so much! You will be here long after I'm dead, you will be here on and on'. Andrew burst out laughing along with everyone else sitting on the veranda. As an expression of gratitude, this sort of statement may seem a bit strange, the irony being somewhat implicit. The gratitude, as well as the irony, lay in that a gift received by someone unable to reciprocate materially is responded to by a call for supernatural agency to 'see' the appearance of something there to be seen, and for that agency to reciprocate. By saying 'you will be here long after I'm dead', Andrew was in fact pretending to be addressing such a supernatural third party, such as the ancestors, although now many people explain it as calling out to the Christian God. The outcry is a means to make the supernatural agency help the giving party in return for their good properties that appear in the act of giving.

I might note that what was funny in this instance was that Andrew is wealthy, and among the most generous both in terms of remittances and in having helped to fund the building of several houses for relatives of his. The very thought that he would be unable to reciprocate something as insignificant as a few betel nuts was ridiculous and therefore funny. The fact that I gave him a handful rather than just one betel nut – as Mbuke people mostly do unless they have piles of them lying around out in the open (which they would try to avoid) – might also have given rise to the laughter. Giving many betel nuts like that might indicate that he is poor also in the sense that others fail to share betel nuts with him generally, indicating that no one has any kind of reciprocal obligations towards him, which is even more ridiculous in his case. In fact, an elderly quite poor man who often came to the household I lived in was often given handfuls of betel nuts and numerous cigarettes 'for later' that he would immediately hide in his bag, and in many ways he had a kind of patron–client relationship with the clan leader (Polongou) with whom I lived. I never observed such extensive giving of betel nut or cigarettes to people who seemed to be 'equals', apart from in situations of more formal exchange or village meetings. In this sense, Andrew was somehow counteracting the insult that the quantity of betel nuts could be seen as from his point of view.

When a person gives fish to an elderly person who is no longer able to go fishing themselves, the giver is said to be doing *mata-moma*, and the elderly person will respond loudly in phrases such as, 'You will not die, you will live long and help me and be a good fisherman'. By speaking loudly, I would argue, the person speaking calls upon an audience beyond the actual giver in such a situation. It was often explained to me that after giving fish to an elderly or unprivileged person, and such a statement had been made, the next time the giver goes fishing they might find it easier, and catch a lot of fish. This has to do with 'the power of the mouth' of that elderly person, the power they have to call upon the agency of a third party (God or ancestors), which might make it easier to catch fish. Similarly, when I went fishing with men from Mbuke they would often start chanting in Titan, *Oh, mambru* ('Oh ancestor/s') if they were not catching many fish, and explain that they were calling upon the ancestors to help them catch more. The calling out from an elderly person as an expression of gratitude is referred to in Tok Pisin as a 'blessing'. Some people say that calling out in this way will make the ancestors help anyone who helps the poor – while others say that the appeal is made to God.

From a material point of view, *mata-moma* involves a quite obvious power relation in that a person receiving something which may be recognized as *mata-moma* is being emotionally experienced by others as a particular (weak) kind of person, which the receiver recognizes by calling out. Andrew had good reason to resist being put in such a position by me that day, although he resisted by pretending not to resist. This was the point of Andrew's joke: he called out for the ancestors or God to reciprocate that which he was unable to reciprocate in a situation in which he so clearly was in fact able to reciprocate, and in a situation in which I might have accidentally indicated that he was poor, both in terms of money and relationships of social obligation to share, because I failed to understand (or played along with) the irony of him saying 'I am a poor, poor man'. The interesting thing here is that Andrew did not include me in a prayer enclosed in his own mind; he shouted it out excessively loudly for other people to hear (not just those present). The 'reward' (used here in Tok Pisin) comes with 'the power of talk' or of 'the mouth' (TP: *paura blo toktok, paura blo maus*), which induces an effect by calling upon a supernatural agency to cause it. That is one of the things which are referred to in Tok Pisin as a 'blessing'.

The idea of 'blessing' shows up in many different contexts, and has been a part of life among the Titan for a long time (see Fortune 1969: 74 et passim; Schwartz 1975). In the Titan language, Mbuke people use the word *tandritanitani*, which means blessing but also curse, as Fortune (1969: 78) noted. According to Fortune, *tandritanitani* literally means 'making come on top of', or more precisely, 'making a ghostly influence possess, or exert influence on a person' (ibid.). In this sense, the statement addresses and calls upon a (particular) third party to cause an effect; the blessing comes from the person who calls upon the supernatural, but the effect comes from the supernatural. Such statements, the words that indirectly cause effect, are not simply words; they are ways of directing some agency's attention to certain appearances. Such words are not simply descriptions of the social world; they refer to and draw attention to 'appearances' of it as well and thereby participate in the dialectics of valuating through which the social world is produced and reproduced. Blessings are statements, but unlike words in other contexts, they are statements which people hope and believe will come true if such a description of persons is reciprocated by the supernatural audience summoned, or otherwise recognized by an audience or third party called upon.

In the eyes of an audience – in this case a supernatural third party – a person may be constituted as a certain kind of person, namely a good one, who deserves to live long. This reflects on 'the good of you', on *tawian*. As I argued in Chapter 2, ensuring a person remains visible while they are away through the giving of remittances clearly reflects an underlying hope that what appears back home will add to this personal value, as indicated in one migrant's statement during an interview:

> You give because of *tawian*, it is the good of you that you are giving and you will get it back here and there, not directly but part by part (TP: *hap hap*). How can I say – *tawian* is like your behaviour or character, like you are a man who sees (TP: *luksave long*) other people, you are not a selfish man.

In the Maussian conception of reciprocity, the most basic formula is one person giving to another, and the other at some point reciprocating. As Rio has pointed out, Mauss seems to see the fact that there are actually three persons involved in the example given by the Maori, Ranaipiri, whose explanation of reciprocity and 'the spirit of the thing given' Mauss drew upon, as an insignificant complication, when it might equally have been a significant aspect in defining the exchange as socially real (Rio 2007: 22–23). As Rio points out, drawing on Peirce (1958: 331), it may be that a gift can never be a gift unless there is a code of behaviour forming an 'outside view' which recognizes that giving and receiving are part of that same phenomenon (gift exchange) (Rio 2007: 20). For Rio, the third party in exchange is such an 'outside view' of an abstracted idea of a whole, the 'social structure' which people themselves imagine; and among the Ambrym (of Vanuatu), agency entails a perspective of a third party which totalizes social structure by 'looking at it' (ibid.: 7). Although I will not discuss his argument in detail here, it points to the importance of an audience that is imagined or physically present. As Graeber has pointed out, the actor acts with an imagined audience in mind, an audience which potentially recognizes the value of the act in itself (Graeber 2001: 76). Such an idea of a third party is quite literally present in regard to *mata-moma* in the responses to it, namely blessings. But the third party, as an audience outside the immediate relation to which actions or statements refer, is equally crucial in curses and gossip among Mbuke people.

In his description of 'Manus religion', Fortune explains the role of ancestral spirits in 'Manus society'.[4] 'Sir Ghosts', as he called them, were protective ancestral spirits of individual houses, often the most recent male head of the house that had passed away.[5] In somewhat functionalist terms, Fortune explained 'ghosts' as agents who oversaw the actions of the living, able to both punish and help them, and in doing so they helped uphold, among other things, a strict sexual morality and the obedient fulfilment of exchange obligations (Fortune 1969: ix). Fortune wrote that when a person came to the house of an offended party to pay compensation for a sin committed against someone in the house, 'this expiatory offering, *kano*, is made, never ostensibly to offended mortals, always ostensibly to offended ghosts' (ibid.: 42). That is, compensation was made to the ancestral spirit of the house against which the 'sin' had been committed. For example, when a young woman of one family had sexually 'sinned' with a particular man while betrothed to another man, compensation was paid to the 'house' of the contracted groom by the young woman's family, but not directly to living members of the household. Wealth, which was shell money and dog's teeth at that time, would be placed on the platform in front of the house of the offended party, who would remain inside the house, and the man from the young woman's family who was in charge of the compensation payment would address the receiver's ancestral guardian spirit: 'the head of the girl's house addresses by name the Sir Ghosts of the house on whose platform he has laid the wealth' (ibid.: 41). Likewise, the anger feared was not that of the living relatives of the groom to be, but that of his family's Sir Ghost. In his address, the man giving the compensation would beg the Sir Ghost for forgiveness rather than the people physically in the house (ibid.). It could be argued that the 'ghost' here is the third party directly being asked to recognize the value of the act of compensation which nevertheless goes to the injured party, the household, while the presentation (appearance) is made to the third party.

Tandritanitani and the Cursing of Relatives

The flip side of 'the power of the mouth' is that this power to elicit supernatural agency does not always call upon a positive effect. The same term, *tandritanitani*, which is used when calling for supernatural agency in response to acts of *mata-moma*, is used in reference to curses cast by aunts and parents in other situations. In his explanation of *tandritanitani*, Fortune describes it as an aspect of specific relationships, namely the cursing power that a woman holds over her brother's children, and he argues that this power might be seen as a remedy for women's disinheritance from the material property of the patrilineal descent group into which she was born (Fortune 1969: 77; see also Schwartz 1975: 318). In this case too, it could be said that the power to call upon a supernatural agency is an ability held by those who are materially in the inferior position.

According to Fortune, *tandritanitani* referred more or less strictly to a power to both curse and bless held by a woman over her brother's children, and other aspects of this specific relation, such as children-of-sister towards children-of-brother (Fortune 1969: 74–75). In the simplest version, the sister holds a magical power over her brother's children, a power which she can use when discontented with her brother or his children, but the same term was (and is) employed when referring to the power of a man's sister's daughter to bestow (bless) his children with fertility (ibid.: 78). In both these instances this 'power' concerns the relation between brothers and sisters, and even though a woman is 'married out' of the immediate patrilineal descent group, she remains part of the group through that power that she holds over her male siblings, those who stand to become leaders of that descent group. The power of *tandritanitani* to both bless and curse is explained by Fortune as the ability to bestow fertility and simultaneously the possibility of being able to cause sickness and barrenness (ibid.: 77). When questioned directly, Mbuke people told me the same version. But in present day Mbuke there is a wider set of relations in which *tandritanitani* is employed to curse, but significantly this occurs within the immediate family between siblings (also of same sex), parents and children, and also still specifically a woman's brother's children. Based on fieldwork carried out in the 1960s, Schwartz likewise pointed out that cursing had become a significant aspect of relations between parents and children (Schwartz 1975: 318), something of which there was no indication in Fortune's account.

In line with Schwartz's account, parents among Mbuke people today are able to curse their children, and this is referred to as *tandritanitani*. Interestingly, Schwartz mentioned this fact in his explanation of how remittances were drawn to the village among the Titans in a discussion of changing 'relations among generations' (ibid.). During the heyday of the Paliau Movement in Manus Province – from the mid 1940s to the mid 1950s – many of the existing beliefs, rituals and forms of exchange had been abandoned (see Schwartz 1962; Otto 1992; Mead 2001), but when Schwartz came back to do further fieldwork in the 1960s he observed that certain 'traits of culture' had persisted, although in new forms (Schwartz 1975: 321). One example of this was *tandritanitani*, which was at the time much more widely used in kinship relations (ibid.: 318). This was when a new flow of wealth had started coming into the villages, namely money from young migrants (ibid.: 319), the development which I sketched in Chapter 1. In 1963, Schwartz observed, this constant flow of wealth (cash) into the village had become an important part of the economy. Schwartz argued that there were two main ways for these remittances to be drawn to the village: one involved 'buying teeth', an exchange between inter-marrying and therefore distinct patrilineages (see Chapter 1). The other involved *tandritanitani*, the magical power which at the time of Fortune's fieldwork was specific to the relation between a woman and her brother's children, and which was in the early 1960s employed in the context of remittances (Schwartz 1975: 318–19; see also Otto 1991: 246 et passim).

Interestingly, Schwartz notes that the power to curse previously specific to the sister–brother's children relationship was at the time also used by parents of young migrants to ensure that they would send large parts of their incomes home. That made such *singaut* (to use the current term) for money difficult to reject, and Schwartz explained that young people were afraid not to meet these demands from parents for fear of being cursed (Schwartz 1975: 320). So when Schwartz asked a young migrant why he did not refuse demands for money, the young man responded that he was afraid to, and that his father had cursed him before – which had caused him to fail an exam and miss out on a job opportunity (ibid.). All the instances of *tandritanitani* curses that Schwartz heard about from 1963 to 1975 (including the 'original form' from a person's father's sisters) were similar to this: they were retaliations in response to requests for money and goods that had not been complied with, and they were all directed directly at the young person, affecting their urban career somehow (ibid.), rather than their fertility, as in the past.

There are a number of things to be noted when comparing the situation which Schwartz describes and the current one on the Mbuke Islands. Cursing is mentioned by many Mbuke people not only as a motivation for remitting but also as a motivation for sharing within the villages more generally. So if one was to call the power to curse a 'culture trait', as Schwartz does, it is true that parts of the 'existing culture' have persisted by changing themselves in a new situation, and what is interesting is that curses do not address the migrant's social standing in the village as such. Instead, as in Schwartz's account, curses are directed at the person's social standing in the urban setting. Curses on Mbuke today take the form of statements like: 'If he cannot send me money he might as well lose his job and come home', that is, curses affect the urban career mainly (see also Otto 1991: 246). This kind of statement is believed to work as a curse and will have an effect on the destiny of the person in question. If quarrels with such relatives are not solved, this is what will happen – and that is what many people fear. They will start losing money and may lose their job. Many Mbuke migrants in Port Moresby were indeed worried about cursing, as the following example indicates.

Every now and then people from the village go and visit relatives in Port Moresby and elsewhere. Among the Mbuke people in Port Moresby these are referred to in Tok Pisin and Titan alike as 'local tourists'. When these 'local tourists' are in Port Moresby, it is expected that other Mbuke people go and 'see' them with a bit of money for them to take home (see also Schwartz 1975: 319–20), especially those who are close relatives of the 'tourist'. In the following example, the one casting the curse is in fact the father's sister of the man in question. This is not always the case, and many examples given to me involved parents.

Ken, a young man, recently had a relative from Manus visit him in Port Moresby, namely one of his female cousins (his father's sister's daughter). Ken was never particularly successful at getting well paid jobs by Mbuke standards, and at the time he was working in a big store. Not long after her arrival, his cousin decided to buy a large number of a particular type of good which was sold in the store where Ken worked. She asked Ken if he could help her get a discount since she knew that employees in that type of store can often acquire one. But Ken explained that he had recently purchased a number of things and used up his annual discount allowance, and thus could not help. The cousin, however, did not accept this excuse. When she was back in Manus she explained to her mother that Ken had refused to help her get the goods she wanted, to which her mother responded: 'Aha! So he wants to have that kind of behaviour towards you. He doesn't like to see (*lele-awian*) you? All right, good, he will waste his money on nothing; he will not have money any more'. The man narrating this to me looked at me gravely, adding: 'That's a curse now. It is going to happen!'

This simple statement, spoken in anger and directed at a particular kind of relative, is meant to affect the person in question; the statement is believed to be a more or less direct representation of the future. Ken went on with his life in Port Moresby, not knowing what had happened, but it was not long before problems started arising. A friend of Ken explained to me:

Now Ken would go working, on and on, and you saw for yourself how Ken's fortnight came up and his money kept disappearing or was used up very fast (TP: '*pinis nating*'. And I don't know if he was misplacing his money or how it happened, but he never had money any more. And I don't know how this works, but I believe that it works that way. Someone in the village might say, 'So you don't want to help me, I think then it would be better if you were to come and live here in the village with me instead'. Okay, now you will see how you will not have money, you will see like: 'Hey! I don't have money now – and I don't even usually drink beer, so why do I have no money? I think maybe I must have hurt a member of my family'. It is like that, the power of talk. And you know at that point, Ken, he felt that he had problems with his money. So he went to the village and they all went and sat down, a little family meeting, and all Ken's relatives, they came, and they asked: 'Who is it that has got a grudge (TP: *bel i hevi*; which here could also mean 'troubled by something he did') against Ken?' And the aunt [Ken's father's sister], she spoke out now: 'I have a grudge against Ken, because he did this thing to my daughter, [and] so I threw this curse at him'. So he said sorry and took a bit of money and paid this wrong, he did this 'compensation' (T: *kanain*),[6] which is not big money, as long as he marks it – like a token or what you call it – it can be 100 kina. And then she said, 'Okay, I accept your apology'. And she would say sorry and hold him and wash him with all sorts of leaves and stuff.

At this point I interjected and asked for an explanation of the use of leaves:

I don't know why they use leaves. But Ken came back [to Port Moresby] and his money was all right again. Because they 'straightened it out' (TP: *stretim pinis*) [...] from the heart! If you just say it (TP: *tok nating*), and [that] it is not from the heart, then the problem will continue to be there, money will still disappear.

As Fortune pointed out, 'the use of the *tandritanitani* curse is always in the open. It is not a curse ever done with concealment' (Fortune 1969: 97). For the curse to work, it is said in the presence of others, and it will be confessed to the victim when family meetings are held. Curses among Titans are always lifted eventually, Fortune noted (ibid.: 98), and this also appears to be the case today. To use the terminology developed in Chapter 2, the cousin 'made appear' a certain relation by asking for help in obtaining a discount, but that appearance was not 'seen' or recognized by Ken when he rejected the request, thereby questioning the relationship. In turn, the curse is a way to pull the rejecting person back into the relationship. The relationships denied or disputed by rejection, and the grudges arising from it, are eventually put back into (some agreed upon) place, 'straightened out', and so the curse is only temporary. The process of cursing leading to a family meeting and compensation such as in this case is a process of negotiating relationships into their right place by temporarily destabilising them. If the request is a 'value question' and the response provides the answer in which requestors have to see themselves in new forms (Strathern 1992a: 187), then cursing and later compensation provides a 'second round' in the dialectics of valuation.

Cursing is taken very seriously and is feared. Indeed, there are some who feel that there is some connection between the fear of a curse and the fact that the curse works. In fact, many Mbuke people told me, 'of course it only works because we believe that it works', although such statements might also have to do with an assumption that such beliefs are not shared by someone like me (in my capacity as a European). It might also be the case that a curse works because it constitutes a disruption of a significant relationship, which in turn negotiates or even disputes the constitution of the person otherwise constituted as part of that relationship. As the case of Ken exemplifies, a curse is a way of disputing the nature and/or existence of a relationship, but it does so as a response to a prior disputing of a relationship, which in the case of

Ken did not 'appear' following his cousin's request for a discount. Blessings work in the same way. The person who blesses another will simply utter a statement in the presence of others (or hope to summon supernatural others by speaking in a particular way), such as, 'You are a good man, you shall live long to help others like you have helped me'. In this case, the person is made into more or something better to fit the personhood (*tawian*) which is made to appear by the unselfish act of helping someone in a hopeless situation.

This, Mbuke people say, is the power of the mouth or the power of talk. 'Talk' or 'people talk' can mean many different things depending on the context, everything from blessings and curses to gossip and rumours suggesting that a person is often reluctant to help, and that they tend to fail in 'seeing' their relations. But the effects of 'talk' differ depending on the relation between the speaker and the person being talked about, and on the form of the 'talk'. Although words are not trusted to reflect what is in the mind of others, they are feared because they reflect what may happen in the future. Polongou's wife Linda, quoted at the outset of this chapter, provided gossip (and her own good name, and her husband's) and cursing as explanations for not refusing to share, which means that although the example given here concerns relations between migrants and non-migrants, the same conflicts arise between people in the villages. In the last section of the chapter I illustrate this by describing some aspects of daily sharing which Linda referred to when uttering her fear of gossip, and other people's fear of cursing.

'Talk' and its Antecedents

'In the village we depend on each other for survival', Linda kept telling me from the very first day I spent on Mbuke Island. And yet many people hide most of the food reserves in their household in strange places around the house to avoid sharing it with others. The main problem is that not everybody depends equally on others for their survival. A few people even openly admitted to me that they depended completely on others for their living; they seldom went fishing, they had no income, they were living on *singaut*, and certainly everyone depends on other people in one way or the other when it comes to getting food every day. This makes it hard for others to have enough for themselves, and causes almost everybody to eventually *singaut* to their migrant relatives 'in *yap*', as well as to neighbours, relatives, and friends in the village. Those who do not have relatives 'in *yap*' in turn *singaut* to those who do or to others in the village generally.

It is not just a matter of the money from *yap* being distributed in the village. In the village, people have started to *singaut* even for fish and sago, which is the staple diet of the village, and according to many informants this is an emerging phenomenon. Part of the situation that might have caused an increase in *singaut* inside the villages is the fact that hunger is becoming a reality for some families, particularly outside the sea-cucumber season, the time of year when the National Fisheries Department allows people to collect and trade in sea cucumbers. At the time of my fieldwork, this was a significant means of income.[7] Sago, the main source of starch in the Mbuke Islands, has become more and more expensive in the markets on Manus Island, where Mbuke people could previously get it through different kinds of barter or exchange (see Chapter 1). One source of sago for which money is not needed on Manus Island still remains, however. This involves occasional long-term exchanges with 'trade partners' (T: *kawas*), or even longer-term exchanges (or sharing) with relatives living there – particularly other Titan villages, and relatives from Mbuke who have moved there. But despite this source, most sago has to be bought with cash. *Singaut* in the villages is the reason most often brought up for the fact that in some of the better-off families (perhaps in most families) in the Mbuke Islands, it has become necessary to hide food.

One of Linda's close relatives, Ben, lived quite close to Linda and Polongou's house, and the two households often helped one another when there were shortages. This is how it was supposed to be, but no longer is, Ben explained. There was supposed to be reciprocity. Ben is an extremely active man, often going fishing, sailing back and forth to Lorengau with goods for Polongou and Linda's store, and he has two wealthy brothers who live and work in Port Moresby. Ben receives rather a lot of remittances – according to himself an average of K3,000 a year, which is more than twice the average amount, and he manages to maintain a good standard of living.[8] This makes him a 'victim' of *singaut*: 'People come around pretending just to drop in, but at the same time their eyes are working, and they notice what you have around. Later they will drop by and ask if you have a little bit of rice you can spare – because they have already seen that bag of rice that is standing in your kitchen'. This has caused Ben to hide things sometimes, or at least try to avoid having them out in the open. The problem is that a person often cannot simply say no, as it depends very much on their relationship with the person asking. Food is not the only thing that people hide – many other items that a person would like to keep may also be involved. There are many examples of hiding things to prevent someone 'entitled' to take them or *singaut* for them from seeing them. As Gustafsson has pointed out for Mbuke, 'Close relatives and cross-cousins visit each other's houses freely and treat themselves to food inside them' (Gustafsson 1999: 66). Other people are more reluctant to visit other people's houses without a legitimate errand (see also ibid.). I take Gustafsson's term 'close relatives' to refer to parents, children or classificatory siblings of the same sex (especially men), and I have often observed how these types of relatives 'treat themselves'. A similar observation has been made by Peterson (1993: 861) among the Murngin of Australia, where the same kind of practice has been described as 'tolerated theft' (see also Jones 1987).

People in the Mbuke Islands often hide food to avoid having to share it with others; but they also hide non-consumables like fishing gear and tools. For example, to begin with I was a bit hurt by the fact that Polongou never used the fancy fishing equipment I always brought him when returning to Mbuke from Denmark, Australia or Port Moresby. I kept trying to buy things that I was sure he would have good use of, but he continued to use his old, half-broken equipment. I was starting to think that there was something wrong with giving such things to him in some way which was unknown to me. I started thinking that by not using it he was trying to tell me to stop buying such things for him, that perhaps expensive fishing gear was not an appropriate form for a son–father relationship. On the other hand, I knew that fishing gear was a perfectly normal thing for those 'in *yap*' to buy for their relatives in the Mbuke Islands, and Polongou was always very happy and thankful when I gave it to him.

I was confused until one day I went into his bedroom – a room rarely visited by anyone other than him and his wife – to ask him about something. On the wall, behind the door, I saw the transparent yellow waterproof bag that I had given him three years earlier after my first stay on Mbuke. In the bag was all the fishing equipment I had ever given him, everything from rolled up fishing line to large spinning baits for catching big mackerel. Most of these things were still in their original packaging and had clearly never been used. He saw me looking at the bag and said, 'I have hidden it, to avoid if the men say, "I'll take this one *amu*" [T: first; in this context: temporarily, see below], or "I like this one". I am not sure if he ever got round to actually using it.

The two pieces of hypothetical direct speech that Polongou used – 'I'll take this one *amu*' and 'I like this one' – are examples of two ways of losing things. The last could be said by a cross-cousin or classificatory brother to whom a person cannot say no directly without insulting them by indicating that the relation is not the way that their action makes appear. The first involves *amu*, borrowing without any specified time of return, which I will discuss further in Chapter 4, and which often leads to the problem that asking for something back indicates a shorter 'distance of relation' than one might want to communicate, and might spark 'talking' and people saying 'that man does not see other people, he does not know who is his blood' and similar accusations.

The fact that such relatives are entitled to take a person's things without them being able to do much about it is a general problem when one wants to protect one's personal property. For instance, a man's brothers (including classificatory brothers, which means that quite a few people may be 'brothers') might simply take his things, and it would be highly problematic to say anything about it, because that might be interpreted as a refusal of the particular type of relation (much like refusing *singaut* for remittances). But other close relatives like parents will also take things without asking in a way that would certainly surprise an outsider – or at least a Danish person – at first. I recall a situation in which a man living in Port Moresby was visited in the holiday by his daughter, who was studying in another big city. She had brought her new mobile phone, which she had bought from a fellow student with her own money, but when her father saw it he said 'it looks like that phone will stay with me for now' (TP: *luk olsem phone hia bai i stap wantaim mi pastaim*). The daughter, who looked rather unhappy about this, rather unwillingly said, 'Okay, but I'll keep it for the rest of the holiday'. The following day I saw the man using the phone, and clearly the daughter had failed to keep her new phone, even for the rest of the holiday.

Cross-cousins are often difficult too with regard to sharing, but often they will not simply take or seize things, but simply show up and one will have to offer them food if it is present. Rather than simply taking fishing gear, they will, perhaps after having spied it in the way Ben mentioned, say, 'I wish I had some fishing line, so I could go fishing'. If the person being visited has fishing line in their possession, they will have to be very certain that the one who said they wished they had some does not know this, otherwise they might gossip about the other person's lack of generosity, or lack of *tawian* –worse still, as we saw in Ken's case, they may be cursed.

So relationships between siblings, parents and children as well as particular cross-cousins are often relevant to attempts not to lose things that one would like to keep. But in practice there are many different types of relationship in which sharing occurs. Neighbours, friends and allies of various kinds are other examples. But relatives of one's patrilineage and those connected to it through their mother are the ones who a person is mostly obliged to help, and they are also the ones with whom a person has often had a life-long close relationship. As I noted in the case of Ben, a person might find it hard to say no to *singaut* if people ask for something that they have seen in their possession. The only good excuse is to say that one does not have what people ask for. The negative value of saying no while lying about having something is reflected in the term *akalouli*, which is a big part of this day-to-day 'game', meaning something like 'saying no based on a lie'. Hiding things in order to avoid sharing is a game that everyone must play if they are not to be ruined and want to get away with saying no without becoming subject to 'talk'. Everybody knows that everybody lies about it, and that everybody is forced to do so to avoid having to distribute all of their food and belongings among the rest of the village. But it can be problematic too, because being marked as a person of *akalouli* means that one will be considered a selfish and greedy person (see Chapter 4) who lacks some of the properties that constitute a good and proper person. It reflects on one's 'person's value', one's *tawian*, and hence has a negative impact on popularity and support. What is interesting about *akalouli* here is that the only legitimate way of saying no is to lie and say that one is simply unable to meet the requests of others. Saying, 'No, I am saving my betel nuts for tomorrow' would not be acceptable, and I have never once heard anyone do this, even though I was part of the daily sharing of betel nut throughout my fieldwork. Everybody knows that one might have some betel nut that one wants to save for the following day, and nobody will question you the following day if they see that you now suddenly have betel nut again (only perhaps jokingly). Clearly a number of strategies for keeping things are necessary, when constantly being confronted with *singaut* in daily life, and trying to avoid 'talk'.

In other words, it is hard to say no, because a person will be considered a bad and selfish person, and relatives will accuse them of 'not seeing them'. They might also spread the word that they are of *akalouli*, because they have seen what kind of person someone is through their actions. If a cross-cousin tells their mother about it, they risk being cursed; but others may spread rumours too, which will make it hard to gain support in a variety of situations.

Disputing Relationships and Putting Them into Their Right Order

Gossip is often the way of questioning other people's willingness to share. This is a way to air one's views in response to people who say no, a way of slandering others to force them to share in the future. Besnier provides a useful definition of gossip: 'the negatively evaluative and morally laden verbal exchange concerning the conduct of absent third parties' (Besnier 2009: 13). Drawing on this definition, cursing might be seen as an extreme form of gossip, morally evaluating others behind their back, but also attempting to make such a statement affect them. It has also been argued that gossip is socially integrating, that its function is to draw lines between acceptable and unacceptable behaviour (Gluckman 1963). In this sense it is a way of pointing out that a person is behaving wrongly by telling others but without telling them in person. But as Besnier (2009: 16–17) notes, this depiction of gossip as a social regulator fails to account for the interests the gossiping person may have in representing others in particular ways.

Rather than focusing on the functions of gossip, we might focus on the consequences of gossip for its victims, Besnier argues (ibid.: 17). Here I might add that what is involved here are consequences not only for the victim, but also for the relation between the gossiper and the victim. Gossip is a particular description of social relations. The knowledge the anthropologist gathers in the field might share many characteristics with gossip, in the nature of both being 'partial theories' (Van Vleet 2003). But in the Mbuke Islands, the theory involved is most often a theory of a sociality of which the gossiper forms part; and if gossip may in popular phrasing contribute to 'character assassination' (Bailey 1971: 1), then the assassin is hit too in that one of their relations is temporarily disrupted.

The interesting parallel to gossip as character assassination in a European context (ibid.) is that both gossip and cursing among Mbuke people are ways in which the gossiper or curser might dispute not only the relations between them and their victim, but also the victim as a person. Rather than assassination, it might be appropriate to call it socially 'injuring' or 'bruising' another, but always while hoping by such means to return relationships back to the right order, an order in which relatives respond positively to *singaut* from particular relatives. When people complain about migrant relatives not 'seeing them', as I discussed in Chapter 2, they often do so through gossip. The similarity between cursing and gossip is that they entail speaking poorly of a close relative in the presence of others, thereby questioning the person and their constitution as a 'good person' and a relative, but with the hope that the words spoken might cause the person to change.

Both cursing and gossip take the form of an utterance of a statement in the presence of others. Steward and Strathern (2004) have pointed out in a similar vein that there are important connections between magic (including sorcery and witchcraft) and gossip. They point out that both themes have received much attention in anthropology but seldom together, although they are often related (ibid.: ix). For instance, accusations of witchcraft often take the form of rumours (ibid.), and similarly the migrant who fears that they have been cursed because they are losing money will often hear rumours about grudges held against them. Gossip and rumour may work as a covert form of sorcery or witchcraft in their absence, Steward and Strathern point out, and as we have seen in the Mbuke case, cursing and gossip play a similar role in social relations. Like sorcery and gossip, two seemingly different things share the fact that 'they focus on the sources of tension in social relationships and the use of cultural themes and historical ideas in transforming these relationships' (ibid.: xi).

Generally, Steward and Strathern show that a focus on fear of and accusations of sorcery and witchcraft are comparable to gossip and rumour in that both challenge relationships and might slander particular persons. I have altered the focus by looking at the very act of uttering a statement which, when directed towards certain relatives, is in fact a curse. I have argued that the statement defines its own context, that is, the context for a statement is partially made by that very statement rather than being a precondition of its occurrence. Arising from a conflict in the context of social relations, both gossip and cursing take the form of statements which represent the potential for dealing with specific disputed relations in the future so that the context is made anew or restored ('straightened'). While Steward and Strathern point out that accusations of wrong-doing (through gossip, for example) polarize the parties involved socially (ibid.: xii), in my case the object (and hoped for outcome) of action is the opposite: through disordering the relation, the intention is to cause the other to acknowledge the relation better, hence to strengthen or 'straighten' the relationship.

Conclusions

Schwartz (1975) argued that cursing played a big part in forcing migrants to send remittances. In his account, *tandritanitani* was the only form cursing took, but here I have shown that gossip also contributes to ensuring sharing. Blessings have also been mentioned because they too ensure sharing, by a similar means, namely by uttering statements about the nature of the giver's or non-giver's person; they are statements which affect the constitution of that person in various ways. Cursing simply takes the form of a public utterance of a statement in a particular way, as do blessings. Gossip is comparable in various ways, and we could even say that cursing is a modality of gossip and slander, even though it is at the far extreme of such 'talk'. Mbuke people also group these kinds of statements as 'talk' in certain contexts, whether they mean relatives that might curse them or others who simply speak poorly of them to others. Likewise, not only do they use the same word for blessing and cursing (*tandritanitani*), they refer to both of them as the 'power of talk' or the 'power of the mouth'. In the context of talk, speech acts produce value by representing actions as reflections of a person's constitution, connoted in the term *tawian*, the value of a person.

Gossiping as well as cursing are ways of disputing, constituting and negotiating relationships by publicly uttering statements questioning a person's willingness to give, and the person is destabilized to different degrees by both. One way of ruining someone's 'good name', their *tawian*, is by gossiping, by saying that 'my brother must think I have died, he never sees me', thereby questioning his ability to 'see' his relations and fulfil the obligations that they entail, and thereby question 'the good of him'. The fear of 'talk' and its extreme, *tandritanitani* (curse), tends to force people to lie, which is a large part of the daily economy of people in the Mbuke Islands. 'Talk' involves attempts with varying degrees of force or draw back a person into recognizing a relationship as part of their person, such as forcing migrants to remit and fellow villagers to share food. The fear of being cursed or being subject to gossip is the fear of becoming socially invisible and making others invisible to oneself, a fear of social relations becoming unstable or invisible.

Cursing, both in the way Schwartz describes it and in the way Mbuke people practise and describe it, needs no spells or other exotic deeds. A curse among the Mbuke is simply a statement, statements about other people's failure to meet their perceived obligations, in the past as well as in the future, as is gossip. *Tandritanitani* blessings are also simply statements about the object of speech, but they are morally positively laden. All three share the feature that the words are believed to cause effects (indirectly), in that they might make a person catch more fish, make a person lose their money, or they might devalue a person's social standing by indicating failure to see social relations in their proper guise, a proper guise which is as much the outcome of these social dynamics as it is their precondition. In line with Rosaldo's objection against certain formulations of speech act theory, individual persons ('autonomous selves') are not simply unconfined authors of the effects caused by particular kinds of 'talk', but rather the outcomes of 'talk' are relationally constituted in the interplay between actors, 'victims' and audiences (whether living persons, ancestors or 'God'). Gossip, cursing and blessing share their reference to that which is hidden, that which is not, but perhaps should be or cannot be, made to 'appear'. Gifts not given, food or money hidden, gifts that cannot be made to 'appear' by reciprocation. 'Talk' addresses an audience which participates in the production of value, whether as ancestral spirits causing effects or fellow gossipers who recognize and spread the word that someone is failing to share.

Notes

1. The Tok Pisin term *rabis* carries connotations of poor, worthless and even bad.
2. As some forms of Christianity are present among Mbuke people, they often equate *mata-moma* with *mari-mari*, Tok Pisin for 'pity' or 'mercy', which among Mbuke people is often associated with some form of Christianity.
3. And in this sense it is perhaps a virtual fantasy, something which can never fully be realized; see Derrida (1992).
4. A noted in Chapter 1, Fortune uses 'Manus' to refer to Titan people.

5. 'Sir Ghost' was translation adopted by both Fortune (1969) and Mead (2001) of *moen palit*, the term for guardian ancestral spirits of particular 'houses' (families). Today, Mbuke people mostly speak more generally about *mambru*, which simply means ancestor, and deny that they have (or believe in) 'house spirits' any longer. But they still often speak of the agency of ancestors more generally, as we can see here.

6. Translating *kanain* as 'compensation' might on further exploration turn out to be misleading and simplistic, but these payments are not the theme of this chapter, and therefore the translation will suffice. It seems likely that what Mbuke people call *kanain* is what Fortune identified as *kano*, an 'expiatory payment' done after a 'sin' had been confessed (e.g. Fortune 1969: 41).

7. This was a bigger part of the economy between 2005 and 2009 than it is now (2015), since the sea cucumber population radically declined due to overfishing. The season during which the fisheries authorities allowed the collection and trade in sea cucumbers became shorter and shorter between 2006 and 2009, and the money to be gained from the activity decreased radically.

8. As noted in Chapter 1, I estimated the average annual amount raised from *singaut* to be K1,200 per household.

4

It's Never Tomorrow

Debt, Selfishness and the Contest of Obligation

———————— ◆●◆ ————————

'They say, "tomorrow I will pay you", but you know, there is always another tomorrow, the next day there is another tomorrow – tomorrow never comes up!' Linda said this laughingly while talking about the many debts people have in the trade store she and Polongou run from their house. But it is serious too, because when people get something from the store while saying that they will pay 'later' – sometimes without ever doing so – it makes it difficult for them to maintain their business. Polongou and Linda receive very few remittances, and since Linda retired from her job as the headteacher of the community school, their most stabile means of income is the trade store. The moral obligation to help kin, to share money and food with others, makes running a business hard because sharing is not necessarily based on reciprocity in material terms but represents the mutual recognition of relationships. Running a trade store is a matter of trying to make the business survive in spite of this, and in spite of the dilemmas in terms of value formation and personhood it involves.

This chapter deals with the relationship between debt and the social obligation to share, and with the negative value associated with 'selfishness'. While in the two previous chapters I have shown that by responding positively to *singaut* the person often strives to reveal themselves as founded in social relationships, predominantly those of kinship, this chapter introduces 'the person alone' as a negative value. As I argue, accusations of selfishness and 'wanting to be alone' provide categories with which to refer to actions that make the person appear not to embody a meaningful sociality – such as that of kinship relations or the community – in which value can take form, but as 'a person alone', connoted by the moral criticism of selfishness. This demonstrates that value is always produced with reference to some audience, whether imagined or concrete. Thus acts that benefit one person only cannot produce value, because they render the inter-personal dialectics of value production impossible. Empirically, I address questions of borrowing, getting things on credit and the conflicts such 'debts' give rise to, especially conflicts affecting trade store owners in the villages. Interestingly, as we shall see in Chapter 5, 'the person alone' (T: *eh mo ye*, lit. 'that man him') is nearly without exception used in sentences concerning greed for money and 'commodity thinking' that causes selfishness, and may hence be looked upon as the Mbuke version of what has been described as an emergence of possessive individualism in Melanesia, which according to Foster (1995b) is precisely associated with the individual acquisition and consumption of commodities.

By rhetorically contrasting a good person with 'the person alone', some trade store debtors manage to conceptually transform specific transactions from being ones initiated by requests for getting things on credit to being what I refer to as generalized sharing. I argue that getting things on credit while later appealing to the obligation to share is an indirect form of *singaut*. A key observation is that, however implicit, a call for getting money or things back is often morally categorized as 'commodity thinking' and selfishness. Even if debt is also by nature a social obligation, often it is rhetorically compartmentalized as anti-social commodity thinking connoted with terms such as 'the person alone', 'businessman' or *ol kong-kong* (Tok Pisin for Asians), who run stores in Manus in which they rarely give credit.

The chapter is structured in four parts. I first introduce the problems that people living in the villages often have when saying no to giving credit, followed by a section about a local concept of sharing which is similar to Sahlins's concept of generalized reciprocity (Sahlins 1972: 194), but which I term 'generalized sharing' to highlight the lack of material reciprocity involved in it. As discussed in the third section of the chapter, such generalized sharing is often rhetorically presented as fundamentally different from debt, which is reflected in the way that jokes that push generalized sharing beyond its conceptual limit (thereby defining this limit) transform it into something radically and explicitly different, something surprisingly similar to debt. The final section of the chapter discusses the relationship between debt and generalized sharing in terms of personhood. Following the Mbuke conceptualization of the person who says no to – or who reclaims – debt as 'selfish', 'greedy' or 'a person alone', I argue that among Mbuke people themselves the social relations needed to practise commodity exchange cannot easily be realized, and in that sense the possessive individual can only be a category of critique.

Trade Stores

Apart from remittances from migrant relatives and the use of that money for various purposes, the most direct engagement with the money economy in interpersonal relationships among people in the villages involves trade stores and other kinds of outlets that some people try to run there. Attempts to make money by selling things to make a small profit in the villages create a situation in which the nature of social relations needed to make money from commodity exchange comes into conflict with kinship obligations and other relations prescribing solidarity and sharing.

One issue of great concern for trade-store owners in the Mbuke Islands involves customers getting things on credit and how to get such debts repaid. In fact, most trade stores and outlets eventually close down when credits have 'eaten up' the store's capital entirely. The Titan word often used for 'on credit' is *amu*, which also means 'first', hence indicating the reference that debt makes to time and to the future in particular, since it implies getting something now and returning it in the future. On the face of it, debt would appear to be a way for a person to consume the fruits of a brighter future.[1] But this future is speculative, and it might in fact never come. It might be assumed that this places the debtor in an unfortunate situation, but since 'there is always another tomorrow' it often mainly places the creditor in a dilemma.[2] One general problem for people running trade stores in the Mbuke Islands is the fear that if they reclaim an outstanding debt from another Mbuke person, this is often taken as an insult and followed by accusations of selfishness.

I asked a wealthy businessman from Mbuke, who has great experience in starting up businesses and making money in Port Moresby, what kind of business he thought would be preferable for a person in the village to start up if they wanted to make money: 'No kind, it can't be done. It will fall down eventually. It will be eaten by *amu*'. I argue here that this is because debt, which characterizes alienated relations between shopkeepers and customers, and the social obligation to share, which characterizes family relations, friendship and in certain situations even fellow 'Mbuke people' as such, are perceived and rhetorically presented as qualitatively different, and not degrees of the same basic mechanism.

In his classic treatment of reciprocity, Sahlins in a sense treated debt and reciprocal obligation on a par by placing them as forms of reciprocity on the same continuum including both trade (balanced reciprocity) and sharing among close relatives (generalized reciprocity) (Sahlins 1972: 191–96). Sahlins points out that the time span of reciprocity is relative to the distance of the relationship between the exchanging parties; that is, there is a longer time span between relatives, and a shorter one between strangers (ibid.:

196–197, 231–232). In this sense claiming reciprocation for a previous transaction will also somehow define the nature of the relationship.

It might perhaps be argued that it is this interconnection between time span and closeness or distance of the relationship that the debtor manipulates – even misuses – on Mbuke when saying 'later I will pay', when reminded of – or establishing – a debt, while often never doing so. That is to say, by endlessly delaying repayment the debtor leaves it to the creditor to define the nature of the relationship by reclaiming a debt. In this sense, the moment of asking for repayment would be a moment of defining the distance of the relationship, and therefore trade-store owners might be reluctant to claim money back. However, I argue here that debt and the social obligation to share are rhetorically contrasted as radical oppositions by trade-store costumers unable to pay, and that it is this difference that debtors take advantage of when they, so to speak, leave tomorrow to never come, and when they force trade store owners to accept *amu* while knowing that it will be their eventual downfall. Rather than the two being acknowledged as being degrees of the same they are rather rhetorically presented as radically different social obligations altogether.

The Titan word *amu* means 'first' or 'before', but has come to refer to acquisition 'on credit' in many contexts. Most people relate it directly to trade stores and other contexts in which money mediates exchange in one way or another. The logic of this is that I get something from you 'before' or now, and in the future I will pay for it or replace it. It can sometimes refer to getting something and replacing it with something identical, a coconut later replaced by a coconut, or a tin of tuna by a tin of tuna. And it may also refer to borrowing something and delivering back that very thing (like a boat). By saying 'can I get it *amu*' then, one is saying, 'can I get it now and return it or pay for it later'. Often it refers to getting something that one would normally have paid for, and then paying for it later, often at an unspecified moment in the future. The time span of the future to which *amu* refers is a key issue here, because it is a future that does not always come, and trying to make it come is often problematic.

The 'wantok system' in Papua New Guinea (PNG), explained in Chapter 1, has nationally become a popular way of referring to nepotism, favouritism and other kinds of 'corruption' in state institutions (e.g. Reed 2003: 165). Similarly, the '*amu* system' has become a way of talking about one of the greatest obstacles to doing business or accumulating money generally in the villages of the Mbuke Islands. One of the better-off men in the village on Mbuke put it as follows:

The '*amu* system' is a system which has become very popular. But some people don't like this system, because people tend to forget, you know? People come around and say, 'I'll get a packet of biscuits from your trade store *amu*'. At that point the man in the store will be all right with it, because he thinks that you will come and sort it out later. But *amu* does not define a time, it doesn't define a day. It defines anytime, any day, for you to come and sort it out. But sometimes it passes into oblivion – and that is why plenty of men who own trade stores say no to *amu*, they say that you have to sort it out, you have to have money. They say 'no more *amu*'.

All the trade-store owners in the Mbuke Islands have a small sign on the wall of their store saying *nogat dinau*, which means 'no credit' in Tok Pisin, indicating that they have reached the point this man indicates. But unfortunately, relatives are harder to say no to than other people, and most Mbuke people are related somehow. The fact that such signs are written in Tok Pisin rather than in Titan might indicate the fact that it is highly problematic to say no to relatives, even on a sign. At some level, using Tok Pisin rules out other Mbuke people as the main receivers of the message on such signs, while many of the visitors coming to Mbuke – to sell their produce from gardens on Manus Island for example – belong to other linguistic groups with whom Mbuke people communicate in Tok Pisin. Claiming back *amu* even after a long time is often morally problematic, and saying that one would like the *amu* back is an indication that the relation is of a different nature from that indicated by the fact that it has not been repaid. It is not crucial what the specific relation is here (unlike in the situation of requests for remittances), because saying no to a request for *amu* in itself reveals an asymmetry in perception of the relation between the person making the request and the recipient of that request. *Amu* is not confined to kinship relations, but may also be relevant to neighbours and friends, other 'Mbuke people'.

One man, also a returned migrant running a trade store, said in an interview: 'It is not *amu* any more. It is just for going now, not for going back. It is dead money now'. According to older informants, a similar system of borrowing used to work well in the past, for two main reasons.[3] One is that it is not usually hard or impossible to return a person's canoe when one has finished using it, or to get hold of a coconut – everyone should have some kind of access, since many of the areas where coconut palms grow, such as the abandoned coconut plantation (to which I shall return in the following chapters) on the Mbuke Islands are not subject to strict ownership or customary land title. The second reason that *amu* was allegedly a smaller problem in the past is that even though some people did not pay off their *amu*, it was not a big problem because the items involved were more easily accessible to everyone, and shortage was allegedly not a problem to the same extent. In the latter sense, *amu* might in practice always have meant – in some relations at least – getting something without ever replacing it.

Money and preserved or dried food (like canned meat, rice and sugar) sold in trade stores have introduced a possibility for accumulation that never applied to the foodstuffs subject to the kind of exchanges involving *amu* practised in the past.[4] In this sense, both money and new types of goods involve a kind of temporality which does not suit the temporality of 'first' and 'later' involved in *amu*.

Now that money and the food that can be purchased with it have become important factors in the village economy, *amu* appears to have changed; or it would perhaps be more accurate to say that it has failed to adapt.[5] The main change in *amu* – for those in an affluent situation – is that people are starting to fail to pay back debts because they are having difficulty with obtaining money. And as one informant put it, 'You cannot go around on the sea and find a tin of tuna'. It seems always to be the case that *amu* is asked for by the person receiving it, not offered voluntarily to them (or forced upon them) by those giving it. People have similar difficulties in saying no to *amu* as described in earlier with regard to remittances and food sharing: many different relations are at play, a 'person's value' and good name (*tawian*) are at stake, you risk being cursed or people may start gossiping, claiming that you are not a generous person or suggesting that you have grown blind to your relationships. But specifically in the context of saying no to *amu*, accusations of 'selfishness' (this being the word used in Tok Pisin) or 'wanting to be alone' are heard, and not simply from relatives who might feel that they have a certain right to a relative's possessions and help, but also by fellow Mbuke people who are not related to the trade-store owner in question in a way that would be of significance in the context of *singaut* for remittances. Running a trade store or a petrol outlet in the village is particularly difficult, because the nature of such businesses is to visibly have the relevant commodity available; this removes the possibility of hiding it or lying about having it. This means that saying no to *amu* means saying no directly, which, as we have also seen, Mbuke people try very hard to avoid when met with various forms of *singaut*. The problem is that in such an environment it is very difficult to do business, because everything will be 'eaten' by *amu*.

So, saying no directly is avoided, which means that strategies of avoiding requests for *amu* often become preferable. The behaviour my hosts had towards potential customers could be understood as strategies for avoiding *amu*. Often, in the morning, while the rest of the family were getting up or preparing food in the kitchen, I would sit smoking on the veranda of the house, and from there I could see the small window into the trade store underneath the house. People arriving at the store would ask me to tell people in the house that they were there, and when I did that, the members of the household would often ask me, 'Who is it?' Only after consideration would they go down to serve the customer or, alternatively, say that I should tell them that they were having breakfast. After a while I started looking after the trade store once in a while, like the rest of the household, and I was told that this was an advantage because people were less likely to ask me for *amu*.

Only very few people succeed in establishing an ongoing business in the Mbuke Islands. Those who do are often people who already have incomes (village schoolteachers, people with a lot of migrant children and so on), and they are generally people with a lot of assets already. They often own a boat or a large outrigger canoe. They do not depend on help from others in as many ways as most people do. When they need to go to town, they will not need to borrow someone else's boat, who in turn might say, 'Now you want to borrow my boat, but last time I asked for *amu* in your trade store you said no' – even though they would probably not be that direct. Owning boats, canoes, fishing gear and such like makes a person slightly independent and free to say no (sometimes, but not to close relatives), and they are in a sense the local petty capitalists who own the means of production and the capital needed to start up a business in the first place. But there are other factors that make somebody able to resist *amu*, such as having other ways of exhausting the obligation to share.

For instance, Polongou has run his and his wife's trade store since they came back to the village in the 1990s, after having been away working for most of their lives. He is one of the petty capitalists just mentioned, but he does not receive much by way of remittances, even though he has a lot of well-educated and working children, since he refuses to *singaut*. If they want to send money, they may, he says, but he tells them not to (I know from experience), and they do not. Even though this is the case, he still owns a boat, two outboard motors, two large outrigger canoes and one of the biggest houses on the island. This is partly due to the fact that he came back with a lot of money when he retired. But lots of people come back with large amounts of money, and only a few manage to keep hold of some of it as Polongou has done. His success is likely due to the fact that he is a highly respected man as a traditional leader (T: *lapan*; TP: 'clan leader') in the village, perhaps making people less inclined to push him towards defining his relationship vis-à-vis them, which he would be forced to if he had to ask for his money back. For his part, he often says that the store belongs to his wife and that it is often she who visits other people about their *amu* in their store, hence helping him to avoid having to appear 'selfish'. Others less fortunate, who have failed in attempts to establish small businesses like his, say that people pay back their *amu* to him because he is respected. In reality, it is probably not that simple though, and it is a constant struggle for him and Linda to keep the store going. It seems that running a store is only possible if you have other assets which can help you fulfil your kinship obligations and other expected acts of generosity. The recently returned migrant I mentioned above, who is also the wife of a clan leader, remarked:

> If you don't give it [*amu*] you will be like an odd man out. People will look at you like you are not a man from Mbuke, eh? Like you are a man from space or something, and that you prefer to be 'yourself only' (TP: *yu yet*). But really, when you come to see the truth of it, there is no reason why you should spoon-feed and look after your family like that. I sometimes think that way. I usually help other people […] but is it really necessary? But if I say no to *amu* then people will go somewhere and say, 'That clan leader's wife is not a good woman, and she hides things'. They will tell stories behind your back you know: 'He is a "clan-leader nothing" [i.e. in name only] because he is not looking after one single man'. People's expectations are like that. But that is not proper, eh? He is supposed to look after the affairs of the clan, but those people, they think he is like a father of theirs who should look after them with food.

For those trying to prevent *amu* from ruining their business there is a great fear of being accused of being selfish and wanting to be *yu yet*. *Yu yet* is Tok Pisin and can be translated as something like 'yourself only' or 'you alone'. The English word 'selfish' is also used occasionally when making such accusations. This means that it is in fact very difficult to resist *amu* because it is viewed as non-sharing, and as I have argued in the two previous chapters, it is potentially damaging for a person's social standing to be labelled a person who does not help others. It is difficult to provide direct, empirical observations of such accusations, since they often occur in rather subtle ways, such as when someone said the following to me when I was reluctant to lend him petrol that I needed for particular purposes: 'Don't get [learn] the behaviour of your … [relative] who wants to be alone (TP: *laik stap em yet*)', hence including criticism of both the other person and me, without accusing either of us face to face. Eventually a person might become an 'odd man out' (a phrase that is a reflection of the recently returned migrant woman's good English skills, not a general term), or in Tok Pisin *yu yet* or *em yet, em yet* ('him/her only, him/her only'), or in Titan *eh mo ye* (lit. 'that man him'), an equivalent of *em yet, em yet*.

The fear of being labelled selfish or as a person who thinks about 'oneself only' means that most people eventually fail to make money from running a trade store. Surprisingly many people I know in the Mbuke Islands explained that they had tried to sell something. Whether they had tried selling loose cigarettes and fishing equipment or tried running trade stores or petrol outlets, all of them said that they had stopped because *amu* had ruined their business. The tendency for these kinds of trade to be unstable is evident by the fact that one in every four houses has a room especially built and designated for a trade store underneath it (houses are built on poles), most of which are not operating.

One trade-store owner said that people take advantage of 'the system'. He suggested that some people do not understand how costly it is to run a store, having to go to town and get the goods and so on, and even if they do, 'they are just living off the system'. In that sense it is not the indebted person that faces trouble among Mbuke people, but the creditor who is 'taken advantage of'. The person who has given a lot out on credit, a lot of tomorrows or 'laters' waiting to come, can do little about it. A person is expected to help their kin and other people in need generally, and part of this involves allowing them to have *amu* until they have the ability of paying it back. Claiming back money indicates that the relation is not close enough for them to have that right. Often the relation is indeed close, and reclaiming *amu* would be a serious misrecognition of a relative. As the woman quoted above indicated, members of the patrilineal descent group (TP: 'clan') of which her husband is the leader will expect him (and members of his household) not to say no to requests for *amu*, because as a leader he should 'look after' others. Trade-store owners are afraid of the consequences of asking debts to be settled, and would rather lose their business than lose their good name and popularity in other aspects of social life. The uneasy paradox, both for the migrant and the wealthy villager, is that even though they might feel that settlement is due, they cannot demand this from a person who they are well aware is unable to provide it even if they might want to.

When, in a context in which others could not overhear his reply, I asked a wealthy man about the situation, he commented as follows: 'Maybe we spoon-feed them too much and now they are used to help and yet more help – one way traffic, yeah!' In abstract terms, complaints about *amu* are frequent, but saying this directly to the debtor is avoided, which is also evident by the fact that most trade stores eventually close down. As one previously cited migrant commented, 'even if you do think somebody should [reciprocate] – I can't say it, it is for them to say'. Not only must one not reclaim a debt too soon after it is established, it appears in fact that one 'can't say it' at all. The same problem occurs when having to say no in the first place. On the few occasions that someone did ask to get something *amu* when I was looking after my hosts' store, I would go upstairs to ask one of them to approve it, since they had often told me that they had decided to say no to *amu*. But not once did they refuse. 'With that guy, it is all right, he is family', they would explain, only to complain later that he did not pay. So the best avoidance strategy was to avoid being confronted with the question, thereby avoiding the necessity of responding negatively. In this connection, having an excuse for not being able to serve customers who were expected to ask for *amu*, or having the anthropologist man the store (making people less inclined to ask for *amu*) were both good strategies. The children who were often sent to the trade store in the morning to buy biscuits and tea bags would even clink coins in their hands when they called out for us outside the kitchen, thus making it clear that they had money to pay.

It is difficult to ask for outstanding debts to be paid, not only because doing so indicates that the relationship in question is not as close as the debtor seems to think, but also because asking someone to give something that they cannot give is rude, a challenge at best, and always potentially renders not only the other person but also oneself as 'not a person from Mbuke'. This means that a number of minor and subtle strategies to avoid being asked for *amu* in the first place are preferable. But one question remains. How do the people who never pay back *amu* get away with it without losing their popularity or 'name' (which is the risk run by anyone who says no to requests)? Why or how can someone 'live off the system' without significant social marginalization as a result? It might be expected, for example, that an endless running up of debts might distort power relations. But this does not seem to be the case. But how did *amu* become 'one-way traffic'? To answer this, I will explore a few aspects of the 'generalized sharing' of daily solidarity in the village, the give-and-take of daily life, in more detail.

Indirect *Singaut*: Turning *Amu* into Sharing

As noted above, Sahlins placed forms of reciprocity on a continuum stretching from generalized reciprocity through balanced reciprocity to negative reciprocity. The first operated in relations of 'kinship due', and as such 'the counter is not defined by time' but is indefinite and determined by 'what the recipient can afford and when' (Sahlins 1972: 194). Negative reciprocity, on the other hand, is described as occurring between strangers or even enemies between whom the social relationship is the opposite extreme from that which pertains to generalized reciprocity; it is 'the attempt to get something for nothing', and reciprocation takes place only if it proves unavoidable. Sahlins compares balanced reciprocity, placed in the middle of the continuum, with trade, which is 'direct reciprocity' (ibid.: 194–95). By introducing the term 'generalized sharing', I simply aim to make the point that contrary to generalized reciprocity, as defined by Sahlins, in which transactions also generate obligations – 'this is not to say that the handing over of things in such a form ... generates no counter obligation' (ibid.:

194) – in daily sharing among the Mbuke, any hopes for future reciprocity are either absent or must be kept entirely unarticulated (cf. Bourdieu 1977: 5). This is how what may appear precisely to be reciprocity, even to Mbuke people, can turn into 'one-way traffic'.

While *amu* is the local term that comes closest to the Western concept of debt (or 'on credit'), it also has other meanings relative to context, as, obviously, do uses of words like debt in other languages as well. For example, the word *amu* is also used with regard to betel nuts: *sin bruei kime amu*, which in Titan means 'one betel nut come-here first'. However, here *amu* does not imply 'I will replace it'. In the Mbuke Islands, betel nut is shared without much discussion (if not hidden) because it is not particularly costly, and transactions in it work in accordance with a kind of sharing of which no one keeps track – people simply give the nuts to each other (at least when others know that they have them), and receive them when they possess none themselves. Betel nuts are the simplest version of what is often referred to as *ang-ang*. In a sense, I would argue that *ang-ang* is the form of giving into which *amu* is transformed by those who claim that any trade store owner claiming money back or refusing *amu* is selfish or 'wants to be alone'.

Angini means '(to) feed (someone)' in Titan. This is something that people naturally do for their children, and many people also feed their ageing parents if they are unable to look after themselves. This is unsolicited sharing. In this sense it means giving without expecting a return, not out of pity but out of obligation and love. The 'return' remains potential, part of an undefined and only potential future in the case of one's children. In reciprocity terms, people 'feed' their parents because they were fed by them as children. Their parents also brought them up and paid their school fees. In this sense there is a clear and logical generalized reciprocity involved: your children will feed you later, and you feed your parents because they fed you before, but the time span is long term and the return may never occur. The reason to reciprocate is not the settlement of a debt but the nature of the relation between giver and receiver. In the case of mortuary exchange, I heard people use *angini* as an argument when money is distributed: 'I used to feed him, so I should have something, they should recognize me'. This means that ultimately the potential future of reciprocation for feeding is after death, and potentially never. The kind of reciprocity involved here may help answer the question of 'one-way traffic' posed above.

Ang-ang is a form of the word *angini*. I was told that, like *angini*, it means giving without any expectation of reciprocity or reward, but simultaneously it is a kind of investment or trying out of a relationship, and is similar to what Sahlins described as generalized reciprocity, in which the time span for reciprocation is very long and undefined. It is what the trade-store owner attempts to reveal ('make appear') that *amu* is not when claiming money back, and it is what the debtor 'makes appear' that it is, by not only endlessly delaying 'tomorrow', but especially by meeting requests for money back by accusing the trade-store owner of 'wanting to be alone'. *Ang-ang* is different from *mata-moma* (pity), in that when one does *ang-ang* it is not a response or appearance of pity but an act of compassion between equals, which means that reciprocation is not ruled out. Neighbours and close family (siblings, parents and so forth) are usually given as examples: you help them, and one day they might (or might not) be able or inclined to help you. But you do not 'return' the favours, you do *ang-ang* because of the good relationship you have with someone else or because you want (or hope) to establish a good relationship. As one of my neighbours on Mbuke put it:

> if I am doing well right now, and I have plenty, then I might feed (TP: *feedim*) you, when I am all right – I might *ang-ang*. If I then get a bit sick or somehow I am in a bad situation, then *lele-awian* is back with you like: 'this man was helping me, back when he was all right, he *ang-ang*[ed] and now he is in that situation, I think I'll go and see him'. That is the way of *ang-ang*.

Note here how material reciprocity is again only potentially present, if the situation permits it – or demands it. It is not a matter of having to reciprocate when something has been received, but a matter of 'seeing' the situation of the other by responding appropriately to it. The good-'seeing' of *ang-ang* is your chance to reveal ('make appear') 'the good of you':

> You see a man and you see that he has a need for something – sago, for example – and you take a bit of sago and you give that to him. You give it out of your goodness (T: *tawian*), like your helping. You see him and you give. That is *ang-ang*. You see like this: 'I have little, but that is okay, we can eat little and still give a little to this man.

Polongou summed it up well with these words on *mata-moma* and *ang-ang*:

> *Ang-ang* is like this: You have something and you give it to someone else. Even though they have not requested it (TP: *ol i no singaut*), you can still take something and go and give it to your sister or your brother. *Mata-moma* is kind of like [this]. For example, a man who is an unwell/inefficient man, because he is a bad man, you feel sorry for him and you give something to him. *Ang-ang* is a bit different from that. *Ang-ang* is something that we usually do with our family. Like if I catch a bit of fish, then I might go and give some of them to [my sister], just to help her out – then

you *ang-ang*, eh? But it does not mean that she is bad and I feel sorry for her or something. It's just that, when family members get a bit of affluence, we can give a bit to our family members.

Even though *ang-ang* is also a characteristic of transactions between non-kin according to many other informants, Polongou's statement makes the difference clear. *Mata-moma* is seeing those who are to be pitied, those who, due to circumstances that you observe, call for the emotion which is giving. *Ang-ang* is also giving without expectancy of reward, also part of the very observation of need, but potentially there might be reciprocation in the future. Although this discussion of reciprocity might sound like a chicken-and-egg situation, many Mbuke people are very vocal in pointing out that *ang-ang* is not like reciprocity in the sense of expecting some kind of material reciprocation at some point. But since people often receive from those to whom they also give, it often looks like reciprocity. Even if a person may act with the past actions of the other in mind, this is because these actions revealed his good properties or a particular relation, not because the score needs to be settled.

By terming this 'generalized sharing', rather than generalized reciprocity, my aim is simply to note the reverse causal principle (transactions do not generate obligations, they are caused by them), because this reversal is what potentially makes it a principle of 'one-way traffic', which is difficult to resist. Reciprocation might become 'a goal' (as Mbuke people sometimes phrase it) for the receiver, but it is a goal that might be missed if the opportunity never occurs, because daily sharing is not competitive exchange, but pragmatic measures taken to make village survival possible, something which is becoming harder as resources become scarcer, the population grows and barter with other groups has broken down as ecological specializations are dissolved. The cause of giving is the emotional and/or kinship bond between giver and receiver, and since an emotional bond often goes both ways (we all hope), then the giving also goes both ways, but only if possible. In 'generalized sharing' then, potential reciprocity is confined to a 'spin off', in a situation where both parties at a different point in time may or may not have something that the other may desire.

To anyone vaguely familiar with the anthropological literature dealing with the concept of reciprocity, it would seem fairly clear at this point that *ang-ang* comes extremely close to what is often meant by reciprocity. That is to say, *ang-ang*, like reciprocity, is a principle of circulation in which transactions take place within social relations that are generally closer and more long term than those of commodity exchange, and in which giving is motivated by relationships between persons, rather than by relations (of value) between things (Gregory 1982). In the Introduction, however,

I confined myself to a narrower definition of reciprocity, drawing on Gell (1992) and saying that what has otherwise been described as general-ized reciprocity may also be looked upon as the 'absence of reciprocity'. A narrower definition of reciprocity is provided by most dictionaries: 'a situation in which two people, countries, etc. provide the same help or advantages to each other' (Wehmeier 2000: 1060). This definition seems to rule out *ang-ang* as reciprocity since it includes 'one-way traffic'. As my intention here is to take Mbuke concepts seriously, they would protest in strong terms if I tried to indicate that they expect something in return. As I have noted earlier, we are not dealing here with a norm of reciprocation but a norm of generosity and a norm of responding positively to requests.

Based on people's definitions of *ang-ang* with regard to day-to-day sharing in the villages, *ang-ang* has to do with sharing among equals, relatives as well as allies beyond one's clan (such as neighbours). In this there is an ideology that people do not give in order to be able to draw on reciprocity (such as the future possibility of borrowing the other party's boat). But underlying this normative meaning there is the following paradox: in order to be equals, and to prevent *ang-ang* from turning into *mata-moma*, there must be the possi-bility of reciprocation. In *ang-ang* lies a possibility of strengthening alliances of various kinds, but this has to remain unspoken. However, through the widespread practice of joking, this unspoken nature is broken, as is often the case with joking among Mbuke people.[6] In a sense, joking which claims that *ang-ang* is balanced reciprocity helps remind audiences that it is not. In joking, *ang-ang* can mean something rather different from giving with unspecified and only potential hopes of reciprocity. It almost seems to be the case that in jokes *ang-ang* becomes a version of properly functioning *amu*. This may reveal the tension that implicit or unexpressed disagreements about sharing might foster.

Ang-ang forms a big part of day-to-day joking, especially that which involves more or less explicit connotations of sex. The joke is that *ang-ang* in fact does demand reciprocation, even though anyone – confronted by my questions – would define it as a kind of giving which did not need reciprocation. The paradox in the joking, or that which makes it funny, is to state what is otherwise not stated. In such joking, *ang-ang* is often explained as 'pulling them closer to you': by giving to a neighbour you might make the relationship closer. The word is used when men go fishing using bait fish and not many fish are caught. They will start throwing bits of bait into the sea, and say that they '*ang-ang* the fish', trying to attract them – something that here they are also trying to do without knowing whether or not they will be successful. The point is that as there are no hooks in the bait, there is no reciprocation from the fish when they receive the bait, like there would be if the bait had hooks in it (fishermen would get the fish in return). What makes the joke funny is that the hook-free bait is soon followed by hooked bait, rendering the *ang-ang* not-*ang-ang*, since reciprocity was supposed to be undefined in time, motivated by the value placed on the relationship, and not on what material benefits the relationship may provide. We could say that the joke breaks down borders between kinds of exchange, or pushes such borders. From *ang-ang* being generalized sharing it becomes balanced reciprocity, tit-for-tat with a short time span.

Another frequent joke I also became subject to myself occurred when relatives of mine had been to the market and bought betel nuts for me. They would sometimes say jokingly, 'Don't go using it to *ang-ang* all the young women'. The point of the joke is that young men might give money, cigarettes or betel-nuts to young women and expect to have certain sexual services in return. The jokes about *ang-ang* all centre on some form of reciprocity so direct that it turns into a kind of buying or barter, which is not the idea of *ang-ang*.

While joking shows that terms for sharing such as *ang-ang* may have a wide semantic range, it also defines their limits, for example by altering generalized sharing, the giving with undefined expectation of reciprocation, into balanced reciprocity.

Reversals between Debt and Generalized Sharing

The social obligation to share with friends and relatives and the debt facing a person who gets something by *amu* are qualitatively different, and rhetorically opposed among the Mbuke. As we see in the case of *amu* and *ang-ang*, the very fact that there is a difference opens up a space for the manipulation of the of the nature of the initial transaction, since the arguments that 'debtors' bring out, such as 'he is a "clan-leader nothing" ... not looking after one single man', refer to relations where *ang-ang* or generalized sharing would be more appropriate, and indicate that the trade-store owner is rejecting such relations by wanting to be 'himself only'. The trade-store owner, on the other hand, may argue that they are not supposed to spoon-feed the entire village, but can do little about it since they would rather lose their business than be considered a selfish person. In addition, 'it is not good to end up being all alone', as the woman quoted above put it. That is perhaps the ultimate threat of being a person seen by others as *eh mo ye* ('that man him') or *yu yet* ('you alone'), being cut off from daily sharing such as *ang-ang*, embodying no imagined sociality and acting in ways that cannot easily be recognized as value producing by any audience.

In cases of *amu* and *ang-ang*, reciprocity is unspecified in different ways, not to different degrees. This obviously overstates a difference, which is precisely subject to continuous social negotiation, but it is precisely by doing this that Mbuke debtors manage to present rhetorically someone's attempt to reclaim an outstanding debt as a fundamentally anti-social act, even if a debt in itself is also a social obligation, especially from the point of view of those to whom it is owned. The two (*amu* and *ang-ang*) are in a sense created as flip sides of what was otherwise one transaction. In *amu*, the idea is that what has been borrowed or purchased on credit will eventually be sorted out, whereas in the logic of *ang-ang* – which emphasises the value of daily sharing and village solidarity – actual reciprocation must remain an unspecified potential; one should give if one has something to give. In this sense, *amu* turns into *singaut*, by turning into *ang-ang*, which otherwise is not on demand. It is in this sense that I would argue that the 'debtor' in the trade store manipulates the situation from *amu* to *ang-ang*, by suggesting that the store owner is selfish when claiming their money back or refusing to give *amu*. When a Mbuke person suggests that a trade-store owner is selfish by trying to claim back money, a radical switch from *amu* to something more like *ang-ang* happens, and indeed the transaction becomes something completely different.

A similar conceptual flip has been described for the Yukaghir of Siberia by Jiménez and Willerslev (2007) in a discussion of the difference between the social aspects of hunting elk and sable respectively. Drawing on Sahlins's model of forms of reciprocity, Jiménez and Willerslev argue that elk hunting is characterized by generalized reciprocity or immediate sharing, while hunting sable – which is a commercial enterprise – is characterized by balanced reciprocity. They argue that these two 'economies' should be seen as defining 'shadows' of one another, and that they should be understood in terms of one another, not in the sense of being binary opposites (as per Lévi-Strauss), but as 'shadows', that which they can become but which they exactly are not (ibid.: 528–29). When the Yukaghirs go hunting for elk, they often need sponsorship (for ammunition and fuel) from wealthy men from the urban centre who come to participate in the hunting expeditions they themselves sponsor. In these, the dependency on sponsors is not visibly manifest, and the meat is shared in a spirit of immediate sharing corresponding to the elk economy (ibid.: 532–33). But as Jiménez and Willerslev argue, this does not mean that 'sharing' (which they also term generalized reciprocity) is conceptually stable or separate from (balanced) reciprocity, because when on occasion the wealthy sponsor makes claims to a bigger share of the meat with reference to having sponsored the expedition, a radical switch happens. The mode of address immediately changes from that of 'brother' to that of 'master', and the otherwise hidden 'shadow' of sharing and egalitarianism, namely hierarchy and dependency (involving balanced reciprocity), takes precedence (ibid.: 533).

This also means that single factors do not simply determine one another on one social level. The distance of the relation does not simply determine the time span of reciprocity, because Mbuke people engage with one another in many different kinds of relations simultaneously, and when taking up *amu* in a trade store a brother may leave the relation of brotherhood 'in the shadows' and engage with the trade-store owner in terms of the a relationship between customer and salesperson. But when he is unable to repay, the other relationship – perhaps radically different but nevertheless encompassed in the same person – between the two of them emerges and stands in front of the other. To put it otherwise: people 'make appear' – and thereby enforce upon others – perspectives which reveal certain kinds of relationships. The action (here a statement) itself demands a certain way for the other to perceive the situation in which it unfolds. What a person asking for *amu* does when resisting claims for repayment is transforming balanced (although delayed) reciprocity into generalized sharing in an instant by invoking a completely different kind of relatedness when suggesting that the store owner 'wants to be alone' or that they are selfish.

In this sense, the model proposed by Sahlins, which as we have seen is clearly useful, is too schematic for this case when it suggests that the time span of reciprocity is relative to the distance of the relation in question, because different kinds of relations are relevant between the same persons, and even to one particular transaction. *Amu* is thus not simply delayed balanced reciprocity, although that is what it looks like, and sometimes that is the way it is described. Indeed, it may actually constitute delayed balanced reciprocity. But it can equally be (in the form of a shadow) or become (as a reversal) something completely different. *Amu* can be debt, but it can also be debt as a figure of speech, as is the case with betel nuts, and *ang-ang* is generalized sharing, but it can in fact also, when stated openly (as in the Yukaghir case), become its conceptual 'shadow', shorter-term balanced reciprocity in which giving is in fact motivated by hopes for more or less imminent reciprocation, as in the case of 'seducing' fish and women.

The Person Alone: The Emergence of Individualism?

Perhaps by coincidence, the recently returned migrant woman quoted above contrasted 'a man from Mbuke' who gives credit to other people while knowing that these may be transformed into transactions of generalized sharing with 'a person alone', a person from outer space who refuses to give *amu*. This image may be helpful in understanding the difficulty of enforcing the appropriate social relations for commodity exchange to operate. The image of 'the person alone', floating alone in space, free from the weight of social ties, is a person whose actions can be recognized as valuable by no one (as the person not paying back would see it). Nor can such a person be said to be 'part' of any meaningful social whole, such as 'Mbuke people'. The act rendered 'selfish' is not part of kinship relations; it exists in opposition to them, and there is no audience which may recognize the value of that act. That is perhaps what is implied by saying that the person is 'alone' and 'from space'. Such actions address no sociality and turn 'the person alone' into a what appears to be a possessive individual, a person who, in Macpherson's words, is ideally 'the individual as essentially the proprietor of his own person or capacities, owing nothing to society for them. The individual … seen neither as a moral whole, nor as part of a larger social whole, but as an owner of himself' (Macpherson 1962: 3).

Within the villages of the Mbuke Islands, people owe many things to one another, not just as debts for unsettled loans but also as obligations to share with family and friends. As I was told, 'in the village we depend on each other for survival', and a person is always entangled in different socialities which are revealed ('made appear') by their actions, otherwise they would be 'from space' and in a sense something similar to the possessive individual, defined by the commodities they consume (Foster 1995b; cf. Reed 2003: 173), constitutes a fiction that cannot be realized, other than in the form of moral critique. Action that can be claimed to make the constitution of a person appear as a possessive individual cannot produce value if value is, as I have argued, tied up with interpersonal recognition. If actions and transactions are valued by the relationships which they 'make appear', then the act embodying the person as 'them alone' is valued as nothing. This absent or negative value produced by acts that may be recognised as those of a possessive individual apply only among Mbuke people themselves in the villages obviously, and more so from the point of view of those who do not run trade stores. On the other hand, various Mbuke people have made successful attempts to start trade stores in Port Moresby and even in Lorengau without going out of business exactly because they are far away from other Mbuke people who might come and ask for *amu*. A Mbuke person in that sense can only have alienated exchange relations with people who are not from Mbuke, to whom they in fact owe nothing. But running such a business away from the islands is like working as a migrant in Port Moresby, making money that in itself has no value – from the point of view of relationality, that is – before it is transacted as 'appearances' of kin relations within meaningful social relationships.

I am not the first to point out that the less privileged manage to use a value placed upon acts of generosity and solidarity for gaining access to the money held by those more privileged in PNG. For instance, Martin has shown how reference to *kastom* has played such a role in Matupit, East New Britain (Martin 2007, 2009). In this case, people argued that money should be shared among kin, leaving moneyed people with a sense of 'spoon-feeding' (Martin 2007: 287) others without getting much in return. While in Martin's case ideas of 'relationality' refer to kinship relations and their concomitant obligations in which the person is profoundly tied up (cf. Strathern 1988; Wagner 1991), when speaking of *amu* it is not only relatives who are expected to share resources, but also friends and neighbours. The dilemma between *amu* and *ang-ang* among Mbuke people with trade stores is similar to that of the elite person in Matupit, there termed 'Big Shots'. But whereas Big Shots try to resist sharing by questioning the relevance of reciprocity (or relationality), Mbuke people do not 'say no' in as direct a way. When Big Shots question the 'limits of reciprocity' when met by requests for money, Martin argues, this is because they are starting to see themselves as owners of the results of their own labour; that is, they are becoming possessive individuals in certain contexts (Martin 2009: 112).

Being labelled as 'a person alone' or *eh mo ye* is comparable to the concept of 'loose body' used among the prisoners described by Reed (2003: 157–159). The prisoners describe a 'loose body' as a kind of person who on arriving in the prison is recognized by no one and who has no social 'bodies' to become part of. These men are described by other prisoners as detached particles waiting for collision (ibid.: 158) – rather like something floating free in space. Being a 'loose body' in the Port Moresby prison is – like 'the person alone' – not something anyone aspires to be. Reed notes that prisoners contrast living independently with old and customary ways (ibid.: 165). In that sense it might appear as though a greater degree of individuation is emerging with the 'modern' situation, much as Foster describes possessive individualism being associated with being part a larger nation and acting as commodity consumers (Foster 1995b: 18, cited in Reed 2003: 173). But both the 'loose body' and the 'person alone' are not conceptions of one's person anyone aspire to, while – even if Matupit Big Shots presumably do not describe themselves using the term 'possessive individual' – Martin demonstrates how they make claims to limits of reciprocity and proprietorship of their own person that are comparable with the person as a possessive individual. For the person living in the villages of the Mbuke Islands, actions making the person appear as an embodiment of no social whole cannot produce value because they make no social relations appear and because such actions conflict not only with kin relationships but also with the solidarity of Mbuke people as a whole, as a 'community' (on which, see Chapters 5 to 7).

The Matupit Big Shots push the 'limits of reciprocity', and similarly Mbuke debtors manipulate the limits of generalized sharing (in the other direction) by altering debt into solidarity, hence indirectly transforming what is initially a form of *singaut* into unsolicited sharing. Trade-store owners resist this practically by trying to work around it. Selfishness is here brought out as a negative category threatening solidarity, and in this sense the possessive individual is a person whose acts have no positive value, since such acts posit the person as cut off from social relations, rather than, as is the case of Big Shots, being seen as a morally legitimate perspective, at least from the Big Shots' own perspective.

This poses an interesting question, in that the tension between 'market' and 'mutuality', as Gudeman (2008) has phrased it, or the disputation revolving around 'the limits of reciprocity', as Martin (2006, 2009) has phrased it, is not simply a tension between the person constituted by networks of kin on the one hand, and on the other the independent individual concerned with individual accumulation (to ensure, for example, that their trade store survives) since there is also an expectancy of general solidarity within 'the community'. In fact, most of the trade-store owners I spoke to in the Mbuke Islands explained their motivation for running a store as wanting to 'provide a service for the community'.

This latter aspect indicates that money and commodity exchange are seen as potentially capable of achieving social ends which are not strictly those of pre-existing clan or family loyalties, but are still in opposition to the ultimately anti-social threat of possessive individualism. Rather than resisting giving, Mbuke migrants – as we shall see in Chapter 5 – are looking for ways to make it less necessary. As some of the statements made by wealthy Mbuke people show, even though individualism is often associated with moral criticism, some people do nurture hopes that expectations of 'spoon-feeding' can be removed, that people in the villages can potentially become more self-reliant. The tendency, especially among migrants and the financially privileged in the village, is to think of or promote the person as a member of 'the community', a person who should in basic ways sustain themselves, but who should be helped by 'services' provided by 'the community' if this proves impossible. Unlike the out-worldly individual of possessive individualism, such a person is a socially responsible individual, a member of a 'community'.

Notes

1. This observation caused Marx to deem debt 'fictitious capital' (Marx 1954: 595, cited in Peebles 2010: 227).

2. As Peebles (2010: 226) has pointed out, many anthropological accounts of debt have emphasized the beneficial role held by the creditor, while the debtor is often seen as being placed in an unfortunate position. But as we shall see here, the opposite may also be the case.
3. Whether or not this is an idealized past that has never existed is hard to say, but whatever the truth of the matter, it does provide an 'analytical opposition' to the present situation for speakers.
4. This difference between foodstuffs in the past and in the present is perhaps a bit overstated (see Woodburn 1998: 48–49); nevertheless, smoked fish does not last as long as canned fish.
5. In a recent discussion of informal debt in urban Mongolia, Pedersen has observed a similar situation in which a changed degree of mobility has provided people with a way to avoid repaying debts, while the practice of lending to neighbours has failed to adapt, leading to debts that are often never settled (Pedersen n.d.).
6. One popular joke, for example, involves making a man say his mother-in-law's name, something which it is taboo for him to do.

5

The Historical Roots of Community as a Level of Organization and as a Concept

——— ◆●◆ ———

In 2011/12, mobile phone coverage finally reached the Mbuke Islands, one of the last places in Manus Province to obtain it. Along with the spread of smartphones in Papua New Guinea (and elsewhere), this meant that many people living in the villages joined Facebook. This in turn caused the level of activity on the Facebook page of the M'buke Islands People's Association (MIPA) to increase radically.[1] The page quickly became a forum for sharing information with migrants about the situation in the village, about deaths and births, and for discussing plans for developing 'the community'. Recently, for example, there was a discussion of the possibility of installing solar-powered streetlights in the villages. Occasionally the Facebook page also acts as a platform for a kind of collective *singaut*, as reflected by the following exchange that took place during a drought.

A man living in the village posted the following on the MIPA page: 'All the water tanks are empty, and we will now have to start drinking ground water, whether or not it is good [for drinking]. The village is dry and the foods in the gardens have died too. Will there be some kind of help or not? We are truly suffering'. Below this statement, a Mbuke man living and working in Port Moresby commented: 'Sorry to hear this, but I think Mbuke Islands has experienced this numerous times before. I think people know that this [situation] comes around from time to time (TP: *dispela save kamap*). So why do people in the village not bring this up at community meetings? We must try to generate some solutions to problems before they start'.

This discussion reveals *singaut* to exist at a more collective level than that described in the previous chapters, while the migrant's response to the request for help reveals one of the motivations that migrants and better-off villagers frequently state for 'community projects', namely to limit the reliance of some villagers on *singaut*. The hope, as the migrant's comment shows, is that concerns and needs should be addressed to 'the community' in advance of problems arising rather than once the problems or needs occur, in which case they often result in *singaut* to specific relatives. This chapter is the first of three where I turn to focus on what I referred to in the Introduction as the value question of 'what about us?' While in the previous chapters we have mainly seen examples of questions and answers concerning specific relationships, in many cases between those with access to recourses and those in need, the following three chapters address the questions concerning 'us' or 'the community' as a social totality.[2]

However, one cannot take for granted the idea that the people of the Mbuke Islands act as a community capable of working together and solving problems as a united entity. As I show below in the example of a development project on Ponam Island, assumptions on the part of development agencies that villages or other geographically confined human settlements in Manus Province automatically constitute social entities capable of acting as a totality can be erroneous. Rather, the idea of Mbuke as a 'community' has emerged through specific historical processes. Meanwhile, we also sense in the Facebook exchange detailed above that Mbuke people are far from being in agreement about the scope and responsibility of 'the community'. As the villager's statement indicates, it may be looked upon simply as a kind of collective individual (cf. Hirsh 2007) to whom *singaut* can be directed, while others (migrants especially) look upon it as a form of organization that could potentially lessen *singaut*.

Disagreements and social negotiations about 'the community' are discussed in Chapters 6 and 7. In this chapter, I demonstrate that 'community' as a category of description and organization among Mbuke people today reflects a level of social organization which has a history of it own in Manus and among Mbuke people. In order to fully understand the way in which the relational person and 'the person alone' can actually appear as similar, but not identical, threats to 'community', as we shall see in Chapter 6, I must first outline some of the history of this kind of social organization, which reaches beyond kin and specific alliances, and of the actual concept of community. The hope that MIPA and its associated company, MIPA Holdings Limited (MHL), will 'benefit the community' is not the first instance of Mbuke people embarking on a venture imbued with hopes for a better future for the many and involving new kinds of socialities. In other words, the attempt to make 'community' 'appear' through the MIPA and MHL ties into a history of similar attempts among the Mbuke and in Manus more widely.[3]

'Community' as a conceptualization of a potential audience or social totality in which action can take place and produce value did not appear out of nowhere. It is obviously an English word, and it has no direct equivalent in the Titan language. The only local word referring to a somewhat abstract social whole similar to it is *lau*, which has been described as referring to low rank, as opposed to the high rank of *lapan* (Schwartz 1963: 65). More generally, it has been described as referring to the followers of a particular *lapan* which, in turn, has been described as both the term for a specific leader – as is currently the case among Mbuke people – and a term for high-ranking families within clans more generally.[4] Whereas *lau* may be described as the constituency of a traditional leader as the term is used on Mbuke, 'community' implies a kind of equality between all members in its organizational appearances such as the MIPA and MHL, of which 'all Mbuke people are members' regardless of specific relations of kin or alliance to specific leaders.

'Community' as a category of description and level of social organization has roots both in colonial history and in local responses to that history. Mbuke has been and still is one of the strongholds of the Paliau Movement (see Schwartz 1962; Otto 1991; Mead 2001), and has also been part of the cooperative movement in Manus, which are both examples of hopes for a new kind of future of involving unity beyond individual and beyond sectarian interests and affiliations (such as those of the clan).

Working Together as a Community in Manus

The idea of 'communities' in Manus, such as the people from the Mbuke Islands working together as an entity, should not be taken for granted; rather, such a level of social cooperation had to be constructed. In many ways the idea runs counter to the usual organization of production and distribution of wealth on Mbuke and elsewhere in Manus. This is reflected in the social tensions and negotiations concerning MIPA and MHL described in the next two chapters, but has also been reflected in examples of externally introduced 'community projects' that have proved very difficult to sustain in Manus villages.

On Ponam Island, for example, a specific 'community project' ran into difficulties because Ponam people usually organized production in terms of kinship, which was not how the project had been conceived. When the National Development Bank of Papua New Guinea (PNG) introduced a project for freezing fish on Ponam Island in 1977 to help people there make money from fishing, the project eventually failed. According to James Carrier, it did so because it was not based on existing kinship relations but was organized through a youth club for all of the youth of the island (Carrier 1988). He points out that, to Ponam, 'non-kin groups are questionable', and they tended to cause conflict because Ponam people had never previously organized things at a social level on any basis other than kinship relations (ibid.: 54). The fact that the project was organized on a 'community basis' involving the entire Ponam population meant that it came into conflict with the ownership of fishing techniques and fishing rights, all of which were held by patrilineal descent groups (ibid.: 48). Ponam people were only willing to work for the project until the loan from the National Development Bank for the freezer unit was paid off, at which time Ponam's good name was no longer at stake. Otherwise, people were generally only inclined to provide their labour if it could be seen as part of a contribution to an actual relative (ibid.: 48).

To Ponam it made little sense to contribute their labour and produce to an artificial entity like 'the freezer committee' that had been set up, and which was similar to MIPA in that it was constituted by representatives from each of the island's clans (ibid.: 9–12). In the distribution of profits, similar problems occurred because Ponam people had no precedent for distributions that were 'island-wide' (ibid.: 17). As Carrier puts it in his assessment of the possible success of other development projects in villages like Ponam, 'A project like the freezer ... cannot be a community-wide project, for such a project cannot be organised along kinship lines: the Ponam kinship system focused on individuals and small groups and their relationships, and not on the community as a whole' (ibid.: 54).

In spite of this failure to work together as a community, Ponam people still seem to have fostered hopes for something like a community-based business. When Carrier described what Ponam people saw as desirable 'development', not only did it involve business and money making, the idea was also that the business was to 'bear the name of Ponam', and money should be made in interaction with other groups outside Ponam (ibid.: 58), thereby positing Ponam as a whole vis-à-vis other groups. One 'dream' that Carrier often heard versions of was that Ponam people should have their own ship bearing the name of Ponam for use in trading with other groups, preferably from other provinces (ibid.: 58). Both the legitimacy of commodity relations mainly with non-fellow villagers, and the concrete 'dream' of running a ship, was a preference and a dream that has come true for Mbuke people, as we shall see in Chapter 6. Although for Ponam, as the freezer project shows, this may have been a difficult business to success- fully realize if it was to involve the whole of Ponam, there seems to have been at least a tendency to hope (in Carrier's words, 'dream') that some day Ponam as a united entity would be able to run a business, even if the particular form of the freezer project failed.

The difficulties encountered by the fish freezer project on Ponam are not entirely unusual in PNG. James Weiner, for example, describes similar 'development projects' among the Foi of Southern Highlands Province. Here, a silk-production project was successful because it could be organized to fit the usual practice among the Foi at the time, where 'productive life centres upon the married couple' (Weiner 1986: 430). By contrast, a cattle-raising project initiated by the local mission faced great difficulties precisely because the price of a single calf made it necessary for nearly all the men of the village to contribute money, and this level of social organization of production suited the existing organization of production poorly (ibid.: 429). Similar difficulties encountered in dealing with concepts of transactions and social organization introduced by outsiders are described in Bainton's rich account of responses to mining among the local population of Lihir, New Ireland Province, where a large gold mine has been developed (Bainton 2010). For example, Bainton argues that while 'compensation payment' was a concept familiar to Lihirians, the idea of royalties gave rise to great difficulties in figuring out how this money should be distributed. According to Bainton, the problem came down to the fact that there was at the time 'no unifying organisation representing the interests of Lihirian landowners' (ibid.: 22). What the case of the Ponam fish freezer and other similar externally initiated projects show is that the assumption that villages or named groups (e.g., 'the Ponam', 'the Mbuke') constitute coherent political entities which are able or willing to work jointly as the development planners had assumed for Ponam should not be taken for granted.

This does not mean, however, that the only possible endeavours for successfully making money or promoting 'development' in PNG are those that can be fitted directly into existing forms of the social organization of productive activities, such as the silk project among the Foi. Ponam did have a 'development dream', in which they would in fact be a united entity doing business and making money in interaction with other groups. Likewise, there are many examples of social movements in Melanesia oriented towards the realization of a great future, sometimes characterized by a desire for radical change. From the 1940s onwards, a variety of indigenous social movements arose throughout Melanesia, all of which somehow aimed at 'the achievement of economic, social and political development through forms of communal action' (ibid.: 43). Some of these have been described as 'cargo cults', even if they differed greatly in material expectations (ibid.). It is beyond the scope of this discussion to go into the rich anthropological literature on 'cargo cults' and millenarian movements in Melanesia.[5] More importantly, describing Manus peoples' desires and social movements for economic and political development in terms of millenarian expectations would for the most part be somewhat misleading: as Bainton rightfully points out, some of these movements – which to outsiders may have looked similar – were better characterized as self-help movements or development associations (ibid.: 43).

Several different 'development dreams' that it was hoped would be realized through 'communal action' did in fact take wing among Manus peoples, especially in the southern part of the province, and long before the MIPA and MHL. Most notable was the Paliau Movement, which started after the Second World War. Many Mbuke people recall those days with a certain degree of nostalgia. That was the time when they used to 'work in unison' (TP: *wok bung*). The story I was often told as an example of this echoes processes that have been described by anthropologists working among other Titan people in the post-war period (e.g. Schwartz 1962; Mead 2001), and it goes something like this:

Back when the Mbuke people first settled around the Mbuke Islands after having broken out from Pere village (around 1900), they constructed houses built on poles on the coral reefs ringing the islands. Houses clustered at two – and at one point three – different locations, each settlement organized around dominant *lapan*s (see Crocombe 1965: 44–62). Each man would build and maintain his own house and canoe. From here they would go on fishing and trading expeditions in small bands of men organized in terms of kinship. But in the 1940s, the Mbuke people, more or less *in toto*, joined the Paliau Movement, an indigenous social movement named after its initiator, Paliau Maloat, who was a charismatic returnee migrant born on Baluan Island in Manus (see Schwartz 1962; Otto 1991, 1992; Mead 2001). The movement was at the time known as New Way. During a visit to Mbuke, Paliau Maloat said to the Mbuke people, 'You are not fish, you should not live on the sea, you should all build your houses on land'. And so they did. Paliau Maloat helped the Mbuke people organize the new combined village on Mbuke Island. Houses were built in straight rows, each house with an identical plot of land around it. All the men of the village helped to build the houses, and only after they were all completed were houses distributed among the households.[6] Hence, in contrast to what one normally expects in a Melanesian village, housing is to this day explicitly organized in terms of a community plan, rather than on the basis of kinship clusters or 'Big Man' (here, *lapan*) affiliation, as it was before. Those, middle-aged Mbuke people often told me, were the days where everyone would 'work together, stay/stick together, obey/listen together, and be happy together' (TP: *wok bung wantaim, stap wantaim, harim tok wantaim, na hamamas wantaim*). This is one of the 'slogans' of the Paliau Movement (now known as Win Neisen) to this day.

When smaller projects, such as the building of a seawall in front of the village on Mbuke during my longest period of fieldwork, fail or face problems, people will often say, 'If we could only *wok bung*, but people are too selfish'. In many ways, *wok bung* is associated with the level of social organization of 'community'. On one occasion, I was visiting and interviewing a man from Mbuke who lives and works in Port Moresby. We were sitting next to his large house in the capital, and at the end of the interview he returned to one of my initial questions about *wok bung* in what seemed almost to be a discussion with himself, a discussion of the relationship between money and *wok bung*:

> *Wok bung* is a way (TP: *pasin*) of the Mbuke people specifically. It was like that in the past and up until now. Like when they moved from Bulatangelou and Sululau and went to Palan Ko-on [the aforementioned move of the villages into one conjoined on the actual land], it was *wok bung* that made them build the houses and the village. I don't know if it was Paliau Maloat who brought it to us, or if it was something that the ancestors also did. I think maybe the ancestors also did it to some extent – I mean, surely these old ancestors must have had something good about them; it was not all bad, not all about eating other people [laughs]. It must have been for their own good too, for their survival. When they went to war [he is referring to internal warfare occasionally occurring between groups in Manus Province prior to colonial 'pacification' in 1912; see Schwartz 1995: 114–15] they must have *wok bung* to defend themselves … I think. But back then it was with the hands! Head and hands working, back then. But all that started fading away when money came along. Now it is not the hands any longer. Now it is money, and money you know – everybody has hands, but not everyone has money. And the different thing about now is this: when people have money, *wok bung* is no longer in their vocabulary. Now it [all] belongs to him/her only (TP: *em yet*). That is growing now in the community, that the men who have money are starting to say *eh mo ye* ('the person alone', lit. 'that man him'). Did you hear this expression, *eh mo ye*? It means like, all of us one-one only, now it is one-one *em yet*, him only. So I mean […] *wok bung* is no more. *Eh mo* means one man, *eh ye* is *em yet*. One man, himself only. So this has broken this *wok bung*. Like I said to begin with, hands – we all have hands and you can go and do the work, and all other men have hands too. Now money came and only some men have money, and if you have no money now, people will not see (TP: *lukim*) you.

So, according to this man, money brought about what I translated in Chapter 4 as 'the person alone', which I discussed in terms of possessive individualism (TP: *em yet*; T: *eh mo ye*). While we saw there how 'the person alone' is rhetorically presented in opposition to the person who lives up to kinship obligations and responds positively to *singaut*, the same negative category is used here as a threat to communal action and the practice of working together as a community. What is interesting here, as the speaker himself indicates, is that the idea of *wok bung* might actually be part of another response to the introduction of money and new forms of organization (the Paliau Movement), and in that sense it is not 'tradition' brought down by 'modernity', but rather different roles played by – and potentials seen in – money, which come into conflict with each other. It should be noted that contrary to what this statement might indicate, there are still many cases of *wok bung* in the Mbuke Islands, although it was possibly even more frequent when the Paliau Movement was at its height and when money played a less significant role in actual survival in the villages. This – perhaps somewhat romanticized – state of affairs, when Mbuke people used to *wok bung*, is neither surprising nor was it unique in the southern part of Manus Province at the time. Many villages enrolled in the 'new way' that Paliau Maloat and his movement tried to bring about, and the movement involved bigger social wholes than ever seen previously.

The Paliau Movement and the Reorganization of Social Relations

One of the things that Paliau Maloat saw as a problem caused by the persistence of traditional social relations was the 'waste' of migrant money on big feasts and on other things in which money was redistributed among relatives, reducing young migrants like himself to 'rubbish' (Otto 1992: 432–23). In the early 1940s, when Maloat was away from Manus as a labour migrant, he instructed the man to whom he usually sent money not to distribute it among relatives as he normally would. When after a while Maloat came home to Baluan, he used the money to start a scheme to help men in the village pay their head tax (a tax imposed on each man by the colonial authorities) so they would not be imprisoned by the colonial administration. Money was placed in a fund for this purpose, and it was meant to help not only other men from Lipan (Paliau Maloat's native village on Baluan) but men from all of the villages and islands around Baluan; thus the scheme involved men not only outside the bounds of kinship affiliation but also those from other linguistic groups (ibid.: 433). As among the Mbuke people today, even at that point people believed that money could play a role in social constellations beyond the clan and even the village. Just as some of the moneyed people among Mbuke people today see *singaut* as unsustainable and 'community' building as an alternative, so did Paliau Maloat see similar uses of money in the early 1940s as a way to stop 'wasting' migrants' earnings.

Paliau Maloat's break with the fulfilment of kinship obligations which defined to whom money was given involved hopes for a different organization of social relations – a way out of the power relations in which *lapans* caused others to be indebted (for example, by funding their marriage payments) or distributed their money in their own name; a break with the sectarianism of families, clans and village segments towards a united community at a larger scale. In the case of the Paliau Movement, building a new kind of sociality was perhaps the most significant hope, and – sixty years later, when achieving the wealth and standard of living of 'white people' that the movement hoped for have not been achieved – its most profound effect. According to Schwartz, a big part of Paliau Maloat's intention with his movement was the 'reorganization of society', and the idea of uniting people beyond clan, village and even ethnic groups was crucial and explicit (Schwartz 1962: 262–66). Even though at that point each village had a *luluai* – a village leader appointed by the colonial government, meant to act as the connection between the administration and the villagers – it was still the case that 'even the smallest villages rarely acted as a unit', as Schwartz points out (ibid.: 262). Paliau Maloat tried to make people organize themselves in bigger units and put their differences and rivalries behind them (ibid.: 264). The aim was not to achieve a bigger and better version of existing social forms – a process Sahlins has termed 'developman' – nor to simply become entirely like 'white people' – in Sahlins's terms, 'humiliation' (see Sahlins 2005; cf. Robbins and Wardlow 2005) – although improvements in wealth, health and the standard of living were indeed striven for and part of the goal. Schwartz writes that the opposition to the state of social relations in the Paliau Movement's programme for change was twofold: 'The program, calling for brotherhood and deemphasizing the differentials between men and between groups, aimed at extending the cooperative alignment of the efforts of individuals beyond individualism, beyond local kin group, to the village and the Movement' (Schwartz 1962: 263).

Such a formulation of objectives might as well have been made concerning the programme of the MIPA and the general hope of 'community'-building among the Mbuke today, and it seems likely that Mbuke people, who were always a stronghold of the Paliau Movement (see Gustafsson 1992), have drawn inspiration from this earlier community-building project. In the Paliau Movement's programme, then, a similar opposition against both individualism and the relational person entangled in kinship obligations may be observed. We will see in Chapter 6 that, as threats to 'community', both individualism (of the *eh mo ye* kind) and kinship loyalties are in certain social situations grouped together as instances of 'selfishness' or 'greed'. In line with the Paliau Movement's opposition to clan and kinship loyalties, villages spanning ethnic divisions were constructed, and in line with the opposition against 'individualism', Paliau Maloat urged the movement's members not to leave the province as 'work boys' (working for Australians and other expatriates in PNG for low salaries): 'Such a plan would rule out the many possibilities for individuation and differentiation of personal experience afforded by the range of the *work-boy* world', Schwartz notes (ibid.: 263). Eventually, Paliau Maloat's hope, according to

Schwartz, was to 'end the internal divisions and to weld the people of each village into a community capable of working in unity' (ibid.: 263). Clearly, a big part of the emphasis on *wok bung* among the Mbuke today started during their involvement in the Paliau Movement, which is what many Mbuke people state, like the man cited above. In Schwartz's study, the use of the specific word 'community' is not necessarily an 'emic' term, as is currently the case among Mbuke people. But it nevertheless refers to the same level of organization – beyond kin affiliation and individual interests.

The village that was built on Mbuke Island was not the only village to be reorganized geographically as a reflection of a new organization of social relations in the Paliau Movement. The oldest Titan village, Pere, was rebuilt in straight rows (see sketch map in Mead 2001: 236) and came to include non-Titans living in the bush inland on Manus Island in the vicinity of Pere. Those Titans living on the reefs offshore moved onto land near the coast, and those living in the bush further inland moved to the same place (ibid.: 236–264), thereby manifesting both materially and socially the hoped for unity of the many different people that Paliau Maloat and his followers worked for. When Mead arrived there for her second period of fieldwork after the Second World War, she observed how all the houses were built in straight rows, and that the village was organized following 'a plan that had all the over-articulateness of wartime housing' (ibid.: 238). The new village was a material reflection of the social organization of foreign army camps, which had been observed in great numbers in Manus during the war and were clearly a source of inspiration. The organization of the village, with identical houses arranged in neat rows, indicated the equality and communal spirit that Paliau Maloat worked for, an indication of the emergence of a new conception of social relations and their organization. In contrast to former times, when settlements around the Mbuke Islands were organized to indicate their inhabitants' *lapan* and kinship affiliation, all the houses were now identical entities within a larger plan of a community: each individual was an equal member of a community, as opposed to the person constituted out of clusters of specific relationships. An organization which had previously been marked by inequality, obligation and partial loyalties was now marked by equality – at least in material terms. The new villages, like the organizational structures of the MIPA and MHL, were in that sense embodiments of the invisible new sociality, a way of making social relations 'appear' in new and perceptible forms.

Mead saw these changes as evidence that a surprisingly rapid transformation can happen from 'stone-age headhunters into a community asking for a place in the modern world' (ibid.: xxxiii). In her account of this new world, she focuses on the all-encompassing character of the changes brought about by the Paliau Movement, indicated in the title of her book, *New Lives for Old*. Here it might be observed that Mead's interpretation of these events is very similar to the 'humiliation' argument presented by Sahlins (2005), in which people embrace radical change to become completely different. Here, however, rather than a sense of humiliation in the face of an 'other' (such as the colonial power) perceived to be superior (ibid.: 24), the emotions that seemed to characterize these attempts at achieving radical change were hope and 'great expectations' (see Chapter 6).

But perhaps the changes were not as complete and radical as Mead's description might lead one to think. In his study of the same changes, Schwartz (1962) came to conclusions of a more complex nature. He presents a thorough examination of the Paliau Movement, in which he asserts that 'many of the differentials of social groups in the old system still had a place, although they were profoundly modified' (ibid.: 263). As I noted in the Introduction, his study suggests that a variety of possible forms of organization of social relations can coexist, involving social perspectives from which things may look very different, and in which value formations are based on different criteria and are manifested as appearances of diverse social forms. A model suggesting the complete replacement of one 'system' (or culture) with another, such as the one Mead gives of Pere village before and after the Paliau Movement, fails to account for social negotiation, disagreement and the diversity of social perspectives that detailed accounts of social change like the one presented by Schwartz indicate. Nevertheless, if we are to take seriously the way in which hopes for change are rhetorically presented, both in the Paliau Movement and in PNG more generally, the notion of making entirely 'new' forms of sociality and indeed personhood has been strongly articulated throughout the country in a variety of social movements (cf. Maher 1961). As Bainton notes for Lihir, people there do not look upon 'development' as transformation but rather as 'total realisation' (Bainton 2010: 11). As I discuss in Chapter 7 there is, among the Mbuke, a sense in which a value-producing act totalizes sociality and 'considers all things', even if other competing totalizations coexist with it.

The important point with regard to the Paliau Movement here is that even though money to buy 'cargo' from white people was perhaps among the ultimate goals, the organization and reorganization of social relations was seen not only as the means to get there, but also as an end. Otto discusses the term *wok*, Tok Pisin for work, and asserts that whereas work is a central category in relation to the production of value (the labour theory of value) in the West (Otto 2004: 211), on Baluan, where Otto worked, hard work is not a virtue in itself. Instead, on Baluan value is created by the distribution – not the production – of wealth (ibid.: 215). In fact, he suggests, part of the aim of the Paliau Movement was freedom from hard work (ibid.: 222), which is also part of its 'official' programme as written on the back wall of the movement's meeting house on Mbuke Island. What Paliau Maloat and his followers sought was the knowledge held by white people, a knowledge that they suspected had been hidden from them, especially 'true knowledge' about God (ibid.). Otto points out that knowledge is a crucial resource in Manus (see also Dalsgaard 2009; Rasmussen 2013: 11–12), and that knowledge from and about God became a part of the Paliau Movement but, as Otto indicates, 'other elements concerned the communal organisation of productive practices and the establishment of new villages with houses in straight rows' (Otto 2004: 223). The reorganization of social relations was explicitly crucial in the movement, and hence knowledge about organization was perhaps equally important to other kinds of knowledge derived from the colonial authorities and other 'outsiders' who have been encountered locally. As Mead pointed out, villages were physically reorganized along the lines of military and police camps that people like Paliau Maloat had seen outside the province as well as in Manus during the war.

In summary, it is likely that the idea of social organization at a higher level than that of kinship, clan or specific alliances has strong roots in the Paliau Movement, and that this was not simply a direct adoption of newly introduced forms of organization, brought about by the colonial authorities, towards which, in fact, the Paliau Movement was in many ways in opposition (Otto 1991: 180). The physical reorganization of villages may be seen as a material 'appearance' – in the terminology developed in this book – of a new social order, in the same way that 'community' among the Mbuke today has to appear in the perceptible forms of 'community projects' or organizational structures like the MIPA and MHL in order to be recognized as existing (see Chapter 6).

Cooperative Societies and the Organization of Production

In the early and mid 1950s, when the Paliau Movement was at its height, cooperatives aimed at helping organize local people's production of copra and sales of trochus shells were established in Manus Province (Otto 1991: 198–99). Even though these were introduced by the colonial administration, they provide an example of similar conflicts to the ones of the MIPA and MHL discussed in Chapter 6. In many of the Manus villages where cooperatives were introduced, they fostered 'enthusiasm and high expectations' (Schwartz 1967: 36). Many people got involved in them, contributing £5 each, which Schwartz suggests people agreed to do because this was one way of ensuring that the money was 'saved from dissipation into the network of kinship and ceremonial exchange' (ibid.: 37). Here again, the expectations were neither hope for individual gain nor for the enlargement of existing social forms such as ceremonial exchange.

The hopes people had with regard to cooperatives were, according to Schwartz, somewhat unrealistic in their assumption that a European standard of living could be achieved, and people were quickly disappointed with them when this failed to materialize. As dissatisfaction grew, people returned to what Schwartz termed a 'particularistic tendency' and tried to organize similar activities to those of the cooperatives (such as copra production) in smaller kinship-based groups (ibid.: 38). The trade stores run by the cooperatives ultimately faced problems under similar circumstances; people started establishing small trade stores of their own, based around smaller groups of kin or even owned by individuals; this, says Schwartz, was better suited to the 'social atomism and individualism that so profoundly characterise this area' (ibid.: 39–40).[7] Paliau Maloat, who was then a powerful man in Manus and was involved in (and strongly supported) the introduction of cooperatives, declared these kin-based and individually run trade stores to be 'anti-social' (ibid.: 41). Here, 'anti-social' refers not only to the new form of personhood that is individualism, potentially accompanied by particular uses of money ('the person alone'), but equally to relational persons, as reflected in a preference for the kinship-based organization of production. Instead of being opposed to each other, the two are conflated as being 'anti-social'. Paliau Maloat suggested as an alternative to the failing cooperative stores that 'each village should open a co-operative trade store with capital to be raised by share holding by all village members' (ibid.: 41).

Cooperatives were introduced in many parts of Manus Province from 1951 onwards, and according to Otto this was done by the colonial administration to counteract local people's dissatisfaction with their own status vis-à-vis colonial administrators after the Second World War, and to increase the indigenous production of cash crops (Otto 1991: 198–99). In the parts of Manus that were most influenced by the Paliau Movement, cooperatives were especially successful because, Otto asserts, 'co-operative development accorded well with the new social models in the Paliau Movement' (ibid.: 199). But the success was, according to Otto, not long-lived in Manus, and between 1967 and 1969 cooperatives started disintegrating, partly because of disagreements about the ownership of land, which was held by patrilineages in most cases (Otto 1991: 202; cf. Carrier and Carrier 1983).

One exception was the Mbuke cooperative plantation (Otto 1991: 200). In the area where Otto worked, the Mouk people's running of the Langendrowa plantation also lasted a bit longer. The people of Mouk, who are a Titan people who had been living around Baluan in houses built over the sea, had been resettled on another island, where the plantation was run. According to Otto, what is fascinating about the Mouk people's running of their plantation was that they opted to run their plantation on a 'communal' basis (ibid.: 205), and that once they were settled at Langend-rowa they built a new village in which 'iron plate houses stood in neat rows' (ibid.), similar to the new organization of Mbuke village described above.

On Mbuke there were similar hopes for a cooperative plantation. A coconut plantation was originally established in the Mbuke Islands by a German trader in the 1910s, when the area was still under German colonial rule. German-owned properties were taken over by the Australian government following the First World War, and until the Second World War the plantation came under the ownership of a company run by two Australians (Crocombe 1965: 5–6). It is perhaps needless to add that these changes took place without consideration of the fact that Mbuke people were also present in the area. When the Australian company started restoring the plantation in 1951 after the Second World War had brought its activities to a stop, Mbuke people initially resisted, but some of them were eventually employed on a contract basis on the plantation. When incomes from tropical products started decreasing, the plantation was sold to the Mbuke people, and hence between 1959 and 1961 Mbuke people bought the land covered by the plantation for £6,000 (ibid.: 9). This was rather more than the original sale price, which according to oral tradition had been two steel axe heads.

In 1955, before the plantation was reacquired by Mbuke people, a cooperative society was introduced in the Mbuke Islands by the colonial administration. Apart from marketing trochus shell and copra, the society operated a trade store on Mbuke Island (where all Mbuke people lived at the time), and according to Crocombe, the 'society was almost universally supported by the people' (ibid.: 8). In 1961, Mbuke leaders of the cooperative finished negotiating the purchase of the plantation from the administration, and it was taken over by the cooperative. The plantation was led by a committee elected by all the members of the cooperative (ibid.: 11), and was worked by them and by other Mbuke men who were all paid in accordance with their efforts (ibid.: 14). All the members of the cooperative took turns in working on the plantation and making money for themselves, and according to Crocombe the cooperative included all Mbuke men apart from nine, who were either disabled or had other tasks, such as church leaders (ibid.). It is unclear exactly when the plantation stopped operating (see also Gustafsson 1992: 14), but it is not surprising that it did so because copra prices dropped and the number of young men available to work on it decreased as they were increasingly becoming engaged in migrant labour at the time.

In about 1968/9, the cooperative was disintegrating because too little money was being made from it (MacGregor 1971: 30–38). MacGregor states that some people were dissatisfied with being forced to sell their copra to the cooperative and, as he put it, 'they wished to be able to choose between selling their copra through the [cooperative] society or directly to the Copra Marketing Board' (ibid.: 32). This situation seems to have been similar to the problems some people saw in the MHL's more recent attempt to buy sea cucumbers from people in the villages and organize their further sale; that is, some people wanted to sell their sea cucumbers to other buyers in Lorengau and thereby obtain a better price than they would from the 'community' company (see Chapter 6).

The cooperative indicates that organizing work at a community level has a history of its own. It also indicates that some of the same conflicts that arise in 'community' organizations among Mbuke people today were also present then: that community-level organization was under threat from both individualism and relationality in the form of kin affiliation and a form of organization of production based on it. Given its significance, I would like to consider, in greater detail, the specific concept of 'community' as such, before concluding this historical overview.

A Note on the Concept of Community

Among Mbuke people, 'community' beyond certain other alliances has been problematic in the past, and it is still constantly under perceived threat from alliances on a smaller scale based on kinship and by individual interests. I have shown that it seems likely that the organization of Mbuke people in a joint entity has its origins in the Paliau Movement, and in the cooperative movement. But in fact when the word 'community' first became part of the political landscape in Manus it was strongly opposed among Mbuke people and other members of the Paliau Movement. This was not because of its encompassment of people beyond clan alliances, but because of the specificities of the situation in which it was introduced.

In 1982, 'community government' was introduced in PNG to replace 'local-level government councils', which in Manus had been associated with and forced through by Paliau Maloat and his movement (Gustafsson 1992: 152–55).[8] This posed a threat to Maloat's power base in the southern part of Manus, where his movement was strong. In the local-level council, Maloat had been the automatic leader because it was introduced through the Paliau Movement, but 'community government' meant that elections had to be held for the post, and this posed an obvious challenge to his leadership (ibid.: 154). According to Gustafsson, the changes occurring in the Paliau Movement at this point were a response to the potential loss of power on Maloat's part (ibid.). Contrary to his previous arguments, Maloat now claimed that following 'the white man's ways' would lead to violence and disrespect for 'the family': 'What is emphasised is the family as a symbol of the larger family of the new world. Until the little family functions in perfect harmony, the large family, which includes all peoples of the earth, cannot be realised' (ibid.: 156).

In other words, at that time the family as an entity was conceived of not so much as a part of a clan but rather as part of a much wider whole, namely that of the whole of humanity. While Maloat and his followers had previously argued that Manus people should work to adopt certain ways of 'white people', he now turned back to what had previously been the 'rubbish ways of the ancestors', arguing that *kastom* should not be abandoned completely (see Otto 1991: 276–78). Gustafsson points out that this change of emphasis did not mean that clans and traditional ceremonies were reintroduced. *Kastom* was here associated with the family, while following 'the ways of white people', such as 'community government', would eventually lead to communism and a move away from the family (Gustafsson 1992: 155). The few people among the Mbuke who supported community government were the slowly increasing number of members of other Christian churches (thereby not supporting Paliau Movement), but Mbuke people in general continued to support 'local-level government', despite the fact that it had been replaced by a new type of modern political leadership at the local level.

There does not seem to be any direct connection between 'community' with these negative connotations and 'community' as it is currently used among the Mbuke, which largely cuts across previous differences in affiliation – or lack of it – with the Paliau Movement. Community as a concept among Mbuke people and in Manus has a complex history and is associated with various things. Currently the concept is often heard among NGO and Australian Aid representatives who talk about 'community development', but in the past it was much more associated with *gavman*, or government institutions (Otto 1991). The current use seems to also reflect NGO usage, but disagreements about its meaning may also play a role in the problems often facing 'community projects'. While exposure to the social organization of 'white people' was, during the early stages of Paliau Movement, somewhat episodic (temporary army camps during the war, for example), the current situation offers constant exposure to discourses of 'community development', 'community involvement', 'rural communities' and so on, and the term is part of the national and regional state bureaucracy, in which many Mbuke migrants are themselves employed. This does not mean, however, that the concept of 'community' has the same meaning for Mbuke as it might among Australian aid workers, or among anthropologists for that matter. Neither can we assume that contemporary Mbuke people agree about the meaning and scope of 'community' as a category of description or as a level of organization, a point to which we shall return in Chapter 6.

Conclusions

Given that terms like 'society' have been identified as problematic in certain contexts, it might be tempting for anthropologists to use words like 'community' instead. But if we do not specify precisely what 'community' refers to, or what it might translate into among the people who are allegedly members of that community, we would miss the point of problematizing concepts like society and community entirely. Furthermore, if well-meaning NGO workers want to promote 'community development', it must first be established whether or not there is actually such a thing as 'a community' where there appears to be one. As I have shown here, this cannot be taken for granted, and the specific concept might even tie directly into previous political conflicts.

By looking at certain aspects of the recent history of Manus, it is clear that a third possibility has been present from the outset of people's involvement with global capitalism alongside the fear of individualization and the possibility of domestication into existing ongoing exchange relationships and kin alliances. Larger community-wide social wholes like the MIPA and MHL have occurred before in the Mbuke people's recent history, and it seems likely that part of the vision of uniting people beyond previous forms of social relations has roots therein. This brief history of a few attempts to strengthen wider social collectives demonstrates that 'community' – or a level of organization similar to it – is not an entirely new idea, nor one doomed to actual failure; rather, it points to the possibility of imagining populations of whole villages or groups of villages as social entities, which has long been an aspect of Manus social life. We should not take the failures of particular community organizations in the face of kinship-based demands or individualism as evidence of the unimportance of the idea of community, any more than we should take the flexible and contingent nature of the formation and disbanding, appearance and disappearance of specific kinship- and exchange-based entities such as clans as evidence of the unimportance of 'kinship' in Manus. A concept of a wider community, although perhaps referred to using different phrases, is not historically new in Manus and has previously been attempted and stood strong, though it has periodically fallen back into clan sectarianism. But the 'instability' of such social constellations should not be seen in opposition to an alleged stability of kinship-based socialities. The number of 'clans' (patrilineal descent groups) on Mbuke, for example, is unclear because they too break into smaller units occasionally and unite into bigger constellations at other times, and whether there are seven or eight clans on Mbuke is a matter of the social perspective of the person you are talking to. In fact, some Mbuke people indicate that some 'break-out clans' actually formed as a direct response to the prospect of wider influence and access to money for clan leaders when the 'council of chiefs' was established as part of the Manus Provincial Government, thus indicating that clans and kinship solidarity are far from an underlying continuity, but are also formed in interaction with other social entities. As I demonstrate in more detail in the next chapter, these different socialities and concomitant conceptions of the person – as either an individual, a member of 'the community' or a kin person of the relational type – do coexist.

I would argue that the MIPA, MHL and their historical predecessors were attempts to creatively use money and specific forms of organization to 'make appear' socialities of a new kind. Rather than viewing money simply as social solvent or as being something which is reassuringly tamed for the remaking of pre-existing social forms, a better starting point for analysis is to turn the focus to the ongoing – and clearly uneasy – tension over the appropriateness of particular kinds of exchange in particular contexts, or what Gudeman (2008: 4) refers to as the 'tension' that characterizes all economic situations. But such a tension can operate along more than one axis of opposition simultaneously, rather than simply the opposition of 'market' and 'mutuality' that Gudeman's account relies on. This is not simply a remaking of the 'spheres of exchange' argument, first associated with the work of Bohannan (1959), in which different objects legitimately circulate in different spheres. It is also not simply the case that one can distinguish different sets of social relations (such as spheres or fields) through or within which things flow (Akin and Robbins 1999: 8). Rather, it is a matter of distinguishing, in accordance with contexts in which it seems legitimate or illegitimate to have certain things flowing or 'making appear', certain social relations that are contested, overlapping and in conflict, even within one person.

Although this historical overview does not do sufficient credit to the historical complexity of the events and social movements described,[9] it does show how the idea of a social totality on a similar scale to the contemporary Mbuke conception of themselves as 'a community' has certain historical roots, and that this is not simply a historical development in which one concept of a social whole replaces the next since, as we shall see especially in Chapter 6, such wholes and related concepts of personhood may simultaneously coexist and be in conflict. The way in which Mbuke people negotiate and value sociality through 'appearances' in action that continuously remould the very sociality that they 'make appear' is the subject of the next two chapters.

The reorganization of the villages in Manus which were under the influence of the Paliau Movement could be seen as a perceptible appearances of a new form of sociality in which parts (households) related differently to their social totality in comparison with the way relations between households were reflected when clusters of houses reflected *lapan* and kinship affiliation. While houses in rows reflected an abstract plan for something similar to 'community', clustered houses reflected how concrete alliances and kinship groups were perhaps the most widespread level of organization in the past. Similarly, an idea like *wok bung* reflects the way in which collective action is a way to make a certain concept of sociality and personhood appear. If such persons and social totalities do not appear, they cannot be assumed to exist: as the migrant man quoted above said, '*wok bung* is no longer in their vocabulary. Now it [all] belongs to *em yet*'. Here it might not be important whether or not *em yet* keeps money in a person's own 'hands', to 'himself/herself alone', or if that money is passed on to their kin relations, since both are 'anti-social' from the point of view of 'community', a sociality in which neither kinds of action produce value.

Notes

1. I am assuming here that the reader is familiar with Facebook. If not, a Facebook 'group' such as that of the Mbuke Islands Peoples' Association constitutes a kind of small-scale homepage similar to that of an individual person on Facebook, but on a group page all members can read, comment and otherwise add contents, including pictures.
2. The word 'community' has been appropriated by Mbuke people, and is part of contemporary speech. Note, however, that while 'community' is a local category, it is one whose meaning, as the discussion below and in Chapters 6 and 7 will show, should not be taken for granted.
3. For further information on the MIPA and MHL, see the Introduction.
4. See Otto (1994: 225–27) for a discussion of these terms.
5. For classic accounts of cargo cults, see e.g. Lawrence (1964) and Burridge (1971). For recent discussions of the issues, see e.g. Jebens (2004) and Bainton (2010).
6. See Crocombe (1965: 44–62) for a similar version of this story, given to him by Mbuke people forty years earlier than when I was told it.
7. Schwartz's mention of individualism probably concerns the sort that is referred to as 'selfishness' among Mbuke when people talk about taking money from the MHL and giving it to their kin or (allegedly) taking it for their own pockets. As I describe in Chapter 6, this is not necessarily individualistic as such, but might also be an example of a relational person being in conflict with the type of personhood needed to be a member of the 'com-

munity', just as individual Ponam were reluctant to contribute to the 'freezer committee' because of their tendency to think that non-kin groups are questionable (Carrier 1988: 54).

8. See also Otto (1991) on the historical development of the Paliau Movement.
9. For more detailed historical studies, see Schwartz (1962) and Otto (1991, 1992, 1994).

6

To Benefit the 'Community'

Value and Community Membership

———————— ◆●◆ ————————

In this chapter I argue that 'community', as the concept is used among Mbuke people, refers to a social whole in which a person can indeed in important respects be seen as an individual, as a member. In 'community', a person can indeed act as a 'part' of a whole, a whole which can be 'made appear' by action and hence produce value. While the migrant giving money to his brother back in the village 'makes appear' by his action the relationship between the two of them, a sociality which they both embody in the constitution of their person, the person doing things to 'benefit the community' embodies in action their own self as part of the abstract whole of 'Mbuke people'. In that sense, the person in 'community' does in fact 'owe' something to 'society', and it is by actions that 'settle' such obligations that the individual appears as a member of it.

In the Introduction I referred to the story of a migrant man who was planning to start a small business when he returned to live in the Mbuke Islands after retirement. In his business, he would buy fish from other men in the villages, freeze it and then sell it in the provincial capital. His initiative was discussed at a meeting among leading Mbuke men, one of whom commented that: 'we must determine if that business is just meant to benefit himself, his family only, or if it will benefit the community'. This statement reflects some of the fears and expectations Mbuke people have regarding the use and making of money, business organization and coop- eration among Mbuke people as a totality more generally, as a 'commu- nity'. As I showed in Chapter 5, such a social totality cannot be taken for granted, and as we shall see in this chapter, the social whole of 'community' often comes into conflict with value formation at other social levels, such as a person as relationally constituted in specific kinship relations or a person suspected of being selfish. The fact that an idea of 'community' is present does not mean that it is a social whole with fixed structures. The 'community', like other socialities discussed here, is continuously made to appear in perceptible forms such as organizational structures that in turn must appear in the form of action conducted in accordance with them, making them visibly manifest in a form that can be socially recognized. This means that rather than being structures in the conventional sense, organizational relations and positions are, like other social relations among Mbuke people, constantly remade by being 'made appear' and recognized or misrecognized by audiences.

The fear that money and the social relations that commodity exchange may bring about might result in the break down of previous social bonds is well known in the anthropological literature (e.g. Bohannan 1959; Robbins and Akin 1999: 8), but it is often countered by reassurances that money may also be useful in the continuation of ongoing social relationships and pre-monetary forms of sociality (e.g. Gregory 1997: 238; Sahlins 2005: 24), as is the case to an extent with remittances among Mbuke people. But could money not be useful in achieving new forms of social relations that are neither anti-social as such, nor continuations of what was there before money had its 'impact'? Could business organization and the forms of money transactions it entails also be useful in making the 'community' appear? It is argued here that the 'community' involves a hope – a great expectation – that projects designed for the benefit of the community may help to constitute and maintain a social whole encompassing 'all' (Mbuke people). The most ambitious examples of Mbuke people's 'great expectations' with regard to how money and business organization might benefit – or make appear – 'community' are perhaps those of the Mbuke Islands People's Association (MIPA) and MIPA Holdings Limited (MHL), the business arm of MIPA. In the running and organization of these 'community' organizations, as well as in the problems they have encountered, there is a reflection of different and contesting visions of money's role and the value of specific acts in social relations, along with contradicting concepts of the person and concomitant forms of sociality. In the case of MIPA and MHL, the person as a member of 'community' is especially relevant, while in sending remittances and sharing food and services in the village the person as a member of kinship groups is more relevant; and finally there is the perspective of the individual person trying to make and keep money individually, as we saw in the case of trade stores in Chapter 4. These different person–sociality constellations in which value may or may not take form in different ways are not clear-cut or agreed upon, which is reflected in how in practice they are often in conflict. This is the theme of this chapter.

MIPA Holdings Limited: Fear and Great Expectations

The 'community-based business' MIPA Holdings Limited (MHL) explicitly aims to make money to be used for improving the conditions of Mbuke people. These improved conditions are aimed especially at those in the villages who face the biggest problems in terms of 'food security' (such terms are often used in these contexts), and who depend most extensively on others. Examples of planned improvements during my fieldwork in 2008/9 to be financed by MHL were building aid posts, funding an 'elderly support scheme' and developing a 'scholarship programme' for particularly bright students in the community schools, and paying school fees for their further education outside the villages. These objectives in themselves constitute a break with the person's otherwise fundamental dependency on and obligation towards kin, which we saw in the first part of the book. This break is conspicuous especially in the cases of school fees and support for the elderly because care for children (including sending them to school) and the elderly is otherwise seen as fundamentally a responsibility of close kin (*angini*). The will among moneyed Mbuke people to allocate money to such initiatives indicates this break as well, since migrants who donate money to 'community projects' could otherwise have used that money for remittances, which as we have seen would have remained tied to kinship relations.

Both MIPA, the community-wide association of all Mbuke people, and its business arm MHL were very much initiated by migrants and former migrants. Unlike Ponam migrants, who, according to Carrier and Carrier (1989), left the maintenance and constitution of social relations and social positions – or, in Gregory's terms 'the social reproduction of persons' (Gregory 1982: 51) – to people in the village, Mbuke migrants organized themselves as a group at quite an early stage of labour migration. One of the social constellations among migrants eventually gave rise to the MIPA. Migrants in Port Moresby organized themselves as a group based on coming from the same group of islands. These new kinds of social constellations were not based on kinship (other than origins more generally), and nor were they maintained through ceremonial exchange or ongoing reciprocal relations in any form. Many of the categories used in these social formations, such as 'youth', 'elderly people' and ultimately 'community' reflect this sense of being beyond the concreteness of kinship and clan affiliation.

As noted in the Introduction, in the 1970s, a club called the Sugarloaf Youth Club was established in Port Moresby by young men and women from the Mbuke Islands who lived and worked there,[1] and even though it was then mainly a club for Mbuke youth in Port Moresby, it was the intention from the outset that the club should 'help the villages' of the Mbuke Islands as a whole. Initially the youth club mainly arranged sports activities for Mbuke people in Port Moresby. But the club also started organizing common meetings, known in Titan as *kame-sos* ('all gather'), where everyone from Mbuke living in Port Moresby would gather, and village issues and 'development' were addressed. These meetings evoked a somewhat abstract whole (all Mbuke migrants), unlike the family and clan meetings which also took (and still take) place among the many Mbuke migrants in Port Moresby. Later, in the late 1990s, when the young people who initiated the club had grown older, the club became central in organizing fund-raising activities for 'projects' in the villages, an example of which was aimed at building a new community school on Mbuke Island. Around that time the club changed its name to the Mbuke Islands People's Association, and as an association it has come to cover Mbuke people as a totality – whether they live as labour migrants outside Manus or whether they live in the villages. In that sense, the migrants have encompassed the people in the villages in 'their own' particular form of 'social reproduction of persons' entailed in that social totality.

Leading members of the MIPA, especially those living in Port Moresby, explained to me that during the 1980s and the 1990s dependency on remittances increased in the villages, and that at that same time, state institutions began failing to provide basic services like schools and aid posts in villages.[2] In the 2000s this made migrant members of the MIPA decide that the association needed an income of its own – apart from that provided by its increasingly frequent fund-raising activities – to provide money for what is now referred to as 'community projects' to benefit fellow 'Mbuke people' back on the islands. At that point a 'business arm' – a company owned by the association – was established. Ambitiously, the business arm was named MIPA Holdings Limited (MHL), and expectations were great. Crucial to both the association and the company is the fact that they include everyone from the Mbuke Islands.

The following explanation comes from an interview with the councillor of Mbuke ward who, before he was elected ward councillor, was chairman of the MIPA in the village.[3] He began by explaining the nature of the MIPA and MHL:

> [The] organization is meant to come up with ideas for helping the people and to educate the people as well as looking after their welfare. That is the whole concept. Individually, people may own areas of land, and MIPA has not drawn this into the association. The property of MIPA is the big areas of sea and the land that belong to the whole of Mbuke people. The idea is that everyone from Mbuke automatically becomes a member of this association. The business belongs to MIPA; that is why

we call it MIPA Holdings, because it is a holding of all of the Mbuke people. Any other business someone might want to start – they have the right to do so, but under MIPA Holdings.

It was mainly highly accomplished migrant men from Mbuke who started up the company and invested large amounts of their own personal funds in starting some of the company's bigger business activities. A recently retired general manager of a large semi-private company in Papua New Guinea (PNG) was one of the men who played a crucial role in the establishment of MHL. He described the motivation to do so as follows:

We decided that we needed a paradigm shift. Before, we always did fundraisings and sent the money to the community school or other projects in the villages, but now we have to go into business so that when our business starts generating an income ... [it] can allocate some of its profits into our community projects. Firstly, this will help the people in the villages by providing them with a means of income [by employing them in the company and buying their produce]; secondly, if the company becomes successful and makes a profit, money can be donated to community projects like water supply, schools or aid-posts [...] This company belongs to all the Mbuke people, and all of the clans are shareholders in this company. And I went into it mainly because I like this concept ... It is not for politics! I have no need to go into politics! ... Rather, it is because ... [of] what I said to my children: 'You look at our family in the villages, they are depending on us all the time, and we must help them to get a means of livelihood. So we must start this so that they can depend on something else'. That is why I am doing this. I'm losing on it, I'm suffering, and I'm sacrificing a lot.

These comments illustrate the fact that a central part of the vision of MHL is that of a new kind of social whole, namely the 'community', while before it was 'family' who depended on migrants. Those who are behind MHL wanted this to change by improving the 'means of income' of not only relatives in the village, but the village as a whole. The vision reflected here is that of a community in which individual members are ensured the possibility of their own 'means of livelihood'. Whether the claims this man makes are also meant to present himself in a certain guise is not crucial here, since such claims still draw upon a number of morally legitimate reference points when taking on the perspective of 'community', such as pointing out that he is personally losing on it, and that he is not using it for his own political ambitions – a point which some Mbuke critics of the intentions of some of these highly accomplished men have claimed.

The legitimacy of MHL and the initial great expectations it generated were derived from the claim that it was intended to benefit all, and it was that claim which was constantly questioned when meetings were held and comments made. Other socialities like clans obviously remained in existence alongside these new 'community' organizations, and were often seen as potential threats to 'benefiting the community'. To counter one such threat, eight directors were appointed, one from each of the Mbuke clans.[4] This was to counteract the perceived threat that the company might only help the leading members or only their clans or families. In other words, to some extent the new social totality is based on already existing social forms such as clans, but it is based on them in order to transcend them: the clans had to be involved in order to try to prevent the sectional interests of clan-based loyalties from undermining benefits to the 'community'. Money, and in particular the large contributions from particular migrants who have been successful in the cash economy of Port Moresby, is central to making this vision a reality, and so money and commodity exchange is seen here as the solution to a changed situation, not only as a threat to existing sociality.

The plan for MHL from the outset was to make money in diverse ways, such as organizing fishing and collecting sea cucumbers around the islands, as well as running a small cargo ship outside the province. But this money was to benefit all Mbuke people, who were all 'shareholders', not any particular individual, family or clan. The hopes and intentions were explicitly stated by leading members of the company and enthusiastically embraced by many Mbuke people, villagers and migrants alike, and they were to organize both work and distribution of money in terms of the 'community' as a whole, rather than in terms of individuals or immediate kinship relations. When MHL first started running the cargo ship in about 2005/6, I experienced a widespread sense of the 'great expectations' that the retired general manager's statement above reflects, the expectation that involvement in commodity exchange, especially in interaction with non-Mbuke people, would bear fruit for 'all'. Most people were proud to tell me that now they were doing something for themselves, since *gavman* (state institutions; cf. Otto 1991) were failing to provide much needed 'services' (like schools and aid posts), and people told me that they were 'tired of waiting for development'. The profits were to go back into MIPA and would be used for 'community projects' providing such services. They would be used to develop the villages as a whole: there would be scholarships for bright students, chosen on the basis of ability rather than kinship relations;[5] there would be a support scheme for the elderly to ensure that all those no longer able to work would be supported by the 'community' so that they did not need to rely on kinship solidarity; aid posts would be built; and some even suggested that there should be laptop computers for all students in the community school. Such great expectations clearly indicated the community-building potential seen in the making of money, a potential that transcended both individual gain and kin solidarity. The fact that some of these things did come to pass, albeit only partly funded by money from the company and partly funded through fund-raising activities in Port Moresby, indicates a widely held will to 'benefit the community' as a whole rather than relatives or oneself.

One of the big business activities of MHL which caused particularly great expectations was the running of a small cargo ship that the company, as a legal entity, had chartered from the Manus Provincial Government. Another less spectacular business activity was the buying of sea cucumbers from Mbuke fishermen and selling them directly to Asian markets, or to buyers in Port Moresby, hence avoiding the Asian buyers in the province who act as middlemen. Both of these activities suffered serious setbacks during my longest period of fieldwork (2008/9), and I shall here employ some of the explanations of these perceived 'failures' as examples of the fears and great expectations regarding activities based on the social whole of 'community' which Mbuke people had during my fieldwork.

Explanations of Failure in Community-based Business

During 2008/9, business activities involving the running of the small cargo ship that MHL had leased were closed down due to factors such as a lack of funds for maintaining both the company and the ship.[6] During the same period, the smaller business activity of buying sea cucumbers in the villages and selling them directly to buyers in Port Moresby or abroad was also abandoned because it failed to provide a profit. Both of these setbacks gave rise to a number of interpretations as to why things had gone wrong. Worries and expectations about community-based business as reflected in criticisms directed against others during and after these setbacks reveal a potential tension between a number of socialities which are envisioned both in action and in accusations or suggestions about what specific actions 'makes to appear'. There were many different perspectives voiced in the criticisms and evaluations of how the business activities had 'failed'. Some claimed that people had been corrupted by selfishness, whilst others suggested that people had been caught up in a conflict of interest brought about by their business engagement with people with whom they were also entangled in other kinds of relationships.

The case of Niniendras – a subsidiary company of MHL, based in the village and intended to buy and resell sea cucumbers that villagers collected – shows the kinds of conflicts that some people got caught up in, and suspected others of being caught up in. Migrants who were involved in MHL told me that one of the reasons that Niniendras was eventually closed down was that the sea cucumbers often did not have the quality that those in the village who had been appointed to grade them had indicated, and hence the company ended up actually losing money, thereby failing to fulfil the expectation of generating money that could be used for 'community projects'. In such contexts, it was argued that the problems with Niniendras were due to the fact that the men grading the quality of the sea cucumbers were caught in conflicts of interest because many of the people who came to sell their produce were relatives of theirs, which made them grade their produce higher than they should have done due to kinship solidarity. Some of the men conducting the grading even admitted to me that they had done this – though they did not admit it in public.

A similar type of conflict is evident in the example of a man who was appointed as one of the 'executives' of Niniendras. 'Tom', a man who has lived his whole life in the village, had become one of the managers of the subsidiary. He was responsible for the part of the money which had been allocated to Niniendras by MHL in order to run activities in the villages. The people in the village who were fit for diving (sea cucumbers are found on the sea bed) collected sea cucumbers from the reefs around the islands, cleaned them and smoked or sun-dried them so they could eventually be shipped off and sold. Tom was responsible for coordinating the buying of sea cucumbers from producers in the villages and getting them to the provincial capital (Lorengau), where they were shipped off to Port Moresby. Mbuke migrants in Port Moresby would then find buyers either there or aboard. On one occasion, two other Mbuke men with a more peripheral involvement in Niniendras approached Tom asking for money from the company for petrol for the journey to Lorengau. Tom did not agree that their journey required Niniendras to pay for it, but he felt that he could not resist, because, as he told me, 'they are very big men [in terms of social status]' (*ol bikpela man tumas*, he said in Tok Pisin),[7] even if he was supposed to be the one with the final say regarding the use of the money that he was administering. Although the two men were not 'big' in Niniendras, they were in other contexts, one of them being the leader (*lapan*) of Tom's clan. Tom was reluctant to exercise his authority over the clan leader, who was actually 'below him' in the company structure. So, encompassed in Tom are different socialities (in this case clan and community), in which he is a person in different configurations which came into conflict in that situation. He knew all too well that using company money for the particular purposes in question would not 'benefit the community', from the point of view of himself as a manager, but he was unwilling to take on that perspective when faced with the risk of 'appearing as' unrelated in the appropriate way (not responding positively to a kind of *singaut*) to the leader of his clan.

Another problem in the running of Niniendras was similar to claims about 'wanting to be alone' directed against trade-store owners who resist giving credit and/or attempt to reclaim debts (see Chapter 4). It is usually young men who collect the biggest number of sea cucumbers because of their superior physical ability to dive deep, where most sea cucumbers of the most valuable type are found. Some of these young men chose to sell their sea cucumbers in Lorengau rather than to Niniendras because the village company paid them less than the Asian buyers in town. Certain middle-aged men, who did not themselves have the same physical ability to collect many sea cucumbers, but who occupied leading positions in MIPA and MHL, often had a somewhat patronizing attitude towards these young men, and blamed them for the failure of Niniendras. For example, one of the middle-aged men who had been in charge of disbursing payment for 'executives' in Niniendras – and who was himself occasionally blamed for having misappropriated money – said about these young men:

> some people did not understand it. They saw that they could get more money [...] from a Chinese [buyer] in town, compared to Niniendras. But the idea of Niniendras was that such things are resources that belong to all of us, so when you come and sell it, it is like: You dive, you sell it and get some money for yourself while someone who cannot dive can also benefit a little from these resources. The young people do not understand this. They do not realise that it is a company for all of us.

He made this statement when I asked him during an interview why Niniendras had failed to make money and had been closed down. The young men, for their part, would respond to such accusations in formulations like, 'I was the one that went diving [to collect the sea cucumbers], so the money from it must be mine'. In that sense, the young men question their obligation towards Niniendras, and thereby the 'community' on the basis of their right to individual economic enrichment deriving from the fruits of their own labour. Thus they see the value of sea cucumbers as being produced by the 'labour' invested in their collection rather than seeing them as 'resources' that young men simply pick up and sell, the perspective of the middle-aged man.

The fact that sea cucumbers became profitable goods, but only for those able to dive quite deep, frequently comes up in discussions among the Mbuke people. During village meetings I often heard someone complaining along the lines of, 'these resources belong to all of us, but only a few are benefiting', a conflict only made fiercer by the fact that many young men spent much of their earnings on alcohol and on enjoying themselves in town.[8] Not only did a (physically) privileged few harvest resources regarded by many people as being owned by the community ('all of us'), they did not then redistribute their earnings in the village. 'When they have finished the money on drinking, they come to us and *singaut* for food!' an angry mother complained to me. This indicates that at least some of the young men did not redistribute the money, or parts of it, among relatives, which otherwise would have made them appear as part of the sociality of specific kinship relations as an alternative to appearing as members of 'community'. Around the time of my fieldwork, sea cucumbers were subject to discussion in the villages perhaps mainly because the young men of the village – those who had not succeeded in becoming remitting migrants and were already often seen as a source of problems (cf. Otto 1991: 221–22) – suddenly became wealthy while at the same time living in the village, and tended to fail to use their money 'wisely' (from the point of view of the older generations). This was the case both in the sense that some of them did not share the money with relatives to the extent that relatives would have liked, and in the sense that they bypassed Niniendras.

I suggested in Chapter 4 that action which embodies no social relations (or addresses no audience) in its unfolding cannot easily produce value. In the present situation, saying that the youths did not spend their money 'wisely' would seem to be a claim that money that in itself has no value other than that which its transaction makes appear, keeps lacking that value when consumed by individuals rather than entering visible transactions. But even if the young men were also somewhat self-critical towards me concerning spending money on alcohol (saying things like, 'I have wasted the money on drinking'), the consumption of beer, most often a social activity in itself, must be assumed to produce value in reciprocal relations among these young men themselves (cf. Strathern 1975: 316). But acts that may be valued in this form of sociality are far from being generally accepted as a source of value when compared to positive responses to *singaut* from relatives or acts that can be recognized as 'benefiting the community'.

There seemed to be a kind of 'gold rush' among these young men when the high price of sea cucumbers suddenly enabled them to access commodities like beer, petrol and even prefabricated materials for building houses, which are otherwise commodities often associated with the wealth made from migration. When it started to become clear that sea cucumbers had been overfished in Manus (and in PNG generally), and that the population of them was dropping, the older generation was quick to use reports by the National Fisheries Department (for whom some migrant men from Mbuke work) as a basis for further criticism of these young men. In the village, young men are often dependent on having alliances with older men – at least when wanting to go fishing outside the inner reefs, out where fish populations are more plentiful, or when wanting to go to 'town' (Lorengau) – since they often do not own big canoes or boats for such activities themselves. When sea cucumbers became such a profitable commodity,[9] the need for alliances with boat and canoe owners became less significant because young men could paddle out in small canoes and collect sea cucumbers, because depth rather than distance from the islands became important (at least initially). Older men who wanted to go on sea-cucumber expeditions further away from the islands (when the areas in the vicinity of the islands became depleted) even needed help from young men when it came to diving.

Niniendras may be seen, perhaps more than anything, as a way for migrants and village leaders to tax the great amounts of money that young men were able to make, but which they were seen as failing to share in any widely recognized value-producing way, by channelling some of the money into the 'community' where the older men themselves controlled distribution through their capacity as 'executives'. The refusal to sell to the company was often addressed as 'selfishness', or what I have compared with 'possessive individualism' (Macpherson 1962), the perspective that one owns the products of one's labour individually while 'owing nothing to society' (in this case to the 'community'), a perspective which is not shared in the vision of MHL as a company providing money for the benefit of the whole 'community'. For instance, during the 'launch' of the 'elderly support scheme', which was intended to be funded in part from income from MHL and Niniendras, this sort of criticism was reflected in a speech made by one of the migrant men who had initiated the scheme:

> We should recognise the hard work of our fathers, some of whom are already our ancestors now. We can use these resources [i.e. sea cucumbers] for ourselves, but there must also be a kind of community obligation to help these people! These are resources that belong to all of us, they belong to the children and they belong to the old people, and if you are the owner of it, you must benefit from it!

Not everyone saw the unwillingness of young men to sell to the company as the main reason for the failure of Niniendras. Another problem concerned the number of 'executives' and their suspected use of company money for unapproved purposes. Many people even suspected that they stole money. A young man in the village made such an accusation in an interview with me:

> They chose the wrong people for the management, they chose people who have already been out working and who have learned to mess up money. When people like that have a lot of money in their hands, they are tempted. Those of us in the village who were appointed to grade the sea cucumbers, we might have misused some of the money, but we did not steal it.

The speaker was among those who had been appointed to grade the quality of the products and pay the producers accordingly. The conflict involved in grading and buying sea cucumbers for resale by the company in the light of kinship relations is probably what this young man means when he refers to 'misuse' as opposed to 'stealing'. Both misuse and stealing are clearly seen as possible explanations for the company's failure, but from his perspective 'misuse' seems more justifiable, perhaps because it is perceived by young men like himself as an obligation – the moral obligation to respond positively to *singaut* – that is difficult to resist, rather than the choice of individual greed or selfishness, which is more often indisputably inexcusable, as we saw in Chapter 4. Here the distinction between individual selfishness and relational obligation is maintained in the light of the opposition of both to the category of 'community', perhaps because from the social position of the speaker (in the particular situation he describes) it is important to make clear that the form of 'misuse' he practised, which after all was a kind of sharing, is perhaps more morally excusable vis-à-vis the needs of 'community'.

Niniendras was a relatively small business, and businesses of equal size were also run by Asians in Lorengau with only a few men working in each. By contrast, Niniendras had employees from all the clans – which was necessary in order to prevent criticism that the company favoured some clans and not others. But this had the unfortunate consequence that more than eight men worked as 'executives', who did 'little more than conduct meetings', especially seen from the point of view of the young men who felt they had done the actual (value-producing) work. I do not know the exact salaries these men were given, but some people I spoke to explained that salaries had been calculated based on salaries in government institutions in the provincial capital. Another problem was that the clan representatives wanted white-collar type jobs and other people – young men – were employed to do the actual grading and packing of sea cucumbers. This might also be what the young man above meant by 'messing up money', that is, rather than the profits of the sea-cucumber trade being channelled into 'community' projects, too much of the money was simply used up in paying salaries to the ('big') men who were employed as company executives.

Opposition to these executives – who were mostly former migrants and clan leaders – did not only come from the younger men who did the diving. Wealthier and older Mbuke people such as former migrants also saw problems in the organizational structure of Niniendras, and harboured suspicions about the motives of the executives. One recently returned migrant directed the blame for the subsidiary's failure at the executives:

> They sold the sea cucumbers [in Port Moresby] but there was never any feedback to all the men in the village. I think people like … [a leading member of MHL], he

is just conning people. Because I have some education I can see this. He is gaining a lot from it, while investing it elsewhere. And he is just using the name of the community, and the little amount of sea cucumbers the community has, for gaining something for himself only (TP: *em yet*). People are too blind to see.

As this statement indicates, fears of individual enrichment at the expense of the 'community' were also expressed regarding the managerial staff running MHL in Port Moresby, and concerned the set of men who had been appointed to positions of responsibility in the running of the company. A large group of these 'executives' were based in the regional shipping centre of Rabaul, East New Britain Province, from where the small cargo ship was run. One widespread suspicion was that these men were 'stealing from the company' for their own personal benefit. The money that had potentially been 'stolen' was not described as having been redistributed through kinship relations; rather, the men were alleged to be 'eating the money' due to the extravagant urban lifestyle that they were suspected of leading in Rabaul. Mbuke people's general preference for white-collar jobs seems to have been a problem here as well, since the Mbuke men working in the shipping section of MHL were all 'executives', working in an office in Rabaul, and according the pay list I saw, they were a much bigger expense in terms of salary than the actual crew of the ship (fifteen men who came along with the lease of the ship and who were not from Mbuke).

Like the young men who refused to sell sea cucumbers to Niniendras, the men in Rabaul were suspected of undermining the company – and hence attempts at building the 'community' – through individual greed that was characterized as 'stealing', though theirs was the individual enrichment of the well-educated elite as opposed to the individual enrichment of young people in the village, who are poor by comparison. The men in Rabaul did not admit openly to misappropriating company funds themselves, something which young men in the villages would sometimes do, at least when questioned directly by me. Instead, they explicitly claimed to be 'doing it for the community', whereas not all the young men saw it as a legitimate claim that their produce should be 'taxed' by the 'community' company. On the other hand, the men in Rabaul did not conceal the fact that they were paid for the work they did, and as one well-educated former migrant told me, 'of course the employees have to get a little money (TP: *liklik toea*)[10] – we are not communists'.

Some people feared that one of the overall managers of MHL was simply trying to build up his own name through MHL. This suspicion was reinforced by he became a candidate to replace the ageing leader of his clan, one of the most powerful clans among the Mbuke people. Some people said that he had appointed persons to leading positions within MHL who might support his leadership later, and that he was trying to establish himself as a *lapan* backed financially by the company. Traditional leadership in Manus has recently been discussed in great detail by Dalsgaard (2010), and for the sake of my argument here it suffices to say that such leaders gain legitimacy both by achievement (such as conducting exchange ceremonies, organizing social events generally, and in the past by sponsoring bridewealth payments among other things) and by hereditary means, by being appointed by their predecessor. The form of inheritance is currently so flexible that the ageing *lapan* can pass on his leadership to the most suitable man within the clan, although the normal preference is for the oldest direct son, and secondarily to a man of the 'head'[11] patrilineage of the clan (in practice this would mean a son, a son of a brother or a younger brother). But sometimes this 'appointing' does not take place (such as when the ageing leader dies before being able to do so), and competition over clan leadership is frequent as a result.

I have discussed the passing on of parts of one's social person, in the case of the right and ability to build outrigger canoes, elsewhere (Rasmussen 2013, 2014). In situations that result in competition over clan leadership, a number of men will try to prove themselves worthy, or in fact 'appear as' leaders, by holding leading and organizing positions in a number of situations. This is often referred to as *kiliwi*, from *liwi*, Titan for 'to pull'. The word *kiliwi* is used when blaming someone for claiming leadership that they have not been appointed to by others. Dalsgaard suggests that those who have not properly received their leadership from their predecessor are referred to as *lapan-kiliwi* in Titan (Dalsgaard 2010: 106). In daily discourse, though, the word is often used about men who try to 'elevate their own name' (or 'pull their own name', as Mbuke people mostly translate *kiliwi*), and try to put themselves in charge of projects even though they have not been appointed at a village meeting or by legitimate leaders, whether they are 'executives' of MIPA or MHL, or traditional leaders. When someone says something during a meeting which is not constructive but only demonstrates his knowledge about some matter, people might say that he is doing *kiliwi* rather than trying to help. In this sense, *kiliwi* is a way to claim leadership or expertise by other than directly relevant means.

However, in MIPA and MHL, this tendency was not a problem confined to managers, but was a general problem revealed in other projects in the villages. For example, many people were suspected of becoming executives in MIPA and MHL with the sole purpose of building up their own name by having a title in the organization, rather than out of any genuine will to help the 'community'. In other words, the legitimacy of any kind of leader, and self- and un-appointed ones in particular, is always questioned on the basis of the intention behind it; and when migrants or former migrants representing MIPA and MHL gave speeches and presented 'development plans', some people said that 'they are just showing off their knowledge'. From the point of view of this interpretation, what some executives of MIPA and MHL are doing is a new version of the contests over 'name and fame' involved in the old form of leadership.

The value of sea cucumbers appears to be derived from very different sources, depending on social perspective. The young men were accused of being a version of possessive individuals (being 'selfish' or 'wanting to be alone') by claiming ownership of the results of their own physical labour and by not sharing the proceeds realized from it among their kin. Representatives of the company (at least in rhetoric), and especially those unable to dive well themselves, looked at the sea cucumbers as 'resources' belonging to the 'community', hence locating value in the actual sea cucumbers rather than in a version of the 'labour theory of value' which the young men adhered to when saying, 'I was the one who went diving' referring to the labour of diving, collecting, cleaning and smoking sea cucumbers, rather than sea cucumbers as a value in themselves that had been subtracted directly from the collectively owned reefs now under the ownership of MIPA, and thereby owned by the 'community' as a whole. From the latter point of view, the theory of value is different when saying 'these resources belong to all of us', and here the normative expectation is that all Mbuke people, the 'community' as a whole, should benefit from the money that can be realized from the sale of their property. The case of MIPA, and more particularly MHL and Niniendras, and explanations of the problems that came to face the latter two, evokes questions about some of the things that Mbuke people hope (and fear) that money and doing business will be useful for.

Coexisting Forms of Personhood as Revealed by Different Uses of Money

The hopes for 'community-based business' were as much about making 'community' appear in perceptible forms as they were about making business or money as such, I would argue. The issue was always what such money and organizational structures might be used for. The very reference made to the 'community' as a whole, rather than smaller groups like families and clans, which have often been the basis for organizing business operations on Mbuke, as they have in other parts of PNG (e.g. Finney 1973; Sykes 2007b), indicates the possibility of imagining – and attempting to act in accordance with – a social totality that goes beyond the specific personalized microcosms of a person's relations. MIPA and MHL instead encompass and contain both persons and kin groups as parts of a more abstract social whole.

This is not to say that Mbuke people oppose the exchange obligations that come with a person's need to maintain significant social relationships, and neither is it to say that individual gain from engagement with the commodity economy is always morally problematic; individual enrichment it is not morally problematic if it does not conflict with kin solidarity or 'community' interests. That is to say, if a person responds positively to *singaut* and donates money to community organizations, then that person's individual wealth is not necessarily morally questionable. Rather, these new forms of organization, in their adjusted form, simply show that Mbuke people – and especially the educated elite – envision another possibility in terms of what money and new forms of organization might be used for, what kind of sociality they may strengthen and 'make appear'. A possibility in which the 'community' might benefit from (or occur in the form of) involvement with the commodity economy, and in this envisioned possibility (community based business) kin obligation and individual selfishness can even appear as a problem of the same kind from the perspective of those trying to 'benefit the 'community'. This break is not clear or total in any way. In fact, a person can simultaneously be a member of the 'community' (concretized by MIPA and MHL), a microcosm of a network of kinship relations and an independent economic actor – although these conceptions of the person are often in conflict.

Summarizing some of the points made by Macpherson, Sykes states that, 'how humans transact wealth is deeply connected to who they are as moral persons' (Sykes 2007a: 220). As the Mbuke case demonstrates, the ways in which people transact (and they do so in different ways in different situations) and the concepts of their constitution as persons are interconnected in significant ways. People can be understood as 'relational persons' in the way I have used the concept, if things exchanged 'make appear' those kin relationships which play a significant role in their constitution as persons. And a person can appear as a 'person alone' (with certain similarities to the possessive individual) if they can be claimed to reveal themselves as not owing anything to others. In community, the individual member is understood as a part of a larger social whole, imagined beyond concrete networks of relationships of which the person is a microcosm. What then is the form of personhood in 'community'?

The argument that money and commodity exchange tends to dissolve social bonds often involves the idea that money brings along a growth in individualism. I have mentioned selfishness and greed (which I compared with possessive individualism in Chapter 4) in the discussion of MHL, in which both the suspicion of 'selfishness' and the direct claim to ownership of one's own productive capacities occurred. Following a number of anthropologists working in the Western Pacific (Hirsch 2007; Martin 2007;

Robbins 2007; Sykes 2007a, 2007b), I thus have argued that possessive individualism is relevant, although in my case mostly as a 'moral grounds for critique' (Sykes 2007a: 255). Sykes states that the perspective of owing nothing to society is that of a PNG person who 'generally inhabits an elite position' (ibid.: 213), which is also the case in Martin's use of possessive individualism in his discussion of 'Big Shots' who try to limit their engagement when it comes to sharing with village kin by posing themselves as possessive individuals (Martin 2007). But they also enforce that perspective upon the villagers in the hope that that these village relatives will acknowledge that rather than asking others for betel nuts (TP: *buai*) 'their own *buai* they must buy' (Martin 2007: 288). In the Mbuke situation, the person accused of appearing as a possessive individual can equally be a relatively poor village dweller claiming that the fruits of their labour are their own.

Robbins queries the relevance of the idea of possessive individualism in the Western Pacific, an idea which Macpherson used to talk about people living in capitalist market societies, or 'the liberal democratic state' (Macpherson 1962: 1). Robbins asks, 'how people who do not live their lives wholly within such societies are able to put those ideas to use' (Robbins 2007: 304). In a number of papers in a special issue of *Anthropological Forum* addressing the relevance of possessive individualism in the Western Pacific (Hirsch 2007; Martin 2007; Wendel 2007; Were 2007; Robbins 2007; Sykes 2007a, 2007b), two authors answer Robbins's question in ways related to the present discussion, saying that possessive individualism can coexist with other concepts of the person (see Martin 2007; Wendel 2007), but they both understand this in terms of the relationship between tradition and individualism, as Robbins (2007: 306) points out (see e.g. Martin 2007: 294). For example, Martin argues that elite 'Big Shots' in Matupit attempt to enforce upon villagers a degree of possessive individualism in order to limit their 'culture of consumption' or the expectancy of 'spoon-feeding' (ibid.: 289–90), which villagers associate with *kastom* (custom, tradition). Martin concludes that this shows 'that there is more than one way to constitute a person in contemporary PNG' (ibid.: 297). This is obviously also the case among Mbuke people. Both the person as a member of community and the person as relationally constituted in specific relations of kinship are morally legitimate bases upon which a person's act can produce value, ways in which a person can 'appear' as a person of *tawian* (T: 'the good of you/him/her'), even if this basis is also contested and transformed by such acts.

In the Mbuke case, something comparable to possessive individualism seems to be reflected in the accusation against a person who 'wants to be alone', but this is not the type of individualism reflected in the idea of the person as a member of the 'community'. As I have made clear above, the perspective of 'community' conflicts with the perspective of young men allegedly owning the fruits of their own labour, and as such owing nothing to society. It might be useful to consider the idea of the 'collective individual', which, in the same sense as the possessive individual, owns itself, but a self including many people. In a discussion of 'having culture' among the Fuyuge of PNG, Hirsch states that this sort of having 'is a form of "possessive individualism", in which it is "collective individuals" (culture) that do the possessing' (Hirsch 2007: 234), and this might be a way of understanding the 'community'. Sykes develops the idea regarding kin-based businesses in New Ireland Province, making the point that a business manager who runs such a company is not a 'Big Man', nor is he simply an entrepreneur. He is rather, Sykes suggests, in his capacity as head of the company, a contemporary form of a possessive individual which she – drawing on Bakan (2004) – calls a 'corporate individual' who has to own his clan, a social form, and is like the group able to act as an individual businessman (Sykes 2007b: 257). In a certain sense, 'community' is similarly a collective possessive individual, as revealed by the fact that business and alienated relations of commodity exchange can from many people's point of view only be legitimate and successful in interaction with non-Mbuke people, as we also saw for Ponam in Chapter 5.

These authors do not discuss whether or not it is the case that with a new form of personhood comes a new form of social whole of which the person is a part, but instead they see wholes as possessed by the person, like possessive individuals posses themselves (cf. Robbins 2007: 306). In the Mbuke case, 'resources belong to all of us', and the person as a part owes these resources to the 'community', which is the possessive entity. If Melanesians are not individuals because they are not part of a pre-existing society, but are embodiments of the constantly changing social microcosm (of concrete social relationships) which constitute them as persons (Strathern 1988: 3; Wagner 1991: 159), then emergent individualism must involve the emergence of some form of social totality. And rather than this being the nation-state (Foster 1995b), which Mbuke people have by their account grown tired of waiting for as a source of development, this social whole might be, as Mbuke people have termed it, the 'community' as a kind of micro-nation (cf. May 1982). In this case, the person can legitimately be an individual as part of the 'community', as part of categories such as 'elderly people' and 'youth' who should be provided with services regardless of the concrete relationships of kinship that they contain in their simultaneous kinship-based relational constitution.

In the case of MHL, and Niniendras most vividly, and in the idea of 'community' more generally, many Mbuke people saw in the appropriate

◆

use of money a potential for a new kind of sociality beyond kinship alliances and individual interests. Alongside these great expectations, however, there was the fear that other interests and alliances might come into conflict with the company. Although measures had been taken to transcend clan affiliations and other threats to 'community' in the organization, these did not disappear but remained as a threat. What was conceived as rightfully belonging to the 'community', what should be shared with family, and what an individual could claim as 'their own' was never fully agreed upon, but generated tension instead. As Gudeman (2008) has pointed out, there is always a tension between 'market' and 'mutuality' in 'the economy'. In Melanesia, this tension is recognisable in that between the two coeval economies of gifts and commodities (Gregory 1982, 1997). This is a tension revolving around the axis between reciprocal obligation and alien-ated commodity exchange, an axis which is not agreed upon. This tension has been described by Martin for PNG as a contest regarding the 'limits of reciprocity'; the social contest of where social obligation ends and where self-reliance begins (Martin 2007). In this case, the tension may analyt-ically be described as at least three-way; it is not between individualism and relationality but between different visions of appropriate sociality and between different concepts of the person, depending on perspective and depending on the sociality that actions revealing the person's consti-tution 'make appear' in particular situations. From the point of view of 'community', kin-based mutuality can be a problem if it conflicts with the good of the 'community'. And the same is true of what I have compared to possessive individuals (people who keep and sell the fruits of their labour for example), persons who are seen by many Mbuke people as being selfish and 'wanting to be alone', because their actions make no sociality 'appear', leaving them to float alone like 'men from space' as one Mbuke phrased it (see Chapter 4).

Attempts by the organizers of MIPA and MHL to make 'community' appear provide a perspective from which types of sociality that would in other contexts be in opposition as individualism versus relationality are both equally problematic. In certain contexts these may even be grouped together as the selfishness that undercuts 'community' even if in other contexts they are in clear opposition. In that sense, both market and (kin-based) mutuality can potentially conflict with 'community'. In fact, 'community' provides a perspective from which this distinction may be less relevant. From the perspective of those agitating for 'benefiting the community' and attempting to implement 'community projects', when the accusation is made that a particular person is 'selfish' or only thinking of 'themselves' it is not necessarily clear whether or not that 'selfishness' refers to individual enrichment or to distributing resources among relatives along the lines of family or clan solidarity. Consider, for example, the criticism directed against one of the leading members of MHL, of whom it was said, 'he is just conning people [...] He is gaining a lot from it, while investing it elsewhere'. Here it might make little difference, from the perspective of 'benefiting the community', whether the 'elsewhere' is his family business or something which will benefit him personally. Likewise, whether the 'self' claimed to be selfish is an individual who cares little about his own kin, or a 'self' who makes his name and his own clan's name big by taking a position as an 'executive' with motivations suspected to be *kiliwi*, perhaps hoping to become a *lapan*, rather than 'benefiting community', may from certain perspectives be of little importance. That same distinction might be of great importance in other contexts, when for example a migrant does not 'see' their own kin while being suspected of pursuing an ostentatious lifestyle in Port Moresby. In other words, various social perspectives might evaluate the same action in a variety of ways, depending on the sociality the one criticizing the action in question sees as appropriate for the potentially value-producing action in the specific situation. For example, someone who allocated personal funds to MIPA, MHL or other 'community projects' might be criticized by their relatives if they felt that they were being overlooked, and that the person's donation to the community could have instead taken the form of remittances.

The perspective on the effect of money and the commodity economy on social relations which can be described using Sahlins' term 'developman', in which continuity is ensured by using money for 'pre-existing' purposes (Sahlins 2005: 23–24), is clearly present in Manus. In a sense, an instance of 'developman' in Manus might appear to be what we have seen in previous chapters on forms of *singaut*, where I describe how money plays a key role in maintaining significant social relationships. But as I also show, the nature of such relationships is highly determined by the new situation of migration and unequal access to money, and it is not simply as case of the continuation of 'pre-existing' practices, as was perhaps the case when (in earlier days of labour migration) ceremonial exchange was used as a means of channelling wealth between persons and groups and as a vehicle for the social reproduction of persons. Whereas reassurances that money has been 'domesticated' (Gregory 1997: 238) may ease the concerns of those who fear the loss of relationality at the expense of some form of individualism, this is not the case from the point of view of 'community'. The persistence of previous kin-based socialities and the forms of leadership they entailed is not what is hoped for, not even on a bigger and better scale; change is what is hoped for, but also what is put at risk by those who choose to allocate funds to kinship relationships or keep money for themselves. Although no one on Mbuke is explicitly against the

◆

idea of 'community', there is no consensus regarding the limits between what rightfully belongs to the 'community' and what does not, as we saw in the case of the young men. This is perhaps the main source of tension in the Mbuke economy. The fears and accusations that arose in discussions of MHL reflect a tendency of 'developman' – that is, that some titles are distributed according to clan membership. But this tendency is feared or seen as potentially negative from the perspective of the 'good of the community'. When some Mbuke people claim that the leading members of MIPA and MHL are simply 'pulling their name', it is an expression of this fear, that is, that attempts to build 'community' are being undermined by tendencies towards something similar to 'developman' with new social positions (company executives) being used in ongoing contests over 'names' that do not benefit the 'community'.

Some Mbuke people dismissed MHL when I asked them about it, and said 'that is just one man's company'. And many people – especially in the villages – were very critical of the fact that the men appointed as leading members of MHL were also close allies in other contexts. These fears show a persistence of kin-based identifications or affiliations alongside the emergence of a concept of the 'community' as a whole beyond such affiliations. In relation to this, people expressed concern about who is employed and what qualifications they have for fear that they might take on the job simply to gain access to funds that they will later distribute along the wrong lines (to family, for example), or that they have been appointed by leaders to earn the appointee's support in other contexts.

In other words, individualism and relationality are not simply two possibilities threatening one another, and the process of individuation is not simply morally problematic and in conflict with all possible social ends. When there are hopes that the 'bonds of tradition' (such as clan affiliation) can be broken or lessened, this is not because Mbuke people share the dream of liberal economists that the freed individual in capitalist society will – in their self-interested pursuit of wealth – indirectly benefit society at large. Rather, what Mbuke people hope is that money might directly help to create a better community in which 'all' are equal members (and in that sense individual parts). Both the 'bonds of tradition' and possessive individuals are threats to money's potential in building 'community'.

Rather than society existing to ensure individual rights to possession, as Macpherson has it (see Robbins 2007: 303), 'society' in the form of 'community' among the Mbuke possesses its individual members. Macpherson's idea of possessive individualism presupposed its existence within capitalist market societies, and in fact he bases his theories on writings about such societies (see ibid.: 302–4). Macpherson's definition of possessive individualism involves 'the individual as essentially the proprietor of his own person or capacities, owing nothing to society for them' (Macpherson 1962: 3). The individual member of the community among Mbuke people is part of a different kind of larger social whole. In a sense, Mbuke people in economically fortunate positions resist the emergence of possessive individualism amongst villagers by attempting to channel their earnings into the 'community', hence trying to make villagers help care for their less fortunate neighbours, an obligation which *singaut* had gradually put on migrants in particular when money became a necessity. This organized resistance against some form of possessive individualism indirectly introduces another kind of individual who does owe something to 'society', which in turn is introduced directly, the 'community'. This is perhaps a paradox in that many of the aforementioned authors describe emergent individualism as primarily existing among elites, describing hopes for the persistence of kin-based solidarity or relationality as being predominant among the 'grassroots' (e.g. Martin 2007: 286). But as in Martin's own case, elites are in fact those able to meet the requirements of *kastom* by presenting shell money – that they have bought with money – at mortuary exchanges (ibid.: 295). Meanwhile, as we have seen among the Mbuke, people living in the villages are often the ones who face subsistence problems, and may therefore fail to look after relatives that they are otherwise obliged to look after, leaving this task to migrants. At least that is how migrants sometimes see it.

The problem of feeling no obligation towards 'society' is something to be overcome, as it may cause selfishness and 'the person alone', but it is not resisted by reference to *kastom* and clan solidarity (as in Martin's account of Matupit) but by introducing and promoting 'community' as a social whole of which the individual is part, and within which the person can act and produce value. Rather than money being at the heart of a dichotomy between either individualism or 'customary' relationality, or a tension between marked and mutuality, specific uses of money can in the Mbuke case be placed in a three-way tension between three aspects of sociality: the relational person acting in and as the sociality of kinship relations; a member of the 'community'; and the 'person alone'. Two of these (which are usually in opposition) can sometimes be conflated when seen from the position of the third. In order for the third option of 'community' to be successful, Mbuke people have to contain and confine certain economic activities within it, and in doing so they have to strive against the forms of transactions that encourage both 'the person alone' and relationality, the two aspects of sociality which are often opposed in the anthropological literature on PNG, but which can often seem similar or even identical from the perspective of those trying to use money to build 'community'. Naturally, these perspectives are never fixed, and the 'three-way tension' exists not only between particular persons in particular positions, but might equally be present in a single person, as they were in the case of Tom (see above). The perspectives and positions themselves may also be contested in the social situations in which they are actualized.

Conclusions

Although the MIPA and MHL clearly draw on forms of organization which have been introduced from outside Manus and PNG, the 'community project' as such among the Mbuke people is not simply the type of development which Sahlins associates with cultural humiliation and abandonment, in which people want to become exactly like the others whom they feel humiliated by (Sahlins 2005: 24). This is not how Mbuke people have gone about it, because clearly the – at least normative – purpose of the organizations they have formed is to benefit 'all' rather than slip out of obligations of sharing among close relatives in order to owe nothing (or less) to others, which is often perceived to be the case among those who introduced capitalism in the first place. Such 'anti-social' ways are something that should be avoided from the point of view of 'community'. Rather, it seems they try to envision a third possibility in which money and other more recently introduced phenomena can be used to build a new kind of sociality which is neither simply 'domestication' nor complete rupture. This is not to say that these two possibilities are not also expressed. Domestication in some manner is expressed in the way money in the form of remittances is useful in maintaining significant social relationships; but there is also the threat of 'building a name' or misappropriating money from the community business. Radical change is perhaps exemplified above by young men claiming that they personally own the fruits of their labour. But from the point of view of 'community', both of these uses of money are potentially problematic, not because they constitute threats to traditions, but because they pose threats to a vision and concrete 'appearances' of a better future for many. This future is a response to Mbuke people's inevitable involvement in global capitalism, in which commodities produced in a PNG village are sold as luxury goods in Asia (sea cucumbers, for instance).

'Community' as the general sense (as opposed to the Mbuke sense of it) is often seen as being threatened by specific uses of money and commoditization. But as the Mbuke case demonstrates, people may also have great expectations that money and the social forms that come with it may also promote, strengthen and even produce 'community' as such. Fears regarding money among Mbuke people may from certain points of view be of the opposite nature, namely that money might fail to break down the dominance of family or clan affiliation, which will undermine the 'community' company, as will greed and 'the person alone'. In the 'community', people are individual members of a somewhat abstract whole, but only in opposition to this are they comparable to possessive individuals. Members of the 'community' are themselves possessed by the social whole of which they form part. Being a 'member' – and this term is in fact widely used in discussions of 'community' – is in itself a relational form of personhood, in the sense that it describes a relation between that person and that in which they have membership. However, this is still a very different form of relationality from that which I have described as relational personhood funded solely by specific kinship relations. Even if members are more individual than dividual, this is not an argument that possessive individuals pursuing their own interests will produce a well-functioning society (community) as a spin-off effect, but a case of people consciously attempting to use money and the organization that comes with commodity exchange as a means to a social end, deliberately trying to harness the anti-social tendencies money is seen to have in the form of both possessive individuals and overt kinship solidarity.

I have dealt here with three different kinds of personhood: the relational person, based in kinship and which is 'made appear' by acts of sharing with relatives; 'the person alone' pursuing their own interests in making their trade store run or harvesting the fruits of their labour in collecting sea cucumbers; and finally, the member of 'community'. Discussions of 'stealing', 'misuse' and 'selfishness' regarding 'community' funds present a situation in which clan solidarity and possessive individuals are threats to the building of 'community' as a wider social order, as well as maintaining the familiar categorical opposition between individual greed and the maintenance and expansion of networks of the social obligation to share. Discussions in this context of 'greed' and 'selfishness' also mark out certain practices and uses of money as antithetical to those that might build 'community', but by contrast will occasionally conflate the familiar distinction between individualism and relational obligation. The MHL employees in Rabaul who allegedly 'eat' the company's money and the young men who bypass Niniendras in order to sell their produce for a better price are both described as 'selfish'. But so too is the MHL manager's alleged attempt at becoming a clan leader by distributing company funds and offices through kinship networks and exchanges. Relationality and individualism are in such situations conflated as the anti-social use of money to benefit a particular person or set of persons at the expense of the 'community'.

Concepts such as 'community' that encompass wider collectives beyond those of kin groups and exchange partners are an important part of contemporary Mbuke life. For a person unwilling to accept 'groups' of an abstract nature in Melanesia (or someone arguing for cultural continuity 'underneath', such as the 'developman' argument), 'community' could be seen as a new kind of dream and aspiration that never truly takes root, to be contrasted with the underlying 'real' social forms of economic individualism or kin-based reciprocal obligation. Critics might point out that MHL and Niniendras eventually went out of business and that people went back to kinship alliances and the like, which admittedly they did: many informants said that it would be better to organise businesses in terms of family or clan in order to make them work. On the other hand, clan and family are not given by nature, and on Mbuke, clan formations do break down and change their make up now and then. In this chapter I have argued that 'community' may be seen as a social whole in which persons are members whose actions form value and are valued because they 'benefit the community'.

Notes

1. The word 'sugarloaf' used in the name of the club is a pet name sometimes used for Mbuke Island itself (where at this time nearly all Mbuke people who were not away as migrants lived).
2. Such claims seem plausible since that was the same period in which the PNG economy started weakening.
3. A 'ward councillor' is a representative at the lowest level of government in PNG. In a sense these are the contemporary form of the *luluai*, who during colonial era constituted the link between villages and the colonial authorities. See Dalsgaard (2010: 57–63) for a detailed outline of the provincial government system in Manus and PNG.
4. In terms of descent from the 'first' seven Mbuke men, there are seven clans among the Mbuke, as I noted in Chapter 1. However, one of these clans has split in two, even if this split is not recognized from all social perspectives. I comment further on this later in the chapter.
5. The criteria used for these scholarships set up by Mbuke people in Port Moresby was interestingly based on 'the way they behave/conduct themselves in the "community"' (*pasin blo en, insait long community*).
6. The authorities declared the ship unseaworthy. It was argued by Mbuke men who managed it that the maintenance of the ship was the responsibility of the owner, namely the provincial government. In the contract between MHL and the Manus provincial government this is quite unclear, and it seemed that both parties saw it as the responsibility of the other party when it became relevant.
7. The phrase can also be translated as 'they are too big men'. Regardless of this, it was still their status within kinship-based political entities rather than in the 'community' to which he referred.

8. See Strathern (1975: 316) for a discussion of the ambiguous status of large-scale beer drinking in urban PNG, an activity which when seen from the perspective of the village appears as simply selfish, but can be understood as one of the exchange routes by which new forms of urban sociality are formed.

9. This happened quite suddenly. Prices paid by Asian buyers in Manus rose sharply from 2005 onwards, but they dropped equally sharply from 2008, when sea cucumbers became scarcer and the fisheries department put limits on the trade in them.

10. The expression *liklik toea* is similar in sense of the English 'chickenfeed'.

11. This refers to how certain families within a clan were of higher rank, known as *lapan*, while those of lower rank are known as *lau* (see Schwartz 1963: 65; Otto 1994: 225). On contemporary Mbuke Islands, the term *lapan* is used for persons who are clan leaders, and *lau* is used for their 'people' or followers.

7

All Things Considered

Organized Action as Appearances of Social Totalities

——————— ◆●◆ ———————

The historical notes provided in Chapter 6 are important for under-standing the emerging social whole of 'community', since clearly its 'appearances' – as the Mbuke Islands People's Association (MIPA) and MIPA Holdings Limited (MHL) – draw inspiration from socialities that occurred during the colonial encounter. Nevertheless, local concepts and practices of social totalization and ways in which totalities of different kinds 'appear' also inform the social dynamics and conflicts which arise when different kinds of socialities constitute the basis of valuation and are negotiated socially. Even if 'they', the people we study, have no con-ceptual counterpart to society, they do have ideas about social totaliza-tion which may be of assistance to an anthropological understanding of the formation of social totalities that we actually encounter in the field. 'All things considered' seems like an appropriate title for the last chapter of a book, but what would it mean to actually try to consider all things? An important organizational skill among Mbuke people is described by many of them as the ability to see things from many points of view si-multaneously, and doing so means making all such perspectives appear in the unfolding of organized action (like 'seeing' implies making visible that which is seen and that which is 'made seen' by others, as we saw in Chapter 2). This valued skill, a skill of valuing in itself, is referred to as *lemwenemweneye*, a local concept or ideology which brings us back to the questions of visual 'appearance', socialities and audiences of action in the formation of value.

An Indigenous Theory of Social Totalization

In this chapter I return to Rio's observation that, 'if we can no longer hope to approach society as a "coherent whole", then we can at least trace empirically how people themselves conceptualize their social life world' (Rio 2007: 1). Rio argues that 'the third party' is a 'viewpoint from where society can take a look at itself' (ibid.: 19), and third parties take on an 'outside view' which 'totalizes' social flows (Rio 2005). During the unfolding of organized action, such as marriage ceremonies among the Ambrym of Vanuatu, Rio shows how the totalizing third party remains peripheral – and even taboo (as is the case for mother's brother to the bride in marriage ceremonies) – to the actual event (ibid.: 413), and only if the event endangers the totality of past and future relationships of which the event (the marriage) forms part does the totalizing third party interfere (ibid.: 416). Contrary to Strathern (1992b: 86), who argues that there is no 'holistic' conception of society in Melanesia, Rio argues that the totalizing outside view of the third party presents a whole beyond any person's specific relationships. For example, sand drawings which accompany the narration of stories eventually totalize in an image in which 'the whole story comes together' (Rio 2005: 409). Only the outside view, the narrator, can see the whole image, the whole story, which is not visible from within the story itself for concrete actors in it (ibid.).

Among Mbuke people, the 'third party' may likewise be seen as the audience of action, but the totalizing party on the other hand is at the centre of events as the organizer of action. Totalization then occurs dialectically between organizer and audience. The person organizing action (usually some form of leader) strives to take into account and make appear all the perspectives looking at the event. The totalizing party, the person about whom it may be said that 'this man opens his eyes and turns around' (ibid.: 410), as people from north Ambrym put it, is at the very centre of activity rather than being peripheral to the event among Mbuke people. The ability to see things from all perspectives simultaneously is referred to by Mbuke people in Titan as *lemwenemweneye*, a noun form of the verb *lemweneani*, which is translated into Tok Pisin as *tingim gut* (consider it well), *skelim olgeta samting* (proportionalize, measure all things), while the personal property of *lemwenemweneye* may be explained like this Mbuke man did in Tok Pisin: 'your character, how you analyse things, and how you "scale it", it is one's person's view of the bigger picture, kind of like wisdom'.

Organized action informed by *lemwenemweneye*, I argue here, is a way of totalizing social relations which may shed further light on my previous claim that acts of valuing simultaneously make claims about, present or dispute the specific sociality in which the act unfolds. In Chapter 2 it was argued that a perspective 'made appear' (by money or requests) helped constitute persons and their relationships in a dialectical or reciprocal process between the concrete parties involved. Chapter 3 introduced an imagined, although often singular (ancestral spirit or God) third party constituting an audience that evaluates (recognizes) the action as mediated from the person who is unable to react personally to a perspective which is 'made appear'. Central to the 'exchange of perspective' discussed in Chapter 2 is the idea that the view of the other always implies the view from the other onto the self, and actions were analysed as appearances of the relationships within which action took place. In this chapter this point is developed further in exploring the perspective which aims to see many perspectives (ideally 'all') simultaneously, allowing this to appear in the unfolding of organized social action, here understood as situations in which more than one person acts and affects the outcome of that which is taking place. The unfolding of action informed by *lemwenemweneye*, I argue, makes appear the totality of involved parties, who in turn recognize or misrecognize that totalization directly by applauding or by making things fail. This kind of totalization has to be made when projects unfold making 'community' appear.

Community Appearing in the Form of a Canoe

After having conducted various bits of fieldwork among Mbuke people over a period of four years, I started to feel a certain degree of reciprocal obligation. I wanted to give something back to the people who had enthusiastically embraced both me and my research projects as a meaningful part of their lives. I decided to sponsor the building of a large outrigger canoe for the 'community'. Since many other projects at the time were organized as 'community projects', and since (as we have seen) 'community' was a meaningful social entity to which donations could be made without these being channelled into kin relations, it seemed appropriate that this was the entity to which I made my donation, hence making me appear not simply as Mwaton (my adoptive name), but also as a person who had criss-crossed kin relations and clan affiliations through my work as an ethnographer. I chose to donate money for the building of an outrigger canoe specifically, because I knew that parents of children attending high school in Lorengau often faced problems financing transport back and forth in conjunction with holidays and weekends, and the idea of a 'community canoe' for such 'community purposes' had been voiced many times by many different Mbuke people. When later the canoe was finished, an example of such a 'community' purpose was transporting building materials for new aid posts in the villages.

It should be noted that the largest of these sea-going and sail-carrying outrigger canoes are up to 18 metres long and can carry up to forty people (see Rasmussen 2013). They are propelled by a combination of sail and outboard engines, hence lowering travel expenses in comparison to fibre-glass dinghies with outboards, which in turn seldom carry more than ten people and their luggage across the open sea in which the Mbuke Islands are situated, while also consuming significantly more fuel. The building of such canoes among Mbuke people involves obtaining an often incredibly large tree, since the main hull is built from a hollowed-out log, which hence determines the size of the final canoe (ibid.: 21–45). Getting logs of the desired size is never an easy task, because big trees of the right species are not found on the actual Mbuke Islands, but must be obtained from allies, friends or family on Manus Island, where large trees of the right strain grow. For the 'community canoe' this was also the case, and the event I shall discuss here was the felling of a tree meant to be used for the 'community' canoe. This event shows some of the features that tend to be involved when organized social action takes place among Mbuke people. Mundane as felling a tree may seem, in this case it did involve *lemwenemweneye* on the part of the organizers, and something being mundane does not necessarily make it socially insignificant, as we have also seen with remittances, food sharing and the running of trade stores.

The building of the 'community canoe' was discussed at more than ten meetings among leading Mbuke men – *lapan*s, the ward councillor, ex-migrants and other 'big' men. Then the project as a whole was launched, speeches were given, and a committee was formed which included a chairman responsible for the organization, and a leader for organizing the actual building, among others. At first this seemed to me – from the point of view of efficacy – to involve a great amount of effort for the task of building one canoe. I knew from other cases of canoes having been built during my time on the islands that it is something which is otherwise mainly a matter of getting the materials needed and organizing the work along kinship lines, and usually a canoe is built by one man, perhaps helped by a relative or two who possess the ability and right to build canoes (see ibid.: 83–95). But this particular canoe was the first 'community canoe', and therefore it was not simply a task of building a canoe, but also, I shall argue, in its unfolding it was an 'appearance' of the 'community'. So building a 'community' canoe is not just about a canoe being built, it is equally about 'community' and what that contains being socially negotiated and contested by different social perspectives. The 'community' on Mbuke Islands was going to build this canoe, which meant that whoever led it, contributed to it, held titles in committees and participated in the actual building of it would 'appear' as having a particular role and position in that 'community'. Not only are actions that 'benefit the community' appearances of persons who conduct that action, constituted as a part of and a good member of that specific sociality, they also reveal a certain position vis-à-vis others within that 'community'.

The first thing we (the 'community') needed to do was to get a large log from someone on Manus Island. A number of Mbuke men had declared that they had a friend, a family member or a trade partner who had a big tree that we could buy at a good price. Many of these men approached me, trying to convince me that their 'road' should be chosen. I kept saying that it was in the hands of the committee set up to organize the building. Since during the period in which these preparations took place I went to Port Moresby and back, I had left the money for the project in the hands of Polongou and Linda, my adoptive parents, since I had been warned against giving it to some of the men leading the project as some of them had a 'track record of messing up money', as someone put it. I trusted Linda and Polongou not to do so, but of course, without having thought about it, in doing this I was behaving like a relational person trusting family over 'community' representatives. I did not on the other hand realize the direct connection between distribution and organization, so I had placed Polongou in a more central place than others thought was appropriate. One day Polongou came to me and said, 'I have a tree, we are going to go and get it organized tomorrow'.

Our first trip to Manus Island involved us going to a village where Polongou's connection to the tree, a man called Soren, lived. We sat outside the men's house of Soren's clan and discussed the matter. 'I want the tree to fall this week', Polongou declared. Without it having been stated at any time throughout the conversation, I learned on our way back to Mbuke that now we had to go fishing because we had to give a large amount of fish in exchange for the tree, even if we were also going to pay money for it. The arrangement in terms of exchange was that Soren's father had given a big tree to one of Polongou's classificatory fathers (FB) many years previously. Both the original giver and the original receiver had died long ago, and the tree, which still grew in the bush, now 'belonged' to the male descendants of the original receiver, one of them Polongou. He could claim the tree (or pay a smaller price than the going rate, which would be paid out of my donation) and then give it to the 'community'. That was the plan that Polongou had now set in motion.

After the 'community canoe' committee (consisting of men across different families and clans) had organized several different fishing expeditions over a few days, using petrol paid for from the money I had given to the project, and once their wives had smoked the fish, we were ready to go back to Manus Island to cut down the tree. Ten men from Mbuke including myself set out on this small journey. After a long walk through the bush, we arrived at the extraordinarily big tree, and now both Polongou and Soren gave speeches marking the exchange of the tree before the actual felling began. At first I found it peculiar that they did so facing the tree, and facing into the bush, only occasionally turning towards the rest of us. Soren faced the tree, and, speaking in Tok Pisin, said: 'You must not ruin the tree. Do not make it rotten or be hollow [a frequent problem with large trees of the specific kind being felled]. The descendants are present and it is organized straight [in the right way]. You should forget this tree now, leave it be. We will take it now, all things are straight'. After that, all men present shouted in unison *Uro!* which means 'thank you' in many Manus languages, and clearly indicated that they agreed with Soren and that they wanted him and perhaps whoever he was addressing (including themselves) to know this. During Polongou's subsequent speech, he said: 'I am Polongou, son of Kusunan, the brother of Chakumai, the rightful owner of this tree. I have come to get this tree for my son [i.e. me] to build a canoe, which will be given to the community'.

When the enormous tree was felled, it broke in two when it hit the ground, rendering it useless for the task at hand. It was indeed rotten and hollow inside. Soren, who stood next to me, said quietly: 'We are wrong now' (TP: *yumi rong nau*). By that I think he indicated two things: 'now things will go wrong in the relationship between the exchanging patrilineages', and at the same time, 'we were wrong, we did something wrong, that is what this tells us'. Those of us from Mbuke returned home, having failed in our attempt to find a suitable log. Everyone agreed that the tree had broken because it was rotten and hollow, but why that was the case with that particular tree in that particular situation was not agreed upon in the villages. There were those who said that it was simply bad luck, but many explanations circled around the problem of whether the arrangements of the transaction, as well as the arrangements of those of us who had gone there to get it, were done properly or not, if 'all things had been considered'. A lot of theories were made about the insufficiency of Polongou's *lemwe-neani*. A dominant one was that the tree broke because the two men who originally exchanged the tree did not approve of the transaction. As a young canoe builder said to me: 'Polongou shouldn't have said that the canoe is for the community. Chakumai [the original receiver] might not approve of that – he is a very strict man, you know'. Like him, many people believed that the original exchangers had disapproved of the arrangements because the tree would then leave the patrilineage to which it had been given, since it was to be given to the community. Another theory was that there might have been people in the villages who did not approve of the way it was organized, because Polongou would get the credit for having provided the tree for the 'community' canoe, thereby depriving others – including the leader of the 'community' canoe committee – of the chance to organize part of a 'community project' and hence appearing like some kind of leader within 'community'. This problem was perhaps also a conflict between the *lapan* attempting to constitute himself and 'pull his name' by being the one to give the tree to the 'community' and the general good of 'benefiting community' as a whole. This key role in obtaining the tree might mean that Polongou would have a particular kind of say in the future use of the canoe, which would potentially run counter to the interests of the 'community'. In fact, these things could be what Polongou was trying to anticipate by saying that the tree would be given to the 'community' via his son (me), not directly by himself.

Another interpretation was that the tree was rotten and hollow because some family members of Soren's – who 'gave away' the tree – did not approve of his giving it away. Polongou is not a direct son, but the son of a brother of the man to whom the tree was originally given, which was seen as a potential problem because that man had sons of his own who may have disagreed with the organization of the felling, as well as the future use of the tree. These are all theories of how *lemweneani* (the process of reaching *lemwenemweneye*) had not been conducted properly prior to action or prior to the event, the felling of the tree. Consensus may have been lacking.

On the subject of canoes, this definition of *lemwenemweneye*, given to me by another *lapan* on another occasion, may be appropriate:

> It is like sailing a canoe; you have to consider all things. You have to look at the wind, the waves, the sky, the clouds, the course, the sail and so on. If you organize the trip you have to consider: whose canoe it is you are using; whose fishing net; whose sail; where did you borrow the motor; who paid for petrol? When you get back with the fish, you have to 'see' (TP: *luksave long*) all these people when you distribute. That is why Titan people are so successful in work [getting educated and highly placed in the workforce]; they are used to thinking about many things simultaneously.

One young man, Kenny, who is currently making meteoric advances in the sphere of village leadership, told me a story about a tree he had recently felled with a group of his friends in order to exemplify what had to be done on such an occasion. The tree he wanted to fell was a very big tree on one of the Mbuke Islands. For a long time it had been said about the tree in question that it could not be felled, that if someone tried to it would sink into the mangrove swamp in which it grew (and thus be impossible to move or cut up), and that because of the swampy area on which it grew it would be hollow and rotten inside. When Kenny and his friends started cutting the tree with a chainsaw, water started coming out of it, and the man operating the chain saw said to Kenny that it could not be used, that it would be rotten and hollow. But Kenny said, 'Just continue, you will see'. So they continued cutting the tree until there was only a very small fragment of the trunk left. At that point Kenny decided to make a small distribution. He gave a few betel nuts and a bit of cash to each of his friends who were helping him fell the tree. Then he said to the man with the chainsaw: 'You cut it now, only with the tip of the blade', and this is what the man did. He simply touched the existing cut with the tip of the blade, and the tree started moving. Slowly the tree fell exactly where they had planned for it to land, without sinking into the mud. 'And the tree was fine ... [W]e cut it up and I used it for a house I was building, and as you have seen, the house is still there'. Kenny continued: 'Polongou should have given a little something to those who had been looking after the tree, right there on the mountain [where we were felling the tree], he should have given a little betel nuts and money to Soren'. That is to say, it is not simply important that Soren had received fish when we had arrived at his village before going into the bush to fell the tree. In conjunction with the actual felling of the tree, recognition of particular relationships had to take place in a visually perceptible form.

The Dialectics of Totalization

For north Ambrym, Rio argues that only the outside view narrating or representing the story in a sand drawing is able to totalize social processes from afar as a third party. Only a particular peripheral person in the ceremony can connect the relationships forged in the ceremony with relationships in the past and the future, and see the whole story from an outside perspective (Rio 2005: 410). In the case of the felling of the tree, Polongou and Soren attempted to *lemweneani* (consider 'all things') by 'making appear' the audience constituted both out of those physically present and the ancestral spirits, who were all assured by them that 'all things are straight'. As Kenny pointed out, by saying that all things are considered must be accompanied by the 'making appear' of those 'things', for example by distribution – something which, from Kenny's point of view, Polongou had not done sufficiently. The organized action in that sense is an attempt, from the centre of its unfolding, to totalize, to take all things into account.

It may even be argued that the dispersed ordering of 'things' in time is dissolved in the unfolding of organized action, such as felling and claiming a tree, since, among other things, the tree's future as the property of the community had an effect on the present too. Likewise, in Rio's understanding of the ceremony, in time previous marriages between the same groups, and future children that the marriage might result in, become present in the perspective of the third party, the overseer, who might break in and correct potential wrongs (ibid.: 414). From the outside view, the third party totalizes the specific events taking place into the whole story of which the particular event is part. At that moment of totalization, the event is not a point on the line of time, not a part meaningfully understood as part of a whole story making time that distributes parts in space, but rather an amalgamation – or appearance – of 'all things' involved. In organizing the felling of the tree, Polongou had to take into account both future and past ownership of the tree in one moment, because as an audience, owners would potentially make themselves present by affecting its transformative actions. Such events then, condense many 'things' that one might otherwise consider 'of the past' (such as dead people) or 'of the future' (what people plan to do with a log). For example, the two men who originally exchanged the tree are in fact there and have agency (in the sense discussed in Chapter 3) in the present; they can cause the tree to be rotten in the middle, and therefore they are addressed as part of the audience. Events of that sort make social relationships appear in visually perceptible guises, confirming and transforming social forms which are otherwise invisible.

When the tree fell and broke in two, rather than this being understood as part of the whole which is the 'story' of the exchange of the tree, it actually *is* 'the whole story' (cf. Rio 2005: 414), a condensation made to appear in an instance. Linear time has dissolved (or its social relevance has) because the organizers (the speakers) have to consider all things, past, present and future, because they might show up in the present and have effects. The organizer must consider 'all' and has to make that consideration seen, which was what Polongou from Kenny's point of view should have done better by making it 'seen' that Soren and his predecessors had looked after the tree by giving betel nuts and cash. The ordering of 'things' in time then is not stable – like things in space they may move temporarily.

This conception of time was also occasionally reflected in the conception of space during navigation among Mbuke canoe sailors. When I travelled with Mbuke men across the open sea in their canoes, they would say, 'not long from now island X will come up, up there' while pointing in some direction. Such a reversed conception of space is not unfamiliar in Pacific peoples' navigation: 'A fundamental conception in Caroline Island navigation is that a canoe on course between islands is stationary and the islands move by the canoe' (Hutchins 1995: 71). Similarly, things from the past and the future are moving in time (and not linearly), rather than the moving entities necessarily being those persons who are visually and physically present in the present. The event is stationary, while its context moves, and hence totalization takes place from within the centre of activity, not only externally. Things are made present – made appear – by organized social action, regardless of where they were/are in their circumstances/ conditions beyond the moment. Whatever some people in the village felt about the specificities of the organization of getting the particular tree for the 'community' canoe, those specificities were (according to some) also able to affect our luck regarding whether or not the tree was hollow and rotten inside.

One could argue that organized action in time dissolves or contracts the time in which it unfolds, making persons and relations from the past come back, or change states as they are 'made appear' by an event that involves them. Ancestral spirits are not always present, because then there would be no point in refraining from saying that the canoe was for the 'community', as Kenny recommended, because the men who originally exchanged the tree would have known this already. As an audience they must be 'made to appear' by being considered in the unfolding of the event. This should not be understood as a time reversal when a person understands the event as part of a total narrative, but, I would argue, as things/persons of 'other times' coming back to social reality and doing actual things, like causing trees to break in two, an event interpreted as a misrecognition of the totalization 'made appear' by the organizer. Like people who make the whole that they embody appear by their actions, events condense and 'make appear' the wider context of which they are totalizing appearances, like a person constituting a microcosm of all its relationships. If Polongou posited himself as the owner of the tree in this situation, there is a potential conflict between the interest of 'community' and him as both an individual and the leader of a particular clan. Is he doing it to 'benefit the community'? Is the community appearing in its appropriate guise when he has put himself in charge and bypassed the chairman of the 'community' canoe committee? One of the theories about why the tree broke was that someone in the villages might have disagreed with this part of the organization of the making of the canoe, such that they themselves or others were not made to 'appear' as the persons in the positions in the 'community' they would have liked.

That is how I interpret the meaning of *lemwenemweneye*: all relations, persons, possessions, claims to possessions, feelings and places in time and space must be considered, and they must be accounted for in the way in which organized action unfolds and reveals them (ideally). Seen from this perspective, the attempt to organize action with *lemwenemweneye* is a microcosm of other things and times out of which it is, in its unfolding, constituted temporarily; the event is a contraction of its own context, the whole story in perceptible form. The organization of the building of the 'community' canoe may in that sense be said to be a perceptible appearance of the 'community'. Just as one can in some contexts see persons as social microcosms of their relationships, one can see organized action as the unfolding of various intermeshed lines in time and space all reaching – and breaching – the surface of social (and visual) reality in a particular moment.

The process of *lemweneani* is, like a navigator's position on the ocean, determined by a total computation of a number of diverse factors; endless numbers of star paths, waves, the colour of the sea, seabirds, cloud formations, all of them condensed into one (the position) in the mind of the Micronesian navigator (Hutchins 1995: 68–69). In the case of *lemwenemweneye*, the computation is not a simple one. In fact it is impossible to consider all things no matter who you are, because other people have other perspectives on the perspective that sees and makes seen 'all perspectives', and some of them most certainly will dispute any suggested total perspective 'made appear' by any event a person might organize. They will do so by words, and they will do so by actions during that very event. Like the reciprocity of perspective involved in 'seeing' and making seen by way of demands for sharing and responses to them (see Chapter 2), a totalizing perspective needs recognition from others, from the audience of action, for its action to be valued as an appropriate appearance of a social whole, in this case the 'community'. But that was perhaps not the specific sociality that the original exchangers would have liked to see 'appear', as indicated by the young canoe builder quoted above. Recognition and misrecognition by the imagined whole of the audience of social action is significant if organized social action is to be a successful appearance, or if it is to be regarded as an appearance of a totalizing perspective.

This demand of *lemwenemweneye* has to do with the fact, I would suggest, that the way things are organized makes the perspective of how everyone is located in the constitution of social relations appear visually. This means that every relation, title of leadership, office held, has to be considered in the process of *lemweneani*. But this is also where such positions are constituted and changed in the first place. It was therefore not insignificant whether the log for the 'community' canoe was a donation from Polongou or from me. From some people's point of view, the fact that Polongou organized the acquisition of the log might constitute a danger to the 'community', because I – by giving him that benefit – had conflated myself as a relative of Polongou's, with myself as a member of the 'community'. From some people's point of view, when donating money to the 'community', I should have left that money in the hands of members of the 'community' canoe committee, rather than in the hands of Polongou. In that sense, my leaving the money in Polongou's hands had been an appearance of an inappropriate sociality. It was not insignificant if Polongou had the chance to appear as the man who gave a canoe to the 'community'. Such are the factors that cause disagreement and make things take time when they are being organized. That is why there are always many theories about why something went wrong, because social positions are never clear and beyond discussion.

When something goes wrong it is because it was not done with *lemwen-emweneye*. The ultimate goal is recognition from a particular audience. When Soren finished his speech by the tree, the other men shouted *uro* not just to make it clear to the ancestors that they were present and confirm Soren in his claim that 'all the descendants are here', but also as a way of recognizing that things were 'made appear' in their proper guise and represented as such by Soren. But not all members of the audience are able to communicate in such direct ways, which made the ancestors, according to one theory, break the tree to express their misrecognition of the claim that the tree was going to leave the patrilineage to which it had been given and instead be 'given to the community'. This change of ownership, in turn, was something which some of those concerned with 'benefiting the community' feared would *not* happen completely with Polongou being in charge of the money. They feared that this fact would later result in certain claims from Polongou not only regarding the use of the canoe but also regarding Polongou's position within the 'community', which the canoe and its organization was an appearance of.

In Chapter 2 I showed how value is produced in a dialectical process of mutual recognition by actions 'making appear' relationships, and in organized collective action a similar dialectic process takes place. Here it is between the organizer and the audiences which such action totalizes, the 'all' of 'all things considered'. In that sense, the 'outside view', the audience, is split from the totalizing party, and it is in the dialectics between an inside and an outside view that forms of sociality are totalized. The question of recognition, also discussed in Chapter 2, concerns in this case the audiences that recognize the totalization manifest in the unfolding of organized action. Organized social actions only become valued as expressions of *lemwenemweneye* that make social forms appear if they receive some kind of recognition from the partly imagined audience which they portray in its unfolding. In this sense the standard of value is the ability to create a socially coherent and 'recognize-able' standard of value, and reveal this in action. This is never simple, and conflicts often arise between different amalgams of persons: clan, family and community interests differ and are perceived as threatening one another, and such threats take on perceptible form in the organization of action.

Conclusions

As seen in the ideal of *lemwenemweneye*, certain socially significant events and the way they are organized 'make appear' a totalization of relationships involved. The totalizing perspective which organized action reflects acts as a amalgamation of 'all perspectives' involved. I have argued that such events are 'appearances', breaching the surface between the visible and the invisible, between agents present and those of the past or elsewhere. Felling a tree, a trivial event in itself, can be a moment concluding a long-term exchange, and as such the moment transcends time and space, since all parties involved – including ancestors and living persons not spatially present – may 'show up' as audiences of action and actively affect outcomes of events in the present. Organizers of events aim to imagine and 'see' all members of 'the audience', whose perspectives are 'made to appear' by the unfolding of the event, like gifts making relations appear. 'All things' refers to all perspectives that may involve themselves in the event as the audience. The local concept of *lemwenemweneye* has here been presented as a totalizing perspective that informs the organization of events, a perspective which makes all perspectives appear in its unfolding in social action.

I have analysed certain organized social actions on Mbuke like this as attempts at appearances of perspectives on all things involved. The perspective known as *lemwenemweneye* involves a degree of totalization of social relations that Strathern and other proponents of similar positions suggest is not present among Melanesians in their conceptualizations of social action since 'there are no principles of organization that are not also found in the constitution of the person' (Strathern 1992b: 86). In this case, on the other hand, the whole is not simply the network of social relations seen from the point of view of the person being imbedded in them, but a totalization of perspectives and relations involved in an event, which may well be beyond the scope of the relations of the person organizing such an event. In kinds of organized action such as the felling of the tree described here, the members of the audience are potentially everyone that may have a perspective on the action in question. The only way of knowing if all things have been considered in such a totalization is by way of recognition from a partly imagined audience – that very sociality which is suggested by the way actions resulting in events are conducted. The totality is 'suggested' by being taken into account, which in itself may be an ideological or political claim that may be strongly disputed by members of the audience, and may be brought out as explanations of failure.

Graeber argues that value must be social, and that actors conduct value-transforming action with reference to an audience, whether concrete or imagined. Society for Graeber is the potential audience of one's actions

(Graeber 2001: 76). For the actor, 'society' – or the social totality – is the audience that recognizes the value of their actions. For the Mbuke organizer, the audience is the entirety of perspectives on actually unfolding social action. In this respect we may argue with Rio that even if people in Melanesia tend not to have a concept of society as a reified bounded entity beyond concrete relationships, they do have ways of totalizing social relationships and social wholes. Although Strathern may be right that persons are conceptualized such that in their constitution they model their social relationships (in some contexts), the significance ascribed to *lemwenemweneye* shows that other and more totalizing ideas of social wholes are present in Melanesia, as elsewhere. If we want to consider the idea of trying to imagine what an 'indigenous analysis of social action might look like' (Strathern 1992c: 150), we might have to consider the consequences of the fact that 'they' do have ways of analysing, by totalizing, their own social flows. In this sense, 'community' is not a bounded totality like 'society' is often seen to be, but a disputed whole, among other socialities, which takes perceptible form in totalizing appearances, such as the cutting down of a tree, and the organization of totalizing appearances is referred to by Mbuke people as *lemweneani*. 'All things' had to be considered, and in the process of considering all things, all things as such are defined because the way all things are organized 'makes appear' those things.

This kind of totalization, which makes certain totalities appear in perceptible form, is perhaps the reason why I felt that the social organization of canoe building seemed much more important than the actual (physical) work. The organization of the actual work might cause future problems in terms of ownership, status and leadership if it were not considered carefully before it took place. It is in the organization of events and the form that such events take that social positions and relations are negotiated socially, within wholes such as 'community'. To sum up, the event organized with *lemwenemweneye* is an 'appearance' in the sense that it is a condensed moment of all things involved, a temporary social whole. But of course, making claims to have 'seen all things' provides the organizer with a possibility of defining what all things relevant are, something others may disagree with.

Finally I should note that the specific canoe, once it was built using a different tree, did in fact many times 'benefit the community', and it was never, as far as I know, hijacked by Polongou. This is not surprising since Polongou was indeed, according to most people, a man of *lemwenemweneye*.

Conclusion

◆●◆

The Last Place of the Last Place

The day after I first arrived in the Mbuke Islands, a young man called Bernard asked me 'What do you want here? Mbuke is the last place of the last place!' Young men like him sometimes referred to Papua New Guinea (PNG) as being, in their view, the last place on earth; the last place to receive development and technology that other parts of the world have long had. And they seemed to feel that the Mbuke Islands are even more 'last' therein.[1] The Mbuke Islands are indeed rather isolated, and they do seem to be at the bottom of the list of places for government organizations to promote development. I initially noticed how the local health clinic and the village hall were falling apart, and I could have concluded that these people were simply victims of laying at the margins of a withdrawing state.

On the other hand, there was a brand new two-storey community school, houses were in a much better condition than I had seen in other Manus villages, and speedboats were lined up at the beach. There was something not particularly 'last' about the place. People living there spent vast amounts of money on petrol for their speedboats, on prefabricated building materials for their houses and on processed food bought in trade stores. As we have seen, Mbuke people should not be confused with the people actually living on those islands. Extensive work migration, and the remittances and need for education which have come with it, have been a part of the lives of people in Manus Province for nearly fifty years. Being a group of approximately 1,500 people, it is extraordinary to observe the number of high-level public and private-sector jobs that Mbuke people occupy in urban centres. As we can see in the hope among Mbuke parents that their children to 'get out before it's too late', described in Chapter 1, education and migration are highly valued among the Mbuke. But as the statement of the young man in the village who felt he lived in 'the last place of the last place' shows, Mbuke people lead highly diverse lives. To state it in excessively general terms: a Mbuke child grows up to either achieve a managing position in the public or private sector of urban PNG, or they grow up to fish with hand lines and fishing spears from a dugout canoe while struggling to 'find money' to buy sago to eat with their catch. This radical difference, along with the decreasing access to food and other necessities that results from a lack of stable means of making money in the village, has led remittances to become an important, if not decisive, part of household economies in the villages. Meanwhile, if on my initial arrival there was something of the 'last place' about the deteriorating community hall and the tumble-down health clinic, these have in the intervening years been replaced by new buildings organized and funded as 'community projects'.

Two overall questions have been addressed in this book: the question of *singaut*, and the question of 'community', both of which are tied up closely with the relationship between migrants and non-migrants among Mbuke people. While in anthropological writings about Manus Province it has often been pointed out that remittances are motivated by the need for persons to be socially reproduced through ceremonial exchange, I have argued that this is no longer the main motivation. I have argued, instead, that sharing on demand has become a significant aspect of social life, not only in the constitution of social relations and personhood, but for actual survival in the villages on the Mbuke Islands, and as a motivation for sending remittances. This kind of demand sharing, which is referred to as *singaut*, is often brought out by elite migrants and wealthier villagers alike as an explanation for promoting the 'community' and 'community projects', through which they hope to find ways to limit dependency on remittances and other people's help in the villages, while also ensuring that those in need are helped, regardless of whether or not they have any relatives to help them. While this diminishing concern with specific kin relationships in such situations would appear to reflect a radical break with the way social relations and personhood are otherwise constituted, I have shown that a concept of a social whole, like the 'community' that exists beyond kin, is in fact one among several coexisting and sometimes contesting socialities in which actions may be valued, personhood constituted and relationships produced and reproduced in a variety of ways.

Value and Sociality

I do not mean to say that among Mbuke people there are a number of fixed social wholes containing respective fixed standards of value that differ radically from each other, or that these various forms of sociality add up to an exhaustive description of the ways in which Mbuke people relate to one another. Taking local conceptualizations as my point of departure,

I have argued instead that actions in themselves envision, indeed reveal and attempt to produce, the specific nature of the sociality within which they unfold. Whether that temporary social whole is a relationship, a set of relationships or the 'community', they are 'made appear' by actions and are therefore continuously reconstituted, negotiated and contested socially. As I showed in Chapter 7, organized social action renders tangible particular social totalities in which personhood and value can take shape. Rather than assuming a priori the existence of social wholes such as 'culture', 'society' or 'community', and rather than as a consequence of not doing so confining myself simply to stories of individual persons, I have tried to show how Mbuke people themselves conceive of – and act with due observance of – certain social wholes, even if these are of a provisional kind. This has the consequence that when actions embody (make appear) the social whole in which that action may be valued, the relevance of that social whole is presented and demands recognition from others. As we saw in the case of the 'community' canoe, different sets of social relations may come into conflict in one particular situation.

Writing in the 1980s, it was clearly useful at the time for Strathern – in her attempt to imagine what an 'indigenous analysis of social action might look like' (Strathern 1992c: 150) – to present Melanesian conceptualizations as being in radical opposition to Western social scientific concepts such as the individual and society (see Strathern 1988). As she put it herself: 'The way I have presented the Melanesian ideas are bound to appear both too abstract and too concrete. But perhaps thus they will make explicit the nature of our own concretenesses and abstractions' (ibid.: 188). Strathern's argument 'makes explicit' our (anthropologists') assumptions about the nature of social life, in the same way that actions (whether transfers of remittances or donations to the 'community') make certain social wholes appear in visual form among Mbuke people. But these social wholes are not agreed upon, nor are they reflections of anything other than the claims that they are perceived as making – by others and by the actor or organizer of action. Strathern's analytical opposition between the Melanesian relational person and the Western individual should not be confused with empirical universality in Melanesia, as she herself points out (e.g. ibid.: 188), and neither should the way Polongou organized the building of the 'community' canoe be confused with a simple representation of the 'community', even if it was his attempt to 'benefit the community' and thereby construe (and constitute) the 'community' in the form of a canoe.

Mbuke 'holism' constitutes a kind of meta-holism basic to the conceptualization of many different temporal social wholes. On a general level I have argued that action that produces value does so while embodying the social whole in which it unfolds, in which a person can be constituted in particular ways, as a particular kind of person. As I argued in Chapter 4, actions that (can be claimed to) reveal no sociality often produce no value or are associated with negative value and moral critique. I have discussed how there may be identified a number of provisional social wholes that are relevant in different situations, social wholes that sometimes come into conflict with each other. The tension of the economy in that sense is not between market (individualism) and mutuality (reciprocity and sharing) alone, but is a multidimensional tension between many different hopes and fears regarding what money and new forms of organization may be useful for. Giving examples of remittances, daily sharing in the village and 'community projects' among the Mbuke, I have shown that certain kinds of transactions come with a certain kind of personhood, and that this involves a certain kind of value ascribed to the act of its giving and that which is given in that particular situation.

Even though social wholes have fallen out of grace as a subject of enquiry in anthropology, I have nevertheless addressed issues of value and personhood here through the lens of temporary social wholes. But this has been done from the point of view of the social wholes that people themselves imagine and create when they conduct their actions in accordance to them, rather than fixed social totalities. In this way I have also addressed the dynamics of social change among the Mbuke.

The Value of Questions and Answers

In a failed attempt at jointly writing an introduction to a special issue about value in an anthropological journal, Otto and Willerslev published their debate about whether or not there can be such a thing as an anthropological theory of value (Otto and Willerslev 2013). Otto argues that anthropology should attempt at formulating general theories of value, engaging with concepts from the history of ideas in the social sciences and producing anthropological theories that could in turn challenge the often more wide-ranging theories of value that other social sciences have been successful in producing. Willerslev, on the contrary, argues that rather than attacking other theories of value with a united overall theory, the task of anthropology is to introduce ethnographically driven concepts to produce guerrilla attacks on the larger entities that constitute coherent overall theories. Willerslev summarizes their different viewpoints as the question of whether we 'allow for the "radical otherness" of the other, or do we subscribe to the view where you accept that there are cultural differences, but basically assume that we share a common humanity that in turn allows us to use our own concepts to talk about the other?' (ibid.: 7).

Since I have not engaged deeply in the history of ideas concerning the concept of value in the social sciences in this book, but instead have focused on exploring the theoretical or analytical potential of local concepts (such as *singaut*, *lele*, 'community' and *lemwenemweneye*), it might appear as though I adhere to the same position as Willerslev (allowing for radical otherness). However, to say that local concepts might be helpful in developing an understanding of value and social change is not the same as saying that we cannot 'use our own concepts to talk about the other'. The task is to continuously challenge assumptions about the world that our own concepts bring along. After all, if some of 'their' concepts are useful outside their 'world', then surely that must also be the case for 'our' concepts.

Willerslev's position ties into a trend in contemporary anthropology, namely the notion that rather than distinguishing between 'the world' and the specific meanings or significances that different people ascribe to it (depending on their social and cultural background, for example), different people in fact inhabit different worlds altogether (e.g. Viveiros de Castro 2004: 3–6; Henare, Holbraad and Wastell 2007: 7–10). In this line of thought, there is, in a sense, no actual natural world to which different people at different times and in different places ascribe a variety of meanings. Latour makes a similar argument in a discussion of the relationship between 'value' and 'facts' from his standpoint in the study of science and technology (Latour 2004: 95–102). The overall problem that Latour identifies is the assumption that 'scientists define facts, only facts, [and] they leave to politicians and moralists the even more daunting task of defining values' (ibid.: 95). In terms of the above points (worlds versus meanings), facts are assumed to constitute insights into the common world to which different people might ascribe different kinds of value according to their 'culture'. The weakness of the notion of value in this sense, Latour notes, is that it always comes late, after the facts have been established (ibid.: 97). As Latour argues, there are human judgments involved in the production of facts; scientists, like others, sometimes conflate what is and what ought to be because the distinction between the two can never be clear, and 'if the public is consulted … it is in the mode of informing, divulging, popularizing, vulgarizing. The public is not asked to go into the laboratory and become perplexed in its turn' (ibid.: 121). While making these points Latour suggests, or defines, a whole new conceptual system ('a new separation of powers') with which to proceed in the scientific process without the mistaken distinction between fact and value (ibid.: 112–116).[2] These may be of great use in reconfiguring the relationship between the scientific production of knowledge and value understood as 'what ought to be'. But obviously if I were to adopt these concepts here, it would only force me to go back to the field to see how they hold up against local conceptualizations.

As Latour states, it is 'impossible to begin to ask the moral question after the states of the world have been defined' (ibid.: 125). He suggests, instead, that others (for example, 'the public') be involved in the actual production of facts through, among other things, repeated 'consultations' involving 'outsiders' in the perplexities encountered along the way while producing scientific knowledge (ibid.: 124–26). Here Mbuke people seem to be way ahead of him. The idea of ongoing consultation can also be derived from the continuous dialectics of value questions and their answers among the Mbuke; the same relationship that is valued is reconstituted and recon-figured in the process. Even if a canoe is given to the community after its making, it is not cut off from its origins in the social organization of its making by entering exchange. Unlike commodities, as defined by Marx, which, by being exchanged, 'acquire one uniform social status' (Marx 1954: 78), the canoe is never alienated from its origins in its making. The specific social organization of its making participates in its fact/value as a gift to the community, indeed participates in the new definition of the 'community'. In the dialectic of questions and answers developed here, that which is valued (such as a relationship) is implied and contested in the dialectical process of its own valuation.

The mixture of fact and value which is already in place when the facts are handed over from scientists to politicians, a mixture that leads Latour to conclude that a new set of conceptual distinctions is called for, is not kept secret among the Mbuke. What is and what ought to be is constantly renegotiated; Mbuke people constantly question assumptions about the social world revealed by specific kinds of acts or specific kinds of words. Furthermore, quite often they realize they do not know the value/facts, and therefore question others. While commodity fetishism, according to Marx, is the process by which the exchange of things renders the social relationships in which they were embedded invisible (Marx 1954: 76–87), the reverse is the case for the transactions I have described among the Mbuke, where the moment of exchange renders relationships visible. Value, of the kind I have addressed here, does not, for the Mbuke, derive from work as such, but from an action's ability to embody answers to ques-tions concerning the specific nature of a relationship or other social form. Actions render value tangible, both the value of a specific entity and the constitution of the context in which it is situated. There can therefore be no separation between fact and value.

Latour's understanding of value coincides with what Graeber refers to as the sociological understanding of value: that which is good, what ought to be. According to Graeber, there are three overall ways of using the word 'value' in social theory: one involves using it in a sociological sense, where it refers to that which is considered good and proper, and in this sense it is often referred to in the plural ('values'). Secondly, the word can be used in an economic(s) sense, the degree to which something is desired, measured by how much people are willing to give up to get it. And finally there is the linguistic meaning of the term – the value of a sign vis-à-vis other signs, or meaningful differences within a system of signs (Graeber 2001: 1–2). I have dealt here with the first of the three, although as I have shown the three are not conceptually separate in this way among Mbuke people: what is considered a good thing to do might be to give a certain thing in a particular manner in a particular situation which then renders the thing in question desirable, and more so than other things given in a different manner and situation, regardless of whether the things are identical as material entities.

As I hope I have shown, I have found that one potential contribution of anthropology is to explore what is considered a good life, what is worth aspiring to, and what an idea like 'community development' might be useful for among – for example – Mbuke people. This book has attempted to account for the dynamics through which the social worlds in which different Mbuke persons' lives play out, how they debate the constitution of that world, and how they change that world, whether by manipulating a relationship or by reorganizing sets of social relations as the social totality of 'community'. When I stated in the Introduction that this book is about asking questions and the value of the answers, this is also to say that social life is uncertain, and we can only hope that others recognize the way we see things. I have shown some of the ways in which Mbuke people explore and approximate their own life worlds in interaction with others.

My understanding of value as a dialectic of questions and answers constitutes a 'guerrilla' theory of value based on specific local conceptualizations. It is not an attempt to formulate a general theory of value for anthropology, even if I do hope that what I have said about value, social change and even remittances and 'community development' will be of use outside the confines of Manus Province and PNG. If Graeber is right that some of the great theories of value, perhaps particularly in the discipline of economics, are based on an assumption about a somewhat cynical human nature, then this account challenges that assumption, like many anthropological accounts have done before it. If there are indeed, as Graeber notes, those who claim that 'no one ever does anything primarily out of concern for others … one is only trying to get something out of it for oneself' (ibid.: 8), and that this is the underlying motivation for all human action, then I hope that this book provides a ray of hope that humans are also able to value acts precisely on the basis of their ability to benefit others.

What would be my answer to Bernard's question, 'What do you want here?' What was I doing on Mbuke Islands? What was I hoping to gain from going to a small group of islands in the Western Pacific? What is the value of Mbuke, from my point of view? I recall telling him that I wanted to experience what life was like in a place that was different from where I grew up, that perhaps I could learn something from it. Even if that was the truth, it was a poor answer, reflecting a selfish choice, since it implied that I would potentially be the only person who had that experience and that lesson: my answer did not conjure any sociality in which my actions could have value other than for my own personal satisfaction. But in answer to Bernard, I would say that this book embodies my attempt at an answer, an answer that others may recognize or dispute – but I have tried to share what I gained, rather than keeping it to 'myself alone'.

Notes

1. Cf. Reed (2003) on the concept of 'last place'.
2. The point that it is mistaken to categorically distinguish between fact and value was also made by Gregory in the field of economic anthropology specifically (Gregory 1997: 7), long before Latour made the point concerning moral judgements coming after the facts have been established.

References

◆●◆

Akin, D., and J. Robbins (eds). 1999. *Money and Modernity: State and Local Currencies in Melanesia*. Pittsburgh: University of Pittsburgh Press.

Appadurai, A. 1986. 'Introduction: Commodities and the Politics of Value', in A. Appadurai (ed.), *The Social Life of Things: Commodities in Cultural Perspective*. Cambridge: Cambridge University Press, pp.3–63.

Austin, J.L. 1962. *How to Do Things with Words*, ed. J.O. Urmson. Oxford: Clarendon Press.

Bailey, F.G. 1971. 'Gifts and Poison', in F.G. Bailey (ed.), *Gifts and Poison: The Politics of Reputation*. Oxford: Blackwell, pp.1–25.

Bainton, N.A. 2010. *The Lihir Destiny: Cultural Responses to Mining in Melanesia*. Canberra: Australian National University Press.

Bakan, J. 2004. *The Corporation: The Pathological Pursuit of Profit and Power*. Toronto: Penguin.

Besnier, N. 2009. *Gossip and the Everyday Production of Politics*. Honolulu: University of Hawaii Press.

Bille, M., F. Hastrup, and T.F. Sørensen (eds). 2010. *An Anthropology of Absence: Materializations of Transcendence and Loss*. New York: Springer.

Bloch, M., and J. Parry (eds). 1989. *Money and the Morality of Exchange*. Cambridge: Cambridge University Press.

Bohannan, P. 1959. 'The Impact of Money on an African Subsistence Economy', *Journal of Economic History* 19(4): 491–503.

Bourdieu, P. 1977. *Outline of a Theory of Practice*. Cambridge: Cambridge University Press.

Bubandt, N., and T. Otto. 2010. 'Anthropology and the Predicaments of Holism', in N. Bubandt and T. Otto (eds), *Experiments in Holism: Theory and Practice in Contemporary Anthropology*. Chichester: Wiley-Blackwell, pp.1–15.

Burridge, K. 1971. *New Heaven, New Earth: A Study of Millenarian Activities*. Oxford: Blackwell.

Carrier, A., and J. Carrier. 1991. *Structure and Process in a Melanesian Society: Ponam's Progress in the Twentieth Century*. Chur: Harwood Academic.

Carrier, J. 1988. *The Ponam Fish Freezer*. Department of Anthropology and Sociology Occasional Paper No. 4. Port Moresby: University of Papua New Guinea.

Carrier, J., and A. Carrier. 1983. 'Profitless Property: Marine Ownership and Access to Wealth on Ponam Island, Manus Province', *Ethnology* 22(2): 133–51.

———— 1989. *Wage, Trade, and Exchange in Melanesia: A Manus Society in the Modern State*. Berkeley: University of California Press.

Carsten, J. 1997. *The Heat of the Hearth. The Process of Kinship in a Malay Fishing Community*. Oxford: Clarendon Press.

Crocombe, R. 1965. *The M'Buke Co-operative Plantation*. New Guinea Research Unit Bulletin No. 7. Canberra: Australian National University.

Dalsgaard, S. 2009. 'Claiming Culture: New Definitions and Ownership of Cultural Practices in Manus Province, Papua New Guinea', *Asia Pacific Journal of Anthropology* 10(1): 20–32.

———— 2010. 'All the Government's Men: State and Leadership in Manus Province, Papua New Guinea', Ph.D. diss. Aarhus: University of Aarhus.

———— 2013. 'The Politics of Remittance and the Role of Returning Migrants: Localizing Capitalism in Manus Province, Papua New Guinea', *Research in Economic Anthropology* 33: 277–302.

Derrida, J. 1992. *Given Time*. Chicago: University of Chicago Press.

Dumont, L. 1980. *Homo Hierarchicus: The Caste System and its Implications*. Chicago: University of Chicago Press.

Duranti, A. 2006. 'The Social Ontology of Intentions', *Discourse Studies* 8(1): 31–40.

Errington, F., and D. Gewertz. 2004. *Yali's Question: Sugar, Culture and History*. Chicago: University of Chicago Press.

———— 2010. 'Expanding Definitions, Contracting Contexts: A Comment on Mosko's "Partible Penitents"', *Journal of the Royal Anthropological JournaloftheRoyalAnthropologicalInstitute* 16: 250–52.

Finney, R. 1973. *Big-men and Business: Entrepreneurship and Economic Growth in the New Guinea Highlands*. Canberra: Australian National University Press.

Foucault, M. 1977. *Discipline and Punish: The Birth of the Prison*. London: Penguin.

Fortune, R. 1969 [1935]. *Manus Religion: An Ethnographic Study of the Manus Natives of the Admiralty Islands*. Lincoln: University of Nebraska Press.

Foster, R. 1995a. *Social Reproduction and History in Melanesia: Mortuary Ritual, Gift Exchange, and Custom in the Tanga Islands*. Cambridge: Cambridge University Press.

———— 1995b. 'Print Advertisements and Nation Making in Metropolitan Papua New Guinea', in R. Foster (ed.), *Nation Making: Emergent Identities in Postcolonial Melanesia*. Ann Arbor: University of Michigan Press, pp.151–81.

Gell, A. 1992. 'Inter-tribal Commodity Barter and Reproductive Gift Exchange in Old Melanesia', in C. Humphrey and S. Hugh-Jones (eds), *Barter, Exchange and Value: An Anthropological Approach*. Cambridge: Cambridge University Press, pp.142–68.

———— 1998. *Art and Agency: An Anthropological Theory*. Oxford: Clarendon Press.

_____ 1999. 'Strathernograms, or the Semiotics of Mixed Metaphors', in *The Art of Anthropology: Essays and Diagrams*, ed. E. Hirsch. London: Athlone, pp.29–76.

Girke, F., and C. Meyer. 2011. 'Introduction', in C. Meyer and F. Girke (eds), *The Rhetorical Emergence of Culture*. New York: Berghahn Books.

Gluckman, M. 1963. 'Gossip and Scandal', *Current Anthropology* 4(3): 307–16.

Graeber, D. 2001. *Toward an Anthropological Theory of Value: The False Coin of Our Dreams*. New York: Palgrave.

_____ 2009. 'Debt: The First Five Thousand Years', *Mute Magazine*. Retrieved 2 March 2015 from: http://www.metamute.org/editorial/articles/debt-first-five-thousand-years

_____ 2011. 'Consumption', *Current Anthropology* 52(4): 489–511.

Gregory, C. A. 1980. 'Gifts to Men and Gifts to God: Gift Exchange and Capital Accumulation in Contemporary Papua' *Man*, New Series, Vol. 15(4). pp. 626–652.

_____ 1982. *Gifts and Commodities*. London: Academic Press

_____ 1994. 'Exchange and Reciprocity', in T. Ingold (ed.), *Companion Encyclopedia of Anthropology*. London: Routledge, pp.911–39.

_____ 1997. *Savage Money: The Anthropology and Politics of Commodity Exchange*. Amsterdam: Harwood Academic.

Gudeman, S. 2008. *Economy's Tension: The Dialectics of Community and Market*. New York: Berghahn Books.

Gustafsson, B. 1992. 'Houses and Ancestors: Continuities and Discontinuities in Leadership among the Manus', Ph.D. diss. Göteborg: Institute of Anthropology, University of Göteborg.

_____ 1999. *Traditions and Modernities in Gender Roles: Transformations in Kinship and Marriage among the M'buke from Manus Province*. Port Moresby: National Research Institute.

Haraway, D. 1988. 'Situated Knowledge: The Science Question', in *Simians, Cyborgs, and Women*. New York: Routledge, pp.183–201.

Henare, A., M. Holbraad and S. Wastell (eds). 2007. *Thinking Thorough Things: Theorising Artefacts Ethnographically*. London: Routledge.

Hirsch, E. 2007. 'Looking like a Culture', *Anthropological Forum* 17(3): 225–38.

Hutchins, E. 1995. *Cognition in the Wild*. Cambridge, MA: MIT Press.

Itéanu, A. 2009. 'Hierarchy and Power: A Comparative Attempt under Asymmetrical Lines', in K. Rio and O.H. Smedal (eds), *Hierarchy: Persistence and Transformation in Social Formations*. Oxford: Berghahn Books, pp.331–49.

Jebens, H. (ed.). 2004. *Cargo, Cult and Culture Critique*. Honolulu: University of Hawaii Press.

Jenkins, T. 1994. 'Fieldwork and the Perception of Everyday Life', *Man* 29: 433–55.

Jiménez, A.C., and R. Willerslev. 2007. 'An Anthropological Concept of the Concept: Reversibility among the Siberian Yukaghirs', *Journal of the Royal Anthropological Institute* 13(3): 527–44.

Jones, N.B. 1987. 'Tolerated Theft: Suggestions about the Ecology and Evolution of Sharing, Hoarding and Scrounging', *Social Science Information* 29(1): 31–54.

Keane, W. 1994. 'The Value of Words and the Meaning of Things in Eastern Indonesian Exchange', *Man* 29(3): 605–29.

Knauft, B.M. 2010. 'Beyond Polarization and Partition in Melanesian Anthropology: A Comment on Mosko's "Partible Penitents"', *Journal of the Royal Anthropological Institute* 16: 244–46.

Latour, B. 2004. *Politics of Nature: How to Bring the Sciences into Democracy.* Cambridge, MA: Harvard University Press.

Lawrence, P. 1964. *Road Belong Cargo: A Study of the Cargo Cult Movement in the Southern Madang District, New Guinea.* Melbourne: Melbourne University Press.

Macdonald, G. 2000. 'Economies and Personhood: Demand Sharing among the Wiradjuri of New South Wales' in G.W. Wenzel, G. Hovelsrud-Broda and N. Kishigami (eds), *The Social Economy of Sharing: Resource Allocation and Modern Hunter-gatherers.* Osaka: National Museum of Ethnology, pp.87–111.

MacGregor, A.M. 1971. 'Langandrowa and M'buke Corporate Indigenous Plantations', New Guinea Research Bulletin No. 43. Canberra: Australian National University.

Macpherson, C. 1962. *The Political Theory of Possessive Individualism: Hobbes to Locke.* Oxford: Oxford University Press.

Maher, R.F. 1961. *New Men of Papua: A Study of Culture Change.* Madison: University of Wisconsin Press.

Malinowski, B. 1983 [1922]. *Argonauts of the Western Pacific.* London: Routledge and Kegal Paul.

Marcus, G. 1998. *Ethnography through Thick and Thin.* London: Sage.

Martin, K. 2006. 'After the Volcano: The Language of Custom and Conflict in East New Britain', Ph.D. diss. Manchester: University of Manchester.

———— 2007. 'Your Own Buai You Must Buy: The Ideology of Possessive Individualism in Papua New Guinea', *Anthropological Forum* 17(3): 285–98.

———— 2009. 'Custom: The Limits of Reciprocity in a Village Resettlement', in K. Sykes (ed.), *Ethnographies of Moral Reasoning: Living Paradoxes of a Global Age.* New York: Palgrave Macmillan, pp.93–117.

Marx, K. 1954 [1887]. *Capital: A Critique of Political Economy*, Vol. 1. Moscow: Progress Publishers.

Maurer, B. 2006. 'The Anthropology of Money', *Annual Review of Anthropology* 35: 15–36.

Mauss, M. 1990 [1925]. *The Gift. The Form and Reason for Exchange in Archaic Societies*, trans. W.D. Halls. London: Routledge.

May, R. (ed.). 1982. *Micronationalist Movements in Papua New Guinea*. Canberra: Dept. of Political and Social Change, Research School of Pacific Studies, ANU.

Mead, M. 1930. 'Melanesian Middlemen', *Natural History* 30(2): 115–30.

———— 1934. *Kinship in the Admiralty Islands*. Washington: American Museum of Natural History.

———— 2001 [1956]. *New Lives for Old: Cultural Transformation – Manus, 1928–1953*. New York: Perennial.

Mihalic, F. 1989 [1971]. *The Jacaranda Dictionary and Grammar of Melanesian Pidgin*. Hong Kong: Web Books.

Mimica, J. 2003. 'The Death of a Strong, Great, Bad Man: An Ethnography of Soul Incorporation', *Oceania* 73(4): 260–86.

Mosko, M. 1983. 'Composition, De-composition and Social Structure in Bush Mekeo Culture', *Mankind* 14: 24–33.

Munn. N. 1986. *The Fame of Gawa: A Symbolic Study of Value Transformation in a Massim (Papua New Guinea) Society*. Cambridge: Cambridge University Press.

Otto, T. 1991. 'The Politics of Tradition in Baluan: Social Change and the Construction of the Past in a Manus Society', Ph.D. diss. Canberra: Australian National University.

———— 1992. 'The Paliau Movement in Manus and the Objectification of Tradition', *History and Anthropology* 5(3/4): 427–54.

———— 1994. 'Feasting and Fighting: Rank and Power in Pre-colonial Baluan', *History and Anthropology*, 7(1–4): 223–40.

———— 1997. 'Informed Participation and Participating Informants', *Canberra Anthropology* 20(1/2): 96–108.

———— 2004. 'Work, Wealth and Knowledge: Enigmas of Cargoist Identifications', in H. Jebens (ed.), *Cargo, Cult and Culture Critique*. Honolulu: University of Hawaii Press, pp.209–26.

Otto, T. and R. Willerslev. 2013. 'Value as Theory: Comparison, Cultural Critique and Guerrilla Ethnographic Theory', *Hau: Journal of Ethnographic Theory* 3(1): 1–20.

Peebles, G. 2010. 'The Anthropology and Credit and Debt', *Annual Review Anthropology* 39: 225–40.

Peirce, C.S. 1958. 'Letter to Lady Welby', in *Collected Papers of Charles Sanders Peirce*, Vol. 8, ed. A.W. Burks. Cambridge, MA: Harvard University Press.

Pedersen. M.A. n.d. 'Debt as an Urban Affect in Postsocialist Mongolia', unpublished manuscript.

Peterson, N. 1993. 'Demand Sharing: Reciprocity and the Pressure for Generosity among Foragers', *American Anthropologist* 95(4): 860–74.

Peterson, N., and J. Taylor. 2003. 'The Modernising of the Indigenous Domestic Moral Economy: Kinship, Accumulation and Household Composition', *Asia Pacific Journal of Anthropology* 4: 105–22.

Polanyi, K. 1957. *The Great Transformation*. Boston: Beacon Press.

Poltorak, M. 2010. 'Review of Suhr, Otto and Dalsgaard, *Ngat is Dead: Studying Mortuary Traditions*', *Journal of the Royal Anthropological Institute* 16: 915–16.

Rasmussen, A.E. 2013. *Manus Canoes: Skill, Making, and Personhood in Mbuke Islands (Papua New Guinea)*. Kon-Tiki Museum Occasional Papers No. 13. Oslo: Kon-Tiki Museum.

―――― 2014. 'Infinity in a Spear: Things as Mediations among the Mbuke (Papua New Guinea)', in D.R. Chiristensen, and K. Sandvik (eds), *Mediating and Remediating Death*. Aldershot: Ashgate, pp.63–73.

Reed, A. 1999. 'Anticipating Individuals: Modes of Vision and Their Social Consequences in Papua New Guinean Prison', *Journal of the Royal Anthropological Institute* 5(1): 43–56.

―――― 2003. *Papua New Guinea's 'Last Place': Experiences of Constraint in a Postcolonial Prison*. Oxford: Berghahn Books.

Rio, K.M. 2005. 'Discussions around a Sand-drawing: Creations of Agency and Society in Melanesia', *Journal of the Royal Anthropological Institute* 11: 401–23.

―――― 2007. *The Power of Perspective: Social Ontology and Agency on Ambrym Island, Vanuatu*. New York: Berghahn Books.

Robbins, J. 2004. *Becoming Sinners: Christianity and Moral Torment in a Papua New Guinea Society*. Berkeley: University of California Press.

―――― 2007. 'Afterword: Possessive Individualism and Cultural Change in the Western Pacific', *Anthropological Forum* 17(3): 299–308.

―――― 2010. 'Melanesia, Christianity, and Cultural Change: A Comment on Mosko's "Partible Penitents"', *Journal of the Royal Anthropological Institute* 16: 241–43.

Robbins, J., and D. Akin. 1999. 'An Introduction to Melanesian Currencies: Agency, Identity and Social Reproduction', in D. Akin and J. Robbins (eds), *Money and Modernity: State and Local Currencies in Melanesia*. Pittsburgh: University of Pittsburgh Press, pp.1–40.

Robbins, J., and A. Rumsey. 2008. 'Cultural and Linguistic Anthropology and the Opacity of Other Minds', *Anthropological Quarterly* 81(2): 407–20.

Robbins J., and H. Wardlow. 2005. *The Making of Global and Local Modernities in Melanesia: Humiliation, Transformation and the Nature of Cultural Change*. London: Ashgate.

Roslado, M. 1982. 'The Things We Do with Words: Ilongot Speech Acts and Speech Act Theory in Philosophy', *Language and Society* 2: 203–37.

Rumsey, A. 2008. 'Confession, Anger and Cross-cultural Articulation in Papua New Guinea', *Anthropological Quarterly* 81(2): 455–72.

Sahlins, M.D. 1963. 'Poor Man, Rich Man, Big-man, Chief: Political Types in Melanesia and Polynesia', *Comparative Studies in Society and History* 5: 285–303.

―――― 1972. *Stone Age Economics*. New York: Aldine de Gruyter.

_____ 2005 [1992]. 'The Economics of Develop-man in the Pacific', in J. Robbins and H. Wardlow (eds), *The Making of Global and Local Modernities in Melanesia*. Aldershot: Ashgate, pp.23–43.

_____ 2011. 'What Kinship Is (Parts 1 and 2)', *Journal of the Royal Anthropological Institute* 17: 2–19, 227–42.

Schwartz, T. 1962. *The Paliau Movement in the Admirality Islands, 1946–1954*. New York: American Museum of Natural History.

_____ 1963. 'Systems of Areal Intergration: Some Considerations Based on the Admiralty Islands of Northern Melanesia', *Anthropological Forum* 1: 56–97.

_____ 1967. 'The Co-operatives: "Ol i-bagarapim mani…"' *New Guinea* 1: 36–47.

_____ 1975. 'Relations among Generations in Time-limited Cultures', *Ethos* 3(2): 309–22.

_____ 1995. 'Cultural Totemism: Ethnic Identity, Primitive and Modern', in L. Romanucci-Ross and G. De Vos (eds), *Ethnic Identity. Creation, Conflict and Accommodation*, 3rd edn. Walnut Creek, CA: Altamira Press, pp.48–72.

Searle, J. 1969. *Speech Acts*. Cambridge: Cambridge University Press.

Shieffelin, B. 2008. 'Speaking Only Your Own Mind: Reflections on Talk, Gossip and Intentionality in Bosavi (PNG)', *Anthropological Quarterly* 81(2): 431–41.

Steward, P.J., and A. Strathern. 2004. *Witchcraft, Sorcery, Rumors and Gossip*. Cambridge: Cambridge University Press.

Strathern, M. 1975. *No Money on Our Skins: Hagen Migrants in Port Moresby*. Port Moresby: New Guinea Research Bulletin.

_____ 1988. *The Gender of the Gift*. Berkeley: University of California Press.

_____ 1992a. 'Qualified Value: The Perspective of Gift Exchange', in C. Humphrey and S. Hugh-Jones (eds), *Barter, Exchange and Value: An Anthropological Approach*. Cambridge: Cambridge University Press, pp.169–91.

_____ 1992b. 'Parts and Wholes: Refiguring Relationships in a Post-plural World', in A. Kuper (ed.), *Conceptualising Society*. London: Routledge, pp.75–104.

_____ 1992c. 'Response', *Pacific Studies* 15(1): 149–54.

_____ 1994. 'Parts and Wholes: Reconfiguring Relationships', in R. Borofsky (ed.), *Assessing Cultural Anthropology*. New York: McGraw Hill, pp.204–16.

_____ 1999. *Property, Substance and Effect: Anthropological Essays on Persons and Things*. London: Athlone Press.

Suhr, C., T. Otto (dirs.) and S. Dalsgaard (co-dir.). 2009. *Ngat is Dead: Studying Mortuary Traditions*, 59 mins. Aarhus: Moesgaard Film.

Sykes, K. 2007a. 'Interrogating Individuals: The Theory of Possessive Individualism in the Western Pacific', *Anthropological Forum* 17(3): 213–24.

_____ 2007b. 'The Moral Grounds of Critique: Between Possessive Individuals, Entrepreneurs and Big Men in New Ireland', *Anthropological Forum* 17(3): 255–68.

Van Vleet, K. 2003. 'Partial Theories: On Gossip, Envy and Ethnography in the Andes', *Ethnography* 4(4): 491–519.

Viveiros de Castro, E. 2004. 'Perspectival Anthropology and the Method of Controlled Equivocation', *Tipití: Journal of the Society for the Anthropology of Lowland South America* 2(1): 3–20.

Wadel, C. 1991. *Feltarbeid i egen kultur.* Flekkefjord: Seek A/S.

Wagner, R. 1975. 'Are There Social Groups in the Papua New Guinea Highlands?' in M.J. Leaf (ed.), *Frontiers of Anthropology*. New York: Van Nostrand, pp.95–122.

———— 1991 'The Fractal Person', in M. Godelier and M. Strathern (eds), *Great Men and Big Men: Personifications of Power in Melanesia*. Cambridge: Cambridge University Press, pp.159–74.

Wehmeier, S. 2000. *Oxford Advanced Learner's Dictionary of Current English.* Oxford: Oxford University Press.

Weiner, A. 1992. *Inalienable Possessions: The Paradox of Keeping-while-giving.* Berkeley: University of California Press.

Weiner, J. 1986. 'The Social Organisation of Foi Silk Production: The Anthropology of Marginal Development', *Journal of the Polynesian Society* 95(4): 421–440.

Wendel, J. 2007. 'Making and Unmaking Possessive Individuals: "Xavier Borrowing" at a Catholic Mission Pacific Islands Secondary School', *Anthropological Forum* 17(3): 269–83.

Wenzel, G.W., G. Hovelsrud-Broda and N. Kishigami (eds). 2000. *The Social Economy of Sharing: Resource Allocation and Modern Hunter-Gatherers.* Osaka: National Museum of Ethnology.

Were, G. 2007. 'Fashioning Belief: The Case of the Baha'i Faith in Northern New Ireland', *Anthropological Forum* 17(3): 239–53.

Woodburn, J. 1998. '"Sharing is Not a Form of Exchange": An Analysis of Property Sharing in Immediate-Return Hunter-Gatherer Societies', in C. Hann (ed.), *Property Relations: Renewing the Anthropological Tradition*. Cambridge: Cambridge University Press, pp.48–63.

Index

◆●◆

www.ingramcontent.com/pod-product-compliance
Lightning Source LLC
Chambersburg PA
CBHW070927030426
42336CB00014BA/2570